Poetics:
Essays on the Art of Poetry

An Anthology from Tendril Magazine

Compiled by
Paul Mariani and George Murphy

Poetics:

Essays on the Art of Poetry

Compiled by Paul Mariani and George Murphy

A Special Issue of *Tendril* Magazine

Managing Editor
George E. Murphy, Jr.

Associate Editors

Jacquelyn Crews   Michelle Gillet
Mark Jarman   Sandy McKinney
Sue Ellen Thompson   Bruce Weber

Contributing Editors

Raymond Carver   Brendan Galvin   Mary Robison
Carolyn Forche   William Matthews   Diane Wakoski
Richard Ford   Mekeel McBride   Joy Williams
Tess Gallagher   Heather McHugh   Tobias Wolff
                    Lisel Mueller

Cover Painting by Kim Drew
Book Design by George Murphy
Composition by Coastal Composition, Box 2600, Ocean Bluff, MA 02065

First Edition.

Poetics: Essays on the Art of Poetry, ©1984 by Tendril, Inc.

Tendril, Inc. is a tax-exempt, non-profit organization supported by funding from The National Endowment for the Arts, The Massachusetts Council on the Arts and Humanities, The Coordinating Council of Literary Magazines, IBM, Digital Equipment Corporation, by donations from private individuals, and by services donated by the editorial staff.

ISBN: 0-937504-06-8
Library of Congress Catalog Card Number: 84-050281

Contents

What Is Contemporary Poetry?

Parts of a Grand Design

Introduction

To paraphrase Robert Hass's "Meditation at Langunitas":

"All the new thinking is about the poem.
In this it resembles all the old thinking."

There are nineteen essays of "new thinking" included in this volume, all written between the last phase of America's interminable war in Vietnam and the present. In 1971, Galway Kinnel asked us to turn to our poetry as to a source of life still unpolluted by the Catch-22 rhetoric of four American administrations. In 1984, at the present "end" of this linguistic continuum we are examining, Tess Gallagher reminds us of the need to properly grieve over our losses: the loss of life, the shocks to the psyche, the solitary condition of the soul. They both know, as William Carlos Williams knew, that it was in the poem that we might be able to find the news we were looking for.

Since it is by language we live *and* die, it has been important for these poets to examine the words we use, the assumptions we make, the images we find ourselves calling upon to shape our visions. After all, we are continually being fed images and their concomitant rhetorics — and something in each of us must either find these acceptable and appropriate to our sense of the world or reject them as foreign matter. There is something in the language itself, as William Stafford reminds us, which acts on us, shaping our responses at least as much as we do the actual shaping.

It is no accident that so many of the essays included here speak of chance, ignorance, silence, absence, the unknown. We live in a universe of radical contiguity, or at least we *believe* we do, which comes to pretty much the same thing in this post-Nietzschian moment. And it is against this silence we find a pond teeming with the spawn of the collective unconscious out of which we wait for those deep images to appear, or—to use a metaphor from the New Physics—a field of linguistic particles continually bombarding the subconsciousness from which the poet attempts to order his or her world.

It is clear to any student of poetry that much has changed in the past century; perhaps more has changed since World War II. We began gathering this collection with one question in mind: What exactly is important to the poet working in America *today*? Briefly, the same issues which have preoccupied the poet since at least the formulations of Plato and Aristotle but, of course, with a difference. These preoccupations include both the proper *subjects* of the poet and the actual *craft* of the poem. More than half the essays here deal with the issues of image and metaphor, diction, rhetorical strategies, syntax, melody, pitch, rhythm, prosody, and—in the case of free verse—with the *melos* of line break and the scoring of the piece. Beyond that, there is the question of the forms which so many contemporary American poems take, what Jonathen Holden astutely calls that array of non-traditional analogical forms which have replaced an older order of pattern. These essays, by many of our best living poets and critics help us to read contemporary poems according to a set of formal assumptions in keeping with our own moment: the conversation, the letter, the confession, the psychological retrospection, the myriad forms which even include the prayer forms of Ginsberg, Lowell, and Berryman.

There are of course disagreements and deep tensions which cut across all of this. There is talk of autobiographical self-indulgence, a concern with any of a hundred linguistic and rhetorical evasions, a distrust of rhetoric itself (co-inciding with and following Nixon's Watergate speeches), a parallel distrust of what are perceived as the elitist Gnostic formulations of the practitioners of the "deep image," a distrust of those *personas* which allow the poet to escape claim-ing responsibility for attitudes which the poet also seems to hold in spite of his own disclaimers, a distrust of the aloof, superior attitude of male poets as different in other respects as Robert Lowell and John Ashbury, a distrust, even, of the whole enterprise we call contemporary American poetry, which some would read as an abberation in the larger scheme of things.

And yet. And yet. No important poet ever represents merely one extreme position. Poets grow into positions, defend them, and then abandon them, leaving the evidence of their deeply-held beliefs behind in poems as intricate and as splendid, often, as those won-derful shells left behind by sea creatures. No sooner is a position taken and an element defined than another poet, good alchemist that he or she is, attempts to combine or alter the formula according to his or her own needs. The one thing it seems we can always rely on is change.

If we read the essays by Sandra Gilbert and Alicia Ostriker correctly, there has been something like progress in one of the most interesting areas of American poetry during the 70's and 80's: the issue of defining the female self among American women poets. Poetry by American women now seems to be in a period of sharp revisionism, of re-assessing the gains and losses in the poetry they have written since the late 1950's. If the issue earlier was necessarily one of eminent domain, of taking that power which was rightfully theirs to take as they could, the issue now, Ostriker says, may have more to do with vulnerability, with searching not for those metaphorical structures we associate with the male, but with the power of the feminine.

On the level of metaphor we might note that this issue of the claims of power and vulnerability is present in the very forms and masks which contemporary American poetry itself has taken. If women poets have suffered the "divided self," a self created in large part by the myths male poets have made for them, (a concept true as well of Black poets in a white society), then the issue among many white male poets has been how best to present one's self-portrait in the disfiguring mirror of the poem.

The autobiographical impulse is still central to American poetry being written today. Every major American woman poet in the last 25 years has had to create a complex self in her poetry. As for American men poets, they have had to decide where they divide on a spectrum of personas which range from the confessional poetry of a Berryman, burning his own body to make light of it, to the lyrics of that beautiful "jaded pastoralist," James Wright, to the seemingly impersonal voices of John Ashbury with their analogues in the two-dimensional planes of American abstract art.

What we hope these essays can do, if read carefully, is suggest what are some of the central concerns of our own moment in a poetic tradition now in its fourth century. These are not, of course, the only essays one could have chosen, and we might easily have presented a volume twice this size covering the same time period. Moreover, there are no essays here by American Black poets or American Indians or American Hispanic poets. And this is, admittedly, part of the very problem of seeing and not seeing in American poetry. Moreover, there are many other practicing poet-critics in the "mainstream" who are likewise not included. But these essays certainly offer a way into the extraordinary maelstrom of energies which *is* contemporary American poetry.

Paul Mariani
George E. Murphy, Jr.

What Is Contemporary Poetry?

Jonathan Holden

Postmodern Poetic Form: A Theory

To appreciate the difficulty a critic faces when trying to find any kind of continuity in contemporary American poetry, one need only thumb through the third edition of A. Poulin's anthology, *Contemporary American Poetry*. It would seem at first glance that the poems of John Ashbery and Imamu Amiri Baraka would have nothing significant in common — no more, certainly, than the graceful, late-modernist, domestic verses of Richard Wilbur have with the chants of Allen Ginsberg — both featured in that anthology — or the male boastings of James Dickey have in common with the recent work of Adrienne Rich. Critics have, of course, tried to locate a pattern in this diversity; but their efforts have been either too tentative or not thoroughly enough thought out. Jerome Mazzaro, for example, in his preface to *Postmodern American Poetry*, gives us the following, vague prognostication:

> Without the technical language of the structuralists, the formulation of the essential differences between "modernism" and "postmodernism" becomes: in conceiving of language as a fall from unity, modernism seeks to restore the original state often by proposing silence or the destruction of language; postmodernism accepts the division and uses language and self-definition — much as Descartes interpreted thinking — as the basis of identity. Modernism tends, as a consequence, to be more mystical in

the traditional senses of that word whereas post-modernism, for all its seeming mysticism, is irrevocably worldly and social. Rather than T.S. Eliot's belief that poetry "is not the expression of personality, but an escape from personality," postmodernists propose the opposite.

Mazzaro's statement that "postmodernism accepts the division" simply ignores the poetry of Robert Bly, Galway Kinnell, James Wright, Gary Snyder and other contemporary poets working in the romantic tradition which Paul Breslin has aptly named "psychological pastoral." When, for example, at the close of "Late November in a Field," James Wright says:

> I have nothing to ask a blessing for,
> Except these words.
> I wish they were
> Grass.

he is, to use Mazzaro's language, "proposing silence or the destruction of language." In short, Mazzaro's formulation simply does not apply to a significant segment of postmodern American poetry. More troublesome, however, is Mazzaro's assumption that the character of poetry is determined primarily by epistemology, by the way in which the poet "conceives of language." Nowhere in the paragraph above does Mazzaro suggest why the conception of language "as a fall from unity" is more significant for a *poet* writing in verse than for any other educated user of "language."

Harold Bloom's approach, in *The Princeton Encyclopedia of Poetry and Poetics* is, like Mazzaro's, epistemological. According to Bloom, "The *stance*" of "the strongest and most characteristic poetry of the late 1960's and early 1970's, a transcendental synthesis of the various native strains," ignores the "bogus" issue of whether to write in closed or open "phrased fields," and, "in order to escape the fall into the confessional," performs "a deliberate curtailment of the revisionary impulse toward an endlessly journalistic scrutiny" of the self, "while simultaneously [à la Emerson] asking the fact for the form." Bloom then adduces some poetic instances and remarks: "Every passage, whether in tone, in cognitive aim, or in human stance, shows the same anxiety: to ask the fact for the form, while being fearful that the fact no longer has a form." If we translate Bloom into plain English, he means to say that the mainstream of postmodern poetry shuns confessional, strives toward organic form, and is therefore transcendental, part of a tradition that goes back to Emerson. Leaving aside the fact that the confessional mode is very much alive and, in the hands of poets like Carolyn Forché and Louise Glück, important, Bloom's thesis, while it embraces Ammons, Ashbery and a few other poets, ignores so much of our best poetry and so radically misunderstands the creative process — a process which is not, as Bloom would portray it, inherently philosophical — that it is largely unconvincing.

Postmodern American poetic form, from the political invective of a Baraka to the elegant assemblages of Ashbery, is *not* founded on epistemological anxiety; nor is it primarily "organic." It is *analogical.* Deprived by the modernist revolution of any sure sense of what poetic form should be, poets have increasingly turned to non-literary analogues such as conversation, confession, dream and other kinds of discourse as substitutes for the ousted "fixed forms," substitues which in many cases carry with them assumptions about rhetoric which are distinctly anti-modernist. Indeed, it is through deployment of such relatively "personal" analogues as conversation and confession that a substantial number of our poets are attempting to recover some of the favorable conditions for poetry which had seemed to obtain before the triumph of modernism.

In order to fully appreciate this analogical impulse behind much contemporary poetic form, one must understand why and in what ways the advent and eventual institutionalization (in universities) of "modernism" had rendered the poetic vocation so much more diminished than it once was. How relatively complacent that vocation had been — how reasonable the assumptions behind it had sounded — is vividly evident in the late Robert Hillyer's aesthetic will and testament, the book length essay *In Pursuit of Poetry* (1960). Hillyer, born in 1895, in East Orange, New Jersey, was eight years younger than Eliot and ten years younger than Pound. Like Eliot, he attended Harvard. Like most of the founders of American modernist poetry, he spent time in Europe: he was an ambulance driver with the French army from 1917 to 1919. But he remained a traditionalist. It was well after the period which has come to be known as "High Modernist" when the *Collected Verse of Robert Hillyer* (1934) received the Pulitzer Prize for Poetry. And when in 1944 Hillyer retired as Boylston Professor Rhetoric and Oratory at Harvard, he was considered a major American poet.

A striking aspect of *In Pursuit of Poetry* is the bitterness with which Hillyer attacks modernism. He deplores the modernists' specialization of poetry, evidenced to him by the rise of the New Criticism, and he laments their usurpation of the genteel tradition to which he, himself, belongs:

> Though the symbolism of T.S. Eliot's poetry and the incoherence of Ezra Pound's *Cantos* have served as damaging models for young men, the more nearly complete sterilization and confusion of recent American poetry 'were accomplished by the New Criticism.

He attacks the modernists' formal innovations such as "free verse," comparing it to "a river the banks of which are removed so that it spreads out without restraint into a marsh," and he rejects what might be termed the pessimistic vision of most modernist poetry, chiding Eliot for his *"self-pity,* a dreadful element in any art," and Auden for being, in such poems as "Miss Gee. A Ballad," completely *heartless"*:

> This general rejection of humanity, this stripping away of a mystery and aspiration is the result of a materialistic, mechanistic point of view so closely allied to the self-destructive elements of the age that the poet's continuous complaints about them become a colloquy between the pot and the kettle .... To mention the human soul in the presence of such poetry would be embarrassing.

The traditionalist conception of poetic form which Hillyer proposes has a cut-and dried quality which any postmodern poet might envy; for Hillyer's conception of the universe provides the very model for traditional poetic form, for meter:

> Intricate though verse seems, it is a more natural form of expression than prose. Verse means a turning, and since the turn must come full circle on itself, we speak of it as a repeating, or recurrent, rhythm, just as in music. Prose rhythm is non-recurrent; hence, verse is more natural because it is closer to the rhythms of the universe — and note that *universe* means a concerted turning . . . we are metrical creatures in a metrical universe.

Hillyer's notion of poetic form and his defense of what we now call the "fixed forms" follow immediately from his view of a "metrical universe":

The main forms . . . have developed through centuries and are the result of endless experiment. Their roots go as deep as the languages, and those that we still have with us are so natural that they might almost be cited as examples of Darwinian survival of the fittest. How foolish it is for defenders of free verse to maintain that these metrical structures are not natural. Free verse has no roots at all, and is itself an unnatural departure from the ebb and flow of all things.

Hillyer classifies the language of poetry into two styles, "the *rhetorical,* heightened and dignified, and the *conversational,* informal and familiar . . . . Each has its dangers as well as its virtues; the first may become bombastic, the second prosaic." The poet's choice of a style must be governed, Hillyer says, by the idiom that is "considered most appropriate for the expression of his idea." Similarly, if — as Hillyer suggests — poetry may be loosely classified into "epic, dramatic and lyric," then certain meters are appropriate to certain modes: blank verse to the English language epic and dramatic modes, "three- or four-stress verse and divided into stanzas" to "pure lyrics." Hillyer sees rhyme as "the one string we have added to the Greek lyre": whereas "it enriches the harmonies of purely lyric poetry, and it makes verse easier to remember by heart," it "remains . . . an adornment and is not essential to poetry, as is demonstrated by the great body of our poetry that is written in blank verse."

Hillyer's conception of the role and the mission of the poet follows, likewise, from his view of the universe as an orderly and essentially benign entity:

A good poet is at home in his countryside and his world, and at one with the spirits and traditions of the past. These truths, however, are but aspects of the one truth that poetry is the highest expression of what is most natural to man in every phase of his life. The single idea of the poet is to create from disharmony, harmony; from formlessness, form . . .

As an illustration, Hillyer says that "the majority of the modern poets" who give him "satisfaction," poets such as "Bridges, Frost, Robinson, Hodgson . . . Yeats, Stephens and Gogarty, regard life, in spite of its dissonances, as essentially a harmony in which they are a part. They are at home in this world."

The posture of alienated romantic, for Hillyer, is very nearly a disqualification from poetry. His metaphor for the sensibility that brings harmony from dissonance is a Wordsworthian one, imaging not the sensibility of an isolated and extraordinary individual but a communal sensibility, collectively attained:

> the poet is the stained-glass window that transmits sunlight just as ordinary windows do, but colors it as it passes through. And the poet should rest content with that; no man is great enough to be both the window and the sunlight. And no man should be so perverse as to be merely a distorting glass.

Implicit in this figure is not only an appeal to tradition, but also the sense of a congregation to share that tradition. Perhaps this is the most enviable aspect of Hillyer's conception of poetry:

> All art, in spite of many modern tendencies to the contrary, is more or less enduring as its intention is more or less communal, granted that the receptive community is the intelligent and responsive part of the general population. That is a minority and always has been.

Elsewhere, Hillyer remarks, rather poignantly:

> There is so little reading of poetry nowadays. One reason for the decline of appreciation is the fact that poetry is so seldom read in family groups any more, or among teachers and pupils as a recreation rather than an assignment. And then, of course, so few people know how to read aloud.

The "decline of appreciation" which Hillyer remarks — the apparent end of a tradition in which a family might, instead of watching television, spend an evening reading aloud from Stevenson's *Home Book of Verse* — is nowhere more tersely described than in Edward Mendelson's introduction to *Early Auden*:

> Among the historical crises faced, and, in part invented, by modernism was a breakdown in what might be called the symbolic contract, the common frame of reference and expectation that joins a

poet with a finite audience, and joins both with the subjects of his poem.

Lionel Trilling is more explicit than Mendelson. He suggests that the debunking of the very communal kind of art that Hillyer defends was a deliberately conceived element of the cultural politics of the modernist overthrow:

> Any historian of the literature of the modern age will take virtually for granted the adversary intention, the actually subversive intention, that characterizes modern writing — he will perceive its clear purpose of detaching the reader from the habits of thought and feeling that the larger culture imposes, of giving him a ground and a vantage point from which to judge and condemn, and perhaps revise, the culture that produced him.

Would any of today's really important poets in America accept Hillyer's comforting view of a metrical universe? Unlikely. But few of them, I suspect, would not envy Hillyer's pre-modernist image of the poetic vocation — of a world in which poetry enjoyed some general popularity, in which the poet could deploy with confidence a repertoire of fixed poetic forms. One cannot, of course, deny the desirability of many aspects of the modernist tradition. One need only open any copy of *Georgian Poetry* to observe that the rhetorical tradition against which the imagists reacted was far staler and more exhausted than Hillyer admits. Moreover, while the great modernist experiments were being conducted, it was inevitable that the experimenters see themselves as specialists, and it is no accident that the metaphor at the heart of Eliot's "Tradition and the Individual Talent" is drawn from chemistry: it required "scientists" to synthesize the new compounds, the new "art-emotions" that would replace the old. But the resulting losses were immense and have not yet been fully tallied. Just as Hillyer complained, the revolution has left the poet in America a bureaucratic specialist isolated in a university as in a laboratory, conducting endless experiments with poetic form, and in an adversary relation to the general culture.

Postmodern poetic form in American poetry is best understood as a reaction to the situation I have described; it is, however, variously also an attempt to recover, or at least pretend that there could now exist, favorable conditions analogous to those which Hillyer so intrepidly took for granted. Such form is not, as critics like Bloom would have us believe, Emersonian. That is to say, it is not "organic"; for Bloom's notion that a poem "ask the fact for form" is no more than the conventional organic theory of poetic form, a restatement, for example, of Denise Levertov's dictum that "form is never more than a *revelation* of content," a restatement in which Bloom has substituted "the fact" for "content." Perhaps oddly, the true notion of form which underlies our postmodern poetry, regardless of whether a given poem is in free verse or accentual-syllabic meter, is quite similar to Hillyer's pre-modernist conception of the "fixed forms." It refers to a category. When "form" is conceived and applied as a category, in conjunction with the word "content," "content" must, likewise, be restricted so as to refer to a category of subject matter. Thus the "form" of a poem is a container; the poem's "content" is what is contained. But, it will be immediately objected, the form of most contemporary poems does not fit any known category. My answer to this is that our poems *do* fit formal categories — categories which poets are quite aware of but which, because the aesthetics of modernism has generated so much (often deliberate) mystification, have remained implicit. One of Allen Ginsberg's longest poems, for example, is called a "sutra." Some of Richard Hugo's poems are in the form of "letters." Much of William Stafford's poetry is a mimeses of conversation. Poets like Louise Glück or Carolyn Forché often resort to a rhetoric, a "form" which, in all its details, resembles psychological and religious confession. Certainly some of Galway Kinnell's poems are attempts to imitate something like "primitive song," a sort of scream issuing not from a specific individual but from an archetypal, prehistoric human.

Whether it pretends to be a sutra, a letter, psychiatric confession, talk, primitive song, or whatnot, when a poem uses some non-literary analogue as a basis for its form, the name of the analogue becomes, in effect, the name of a category of form. To talk sensibly about postmodern poetic form, instead of resorting to vague, "organic" mystifications, all we need do is: 1) *to recognize that postmodern poetic form is predominantly analogical;* 2) *to extend the range of categories by which we refer to poems, using the analogues to name these categories.* In fact, if an analogical poem is any good, the name of its formal "category" will **tell** us far more about the poem than even a term like "sonnet" or "villanelle." Consider the following poem by Gary Gildner:

FIRST PRACTICE

After the doctor checked to see
we weren't ruptured,

the man with the short cigar took us
under the grade school,
where we went in case of attack
or storm, and said
he was Clifford Hill, he was
a man who believed dogs
ate dogs, he had once killed
for his country, and if
there were any girls present
for them to leave now.
                       No one
left. OK, he said, he said I take
that to mean you are hungry
men who hate to lose as much
as I do. OK. Then
he made two lines of us
facing each other,
and across the way, he said,
is the man you hate most
in the world,
and if we are to win
that title I want to see how.
But I don't want to see
any marks when you're dressed,
he said. He said, *Now.*

    I suggest that the term "conversation" poem will tell us a great deal about "First Practice." It tells us that the author is speaking in his own person, directly to the reader. It tells us that, if the poem is going to be a successful mimesis of conversation, the prosody will have to seem relatively artless, yet be pronounced enough to lend the poem unity — be blank verse or very skillful free verse. It tells us that the subject matter of the poem will be relatively quotidian, and that the poem's authority — what holds our interest in it and commands our respect — will have to come not, as in confession, from the speaker's unusual suffering, not, as in a mimesis of primitive song, from the grand claims of the unconscious, nor from the speaker's literary expertise, but simply from the speaker's way of telling, his ethos, his sheer inventiveness (for this reason, the conversational analogue, though the most prevalent one in the early '80's, is the most difficult one, because it places extreme demands on the speaker to be casually brilliant.)

    "First Practice," then, is, in form, a "conversation poem" whose content is a reminiscence about high school football. Without the notion of an analogue, however, it is nearly impossible to describe this poem's form at all, let alone account for it. Is it a "lyric?" No, not in any conventional sense of that word, although it is around the length of a lyric, and its line-length, though irregular, is about that of trimeter, a meter which Hillyer conventionally associates with "lyric." Because there is no category which will simply identify this poem, we must, in order to describe it, begin by enumerating its characteristics. It is narrative, in two stanzas, in the first-person singular, past tense; it is rather short, in free verse and in conversational diction. The more we list characteristics, the more we implicitly regard the poem's "form" in what Robert Pinsky would call a "nominalist" manner — not as a category but as a unique thing-in-itself — and are drawn toward an organic conception of the poem's form. Our analogical account of its form, however, is far more accurate (as well as economical) both as to the poem's intention and final result than an "organic" account could ever be, and the reason is simple. The very term "form" as Bloom deploys it or as organicists such as Levertov do acquires such a range of reference that it becomes meaningless.

An ideal example of the limitations of the organic position is Denise Levertov's essay, "Some Notes On Organic Form." Levertov begins as follows:

> For me, back of the idea of organic form is the concept that there is a form in all things (and in our experience) which the poet can discover and reveal.

She then suggests that "poets who use prescribed form" believe that "content, reality, experience is essentially fluid and must be given form" whereas poets "who look for new [forms]" have "this sense of seeking out inherent, though not immediately apparent, form . . . ."

> A partial definition, then, of organic poetry might be that it is a method of apperception, i.e., of recognizing what we perceive, and is based on an intuition of an order, a form beyond forms, of which forms partake, and of which man's creative works are analogies, resemblances, natural allegories.

For Levertov, poetic composition happens as follows:

> . . . first there must be an experience. . . or constellation of perceptions . . . felt by the poet intensely

enough to demand of him their equivalence in words . . . .

So — as the poet stands . . . contemplating his experience, there come to him the first words of the poem: . . . The pressure of demand and the meditation on its elements culminate in a moment of vision, or crystallization in which some inkling of the correspondence between those elements occurs; and it occurs as words . . . .

According to Levertov, as the process of composition proceeds,

. . . content and form are in a state of dynamic interaction; the understanding of whether an experience is a linear sequence or a constellation raying out from and into a central focus or axis, for instance, is discoverable only in the work, not before it.

Levertov's account describes very accurately what certain stages of composition in free verse feel like. The main strength of her argument lies in her attempt to be, at all times, as specific as possible — for example in her distinction above between "linear sequence" and "constellation"; but her very willingness to be specific reveals the impossibility of the organic argument. Consider, for example, her remarks on the sonic aspect of composition:

Rhyme, chime, echo, reiteration: they . . . often are the very means, the sole means, by which the density of texture and the returning or circling of perception can be transmuted into language, apperceived. A may lead to E directly through B, C, and D; but if there then is the sharp remembrance or revisioning of A, this return must find its metric counterpart. It could do so by actual repetition of the words that spoke of A the first time . . . . Or it may be that since the return to A is now conditioned by the journey through B, C, and D, its words will not be a simple repetition but a variation . . . Again, if B and D are of a complementary nature, then their thought- or feeling-rhyme may find its corresponding word-rhyme.

Levertov then summarizes all the specific formal possibilities so painstakingly enumerated above:

> In organic poetry the metric movement, the measure, is the direct expression of the movement of perception. And the sounds, acting together with the measure, are a kind of extended onomatopoeia — i.e., they imitate not the sounds of an experience (which may well be soundless, or to which sounds contribute only incidentally) — but the feeling of an experience, its emotional tone or texture.

Her conclusion: "Form is never more than a *revelation* of content."

Levertov's argument has immense charm; but for us to wholly accept it requires inordinate faith. If, as she implies, each experience were unique, then each poem — which is the organic crystallization of an experience — would have a unique set of formal requirements for its expression, requirements which could not be anticipated. There would be an *infinite* number of ways in which "A may lead to E." This is one reason why organicists invariably use the word "form" as a blank check that can refer to *any* element of a poem. In a good poem, there are too many factors at work to be spelled out. But that is not the only reason. The organic argument, *per se,* is so extreme that, tested against any specific poem, it will not stand up. If we actually examine one of Levertov's strong poems — a poem written around the time when she conceived "Some Notes On Organic Form" — we see that, although elements of its form *do* reinforce its content, that its "form" and "content" are by no means indissoluble, that we can always discover arrangements of the poem which do not substantially alter its content. We discover, in fact, that its "content" is rather abstract. Consider, for example, her poem "Losing Track":

> Long after you have swung back
> away from me
> I think you are still with me:
>
> you come in close to the shore
> on the tide
> and nudge me awake the way
>
> a boat adrift nudges the pier:
> am I a pier
> half-in half-out of the water?

and in the pleasure of that communion
I lose track,
the moon I watch goes down, the

tide swings you away before
I know I'm
alone again long since,

mud sucking at gray and black
timbers of me,
a light growth of green dreams drying.

After the initial reading our attention is directed entirely toward the question of the poem's "content" rather than toward questions of form: we ask, "What is the poem about?" If the poem is the "crystallization" of an experience, what is the *type* of that experience? Implicit in this question is the assumption that each experience, although in many senses unique, may fit into a recognizable category; for indeed only to the extent that a poem admits the categorization of experience can it become a public rather than a wholly subjective utterance. With another reading, we conclude that "Losing Track" is about a love affair, the speaker's dazed paralysis, her helplessness, her enchantment by the intermittent sexual "communion" with "you," so that even when he is gone, she is preoccupied with him, passive: she waits for the tide to come in, the boat to return. But we also see that this "content" would be just as recognizable if the lineation of the verses were different, if the text were written in prose, if the stanza breaks were eliminated, if the order of the sentences were different, or even if some of the diction were changed. In other words, the poem's content is largely (though not entirely) independent of its form.

It will immediately be objected that when Levertov says "Form is never more than a *revelation* of content," she means by "content" something roughly akin to "feeling" — that the essence of poetry is its ability to transmute directly into language the emotional tone of experience. True enough. The problem is that Levertov's organic argument overstates its case by focusing *exclusively* on the particularity of an experience and therefore treating "content" as if content consisted exclusively of ungeneralizable "feelings." No one would argue with Levertov that unless "the feeling of an experience" has, by some mysterious process, been transmuted into language, the verse format will seem to lack a raison d'être and the resulting poem will be a failure. "Losing

Track" succeeds marvellously. With its repeated vowel-sounds, its line-breaks that make the voice crack, make the breath catch in an almost-sob, it moans and sings like blues, while its archetypal imagery of "tides," "moon," and "water" evokes the depth of the speaker's awakened sexuality, which connects her physically, like a pier, to the earth, to the sea, to the rhythms of the universe, to the world's body. We might be correct to say that in "Losing Track" prosody is no more than a "revelation of emotion"; but also to claim that its "form is no more than a revelation of content" is to blur crucial distinctions.

Although organicists such as Levertov doubtless believe in the organic argument while they compose, "organic form," like the "conversation poem," is best regarded as a prescribed type of form rather than as a method of invention. A poem whose form is "organic" is an imitation of a recognizable, indeed almost conventional type of psychic process, one that is non-rational, affective, intuitive, and (paradoxically) sub-verbal. The finished organic poem must, therefore, display the predictable tokens of such a process: it is often in the present tense, in the "lyric" radical of presentation, with the speaker talking or musing to him or herself; its prosody is apt to be flexible; its overall shape is apt to be rather plastic, and its diction is apt to be unstudied. In short, it must conceal its artifice.

"Organic," then, is itself the name of a category that can be applied to a kind of rhetoric — a rhetoric of artful spontaneity and one which is commonly associated with the traditional lyric, such as "Ode to a Nightingale," in which the speaker, overflowing with sub-verbal "feeling," sings to himself or herself. Another good contemporary example of this type of poem would be Ted Kooser's "A Summer Night":

> At the end of the street
> a porch light is burning,
> showing the way. How simple,
> how perfect it seems: the darkness,
> the white house like a passage
> through summer and into
> a snowfield. Night after night,
> the lamp comes on at dusk,
> the end of the street
> stands open and white,
> and an old woman sits there
> tending the lonely gate.

As in the Levertov poem, here, too, because the poem's content consists of feelings which are predominantly sub-verbal, we find a heavy reliance upon imagery to evoke the unspoken, subliminal deathliness as well as the profound melancholy of the evening. Tone and emotion are not, as in Gildner's "First Practice," conveyed primarily by means of voice and line-break but rather as they have to be, by means of imagery; for imagery, as Stanley Plumly has pointed out, is voiceless. It is this voicelessness which, together with the countless past echoes that make up the lyric tradition, gives the speaker of lyric his or her oddly generic quality.

"Lyric," then, like "conversation poem," is a category of poetic form, one that carries with it certain assumptions as to the nature of the speaker, type of subject-matter and type of rhetoric. Whereas Gildner's conversational analogue dictates a persona who is a particular (and rather ordinary) person, a quotidian subject-matter and a conversational rhetoric, the "lyric" category dictates a generic persona, sub-verbal subject-matter and an organic rhetoric deploying a high degree of imagery. Indeed, it is as hard to imagine Kooser writing "A Summer Night" without knowing in advance what general type of poem he had in mind, as it is to imagine Gildner writing "First Practice" without having decided in advance to make his poem a mimesis of conversation. It is in this sense that our poetry is still "fixed form." Analogues, each with its structures as to decorum, have replaced "the fixed forms."

This analogical basis for poetic form is what characterizes postmodern American poetry, if we take "postmodern" to name a literary period beginning after World War II. Historically, it is apparent that whenever the raison d'être of "fixed forms" is in question, poets wistfully propound impossible "organic" notions of poetic form to replace the seemingly dead vixed forms, while instinctively reaching for non-literary analogues as a fresh basis. The romantics, we recall, were attracted both to organicism and to analogical poetic forms: "conversation poems," precisely, or "lyrical ballads." Similarly, it is hardly an accident that Pound, wrestling in a later age with the amoebic growth of the *Cantos,* would invoke the analogies of "fugue," and "ideogram," that Eliot's *The Waste Land* invokes the collage as a formal analogy, that *The Four Quartets* invokes a musical analogy, or that *Paterson* would contain a high proportion of undigested, non-literary material. Indeed, analogical poetic form may be regarded as a manifestation of a general literary principle: the further a poem deviates from fixed-form conventions and a traditional prosody, the more it will be compelled to seek, as a basis for its form, some non-literary analogue. The self-evident quality of this principle may be appreciated if we reword it slightly. If a work of literature does not invoke, as the basis of its form, literary conventions, then, if it is to have a form, by definition that form will have to be non-literary. Thus, for example, before the "novel" in English was sufficiently developed to be the name of a genre, it tended to be a mimesis of something else, such as journalism, romance, epistolary correspondence, spiritual autobiography. Thus it is that, in any epoch, in proportion to the degree that free verse becomes normalized, the analogues underlying poetic form tend to become non-literary.

Just so, *postmodern* poetic form is *analogical* poetic form with a vengeance: though on the one hand it represents a refinement of the analogical approach to form implicit in poetry of the High Modernist period, on the other hand it evinces considerable dissatisfaction with the impersonality of modernism. Postmodern formal strategy consists, therefore, not only of extending the range of formal analogues, but also of clearly favoring "communal" analogues such as confession and conversation over such impersonal analogues as the "fugue," the "ideogram" and the "vortex." We can, in fact, order the prevalent formal analogues along a scale, to borrow Al Poulin's term, of their degree of "personalization." In the admittedly over-schematic taxonomy that results, the outlines of three domains emerge distinctly and in a significant arrangement. Near the middle of this scale, we can locate and define a large, stable body consisting of a rather conservative type of poem that is "lyric" — a poem like Levertov's "Losing Track" or Kooser's "A Summer Night," spoken by a generic, literary "I" and deploying a traditionally "organic" rhetoric. The generic quality of the "lyric" voice may be regarded as an implicit norm, rejected on the one hand by modernists such as Pound and Eliot as being too personal, modified, on the other hand, by such postmodern "confessional" poets as Lowell, Hugo, and Berryman so as to incorporate a broader, more particularized and more topical range of personal experience. To one side of the lyric norm, in the direction of greater personalization, may be located two types of poem — the "confessional" and, furthest from the center, the "conversational." The "confessional" poem, as its very name would imply, is a poem whose form is derived by analogy from the ritual of "confession," a ritual which, in its religious aspect, is Roman Catholic and which, in its secular aspect, is psychoanalytic. It is a mimesis of testimony, in which the speaker either addresses the reader (often defiantly) or addresses some other person. The sense in which "confessional" may be regarded as a greater personalization of lyric may be appreciated if we imagine a blasphemous version of Keats' "Ode to a Nightingale," in which the speaker explicitly complained, in the first person, about his sexual needs, his medical problems, his *thanatos*. By particularizing the agenda of the inner life, placing its items in history and attributing psychological cause and effect to feelings — feelings traced back to specific origins, as elements of a unique autobiography — the speaker would lose much of his generic quality and, because the subject-matter was no longer subverbal, would be no longer singing to himself, but complaining aloud to a listener.

Whereas the authority of the lyric voice finds its source in tradition, the authority of the confessional voice finds its source in the authenticity of the speaker's testimony — a testimony which must, however, transcend the narrowly personal: to some extent, the persona's story must acquire, like a saint's life, a mythic significance. The persona must become a ritual scapegoat. Carolyn Forché's long poem "Return" might serve as a paradigm of how, when the confessional analogue is successfully applied, the poem negotiates these paradoxical demands. The poem's journalistic "witnessing" for conditions in El Salvador has authenticity; yet for all the particularity of exposition, Forché is able, at the end of the poem, to convert her individual suffering into a prophetic stance:

> Your problem is not your life as it is
> in America, not that your hands, as you
> tell me, are tied to something. It is
> that you were born to an island of greed & grace
> where you have this sense of yourself
> as apart from others. It is not your right
> to feel powerless. Better people than you
> were powerless. You have not returned
> to your country, but to a life you never left.

Just as lyric modulates into confessional, so does confessional modulate into conversation. To the extent which the persona of confessional relinquishes the claim to mythic status and extraordinary suffering, he or she becomes further particularized. The conversation poem such as "First Practice" is at once the most personal and, because its subject-matter is quotidian, the most difficult type of poem to write. Its authority depends not on tradition or on authenticity but entirely upon the artistic inventiveness of the poet who, speaking in his own person, must sustain brilliant conversation. Gildner's "First Practice," a narrative conversation poem of voice, is a good paradigm of what Stanley Plumly has labelled "the prose lyric." To the degree that a conversation poem abandons narrative, it becomes discursive, modulating into the mode which it is now fashionable to call "meditative," a mode often shown to its best advantage by such poets as Marvin Bell, William Stafford, William Matthews, and Jorie Graham.

To the other side of the lyric norm, in the direction of impersonality, may be grouped respectively and in descending order of personalization those types of poems which, in various ways, elaborate and extend the modernist impulse to produce poems as objects which can exist independently of their author's implied biography. Immediately to the impersonal side may be placed what, for convenience, I will call "deep-image" poems. The "deep-image" mode, like the "imagist" movement fifty years before it, may seem in part as a reaction against personalization in poetry, recalling, in its revulsion from confessional, T. E. Hulme's earlier dictum to the "romantic" poet to "End your moan and come away." The deep-image poem attempts to treat of the self, but of a self even more generic than the self implicit in lyric. The persona of the deep-image poem is, in fact, scarcely human. The three most prevalent analogues underlying "deep image" poems are: 1) that of a modern man screaming a prehistoric, primal scream; 2) that of a modern man dreaming in prehistoric symbols; 3) as some of W. S. Merwin's poems purport to be, that of the earth itself, speaking through the poet. All three of these analogues recall Galway Kinnell's well-known formulation: "If you could keep going deeper and deeper, you'd finally not be a person either; you'd be an animal; and if you kept going deeper and deeper, you'd be a blade of grass or ultimately perhaps a stone. And if a stone could read, [poetry] would speak for it."

Within the "deep-image" tradition, the same paradox that underlies lyric — that of rendering sub-verbal material by means of language — becomes increasingly acute the further we modulate from lyric in the direction of the inhuman. By far the best poetry in this tradition is by Kinnell — poems which, like "Under the Maud Moon," deploy what I would call "primitive song" as a formal analogue. The less human, the less personal the formal analogue, the weaker deep-image poetry becomes. Consider, for example, Robert Bly's "The Hermit," a poem which deploys archetypal dream-vision as its formal analogue:

> Darkness is falling through darkness,
> Falling from ledge
> To ledge.
> There is a man whose body is perfectly whole.

He stands, the storm behind him,
And the grass blades are leaping in the wind.
Darkness is gathered in folds
About his feet.
He is no one. When we see
Him, we grow calm,
And sail on into the tunnels of joyful death.

Like a dream, the poem presents images. But whereas images in actual dreams have a powerful affect, a "numinosity" which, according to Jung (Bly's model), is proportional to the charge of "psychic energy" which they carry, such images, dried out on the printed page, are reduced to abstractions. Because language cannot render the feeling of numinosity, the poet tries, futilely, to tell us what to feel — "calm" — as we read.

The least successful formal analogue in the deep-image canon consists of the mimesis of the earth's "speech" itself, a wordless speech which is articulated verbally by the poem, with the poet, who does not appear directly, serving as a passive medium. Such a poem is W. S. Merwin's "Eyes of Summer":

All the stones have been us
and will be again
as the sun touches them you can feel
sun
and remember waking with no face
knowing that it was summer
still
when the witnesses
day after day are blinded
so that they will forget nothing

The vocabulary of the earth is elemental to the point of dullness. Translated into human words, it has the force of stale, romantic doctrine.

All three of the principal "deep-image" analogues, "primitive song," "Jungian dream-vision," "Voice-of-Earth," deal with a single type of subject matter: they purport to put us back in direct touch with a primeval mode of consciousness. As all analogues do, these carry with them certain obvious requirements as to prosodic and rhetorical decorum. Primeval consciousness, approached directly instead of through the medium of civilized institutions, does not express itself by means of heroic couplets, in a polysyllabic, abstract vocabulary or in subordinate clauses, but through free verse, through what Paul Breslin has called "a studied plainness of vocabulary," through archetypal dream-symbols, and through simple (in the case of Merwin's poem, deliberately suppressed) grammar. The decorum dictated by deep-image analogues is that of an organic rhetoric carried too often beyond the point of diminishing returns. Kinnell's "Under the Maud Moon" is successful precisely because it avoids the fallacy of imitative form. Instead of insisting on an innocence of vision commensurate with a primitive analogue, it accepts the paradox inherent in the very notion of rendering sub-verbal subject-matter in language. It deploys the primitive-song analogue as a nostalgic but *sophisticated* commentary on the human fall. Kinnell takes up his analogue longingly; but his best poems implicitly criticize the very analogue they are imitating. Consider, for example, the following passage from "Under the Maud Moon":

> The black
> wood reddens, the deathwatches inside
> begin running out of time, I can see
> the dead, crossed limbs
> longing again for the universe, I can hear
> in the wet wood the snap
> and re-snap of the same embrace being torn.
> The raindrops trying
> to put the fire out
> fall into it and are
> changed: the oath broken,
> the oath sworn between earth and water, flesh and
>   spirit, broken,
> to be sworn again,
> over and over, in the clouds, and to be broken again,
> over and over, on earth.

In this passage, Kinnell's attitude toward the purely physical world — that world which Bly and Merwin purport to accept, without qualification — is far from comfortable. The speaker's longing for it is counterbalanced by fear of it, and his sense, hunched before the fire, of being in a starkly elemental position, is counterbalanced by his clear consciousness of how far *outside* natural process (epitomized by the fire) he stands. Bly's "The Hermit" and Merwin's "Eyes of Summer," on the other hand, by taking too literally the epistemological demands inherent in their formal analogues, lack the tension generated by the necessarily paradoxical nature of achieved poetic form.

Continuing to extend our taxonomy, we may locate, contiguous with the deep-image category but in the direction of greater impersonality, poems whose forms are based upon what might be regarded as "literary" analogues: narrative poems such as Louis Simpson's Chekhovian pieces, in which the speaking voice resembles that of a novelist; dramatic monologues such as Robert Pack's recent work, in which the poet's voice vanishes altogether; the late-modernist "essay" poems such as Richard Wilbur's famous "Love Calls Us to the Things of This World," highly-crafted pieces, rich in literary diction and allusions, displaying conspicuous literary artifice, and spoken by a literary expert, a specialist. Whereas even in Merwin's "Eyes of Summer," the author retains a faint, vestigial presence as a character in his own poem, in the three types of poem above, the poet has removed himself fully as a character, and we are conscious of him only as a peripheral presence, as "The Author"; and it may be noted that, once an author has removed himself from his poem the requirements regarding prosodic and rhetorical decorum are simplified. No longer does the speaking voice have to take into account such factors as the need to sound spontaneous, sincere, "authentic." The ethos of the author is no longer directly on trial. Whereas poems based upon non-literary analogues present acute epistemological paradoxes — requirements for calculated spontaneity, for sophisticated primitivism, for mythologically resonant banal detail, for ordinary conversation with the force and staying power of art — the conventions associated with literary analogues render these modes of discourse far easier to manipulate without committing the fallacy of imitative form.

At the farthest end of the scale, absolute in their impersonality, may be grouped poems which are spoken by *nobody,* poems in which our sense even of the author's presence as a central consciousness all but disappears. These are poems in the so-called "post-modern*ist*" mode, for example, many of Ashbery's — poems which are asserted as objects and whose forms depend *entirely* upon analogues, in that they passively recapitulate all the possible modes of discourse, literary or otherwise. Such poems, placed beside the achieved conversation poem, reveal, in stark outline, the fundamental choice confronting the poet working in America today. It is a choice between analogues, between forms which, as we have seen, range from the communal to the impersonal. Curiously enough, this choice ends up being not an epistemological one but an ethical one: whether to trust the self and presume to impose upon the world, by sheer force of character, an individual aesthetic and ethical order, or to continue the modernist hegemony of Eliot and Pound, to retreat in an elitist disgust from modern civilization and indulge in the facile despair of the parodist, recapitulating all the bad languages that comprise our environment, holding our own civilization up before us as if the sad facts could only speak for themselves.

Paul Breslin

How To Read the New Contemporary Poem

To generalize about contemporary poetry is difficult, for we live in an eclectic age without a unified period style. Nonetheless, over the last seven or eight years there has been something in the air, more extensive than a school or group style, roughly comparable to the "confessional" poetry of the 1960's, in its ability to attract widespread imitation among younger poets and indiscriminate praise among critics. Usually known as "surrealism" or "the new surrealism," this idiom has existed since the early 1960s, but only at the end of the decade did it emerge as a widely shared and widely admired common style. The so-called confessional poets were having their day from 1959 to somewhere around 1968 or 1969; the surrealists have been having theirs ever since. The term "surrealism" is even less helpful here than the term "confessional" was earlier. It suggests that the unity of the current poetics derives entirely from technique, rather than from a shared set of implicit assumptions about poetry and reality. It fails to explain why Gary Snyder, who is not a surrealist at all, belongs in some respects within the definition, while such accredited surrealists as Philip Lamantia and Michael Benedikt belong outside it. The best-known poets writing in this style are W. S. Merwin, Robert Bly, James Wright, Galway Kinnell, Mark Strand, James Tate, and Charles Simic. In addition to Tate and Simic, who are still in their thirties and already well known, the younger poets of the new style include Peter Everwine, William Matthews, Gregory Orr, Richard Schramm, Greg Kuzma, and many others less advanced in their careers.

It is clear, from what people say about contemporary surrealism when they are trying to be nice, that such poetry is supposed to be terribly mysterious, profound stuff. Richard Howard says that Charles Simic's poems "come to us . . . from an enormous otherness, a distance beyond words, wrought out of remote elements of the imagination of the hinterlands." "Crunk," the pseudonymous reviewer of Robert Bly's magazine, *The Sixties,* assures us that James Wright ". . . goes long distances when he starts, and gives the impression of someone obeying ancient instincts, like some animal who spends all summer with his herd, and then migrates alone, travelling all night, drinking from old buffalo wallows." Mark Strand says that "the perils of the present, the terrifying compromises we make with the moment, the whole provisional nature of being when the self is mistrusted or simply not there, are what James Tate's work is about." The new poetry, whether surrealist or not, is a poetry of mystery — or mystification.

The kind of poetry in which meaning is explicitly stated, in other words poetry that has an argument, is not very prominent in our century. The more usual approach has been to juxtapose images and symbols so that the reader must draw the implicit connections for himself. In such poetry, context is all-important: the pattern in which the parts are arranged draws out and emphasizes certain meanings while excluding others. Such poems may be mysterious, even obscure,but if they are any good at all, they contain at least the seeds of their own interpretation. One may have to read very closely and, in the case of Eliot or Pound, trace some recondite allusions, but if one does so, one finds that the apparently disjunct parts of a poem converge on some intelligible meaning. Certainly the poetry of the 1970s, though not easy, is no more difficult than that of the early twentieth-century masters. But it is difficult in a less rewarding way. Its coherence has little to do with any context or relationship established within a particular poem, but comes instead from a shared set of rhetorical and ideological formulas that can be rearranged to make any number of more or less interchangeable poems. It has a stock rhetoric of portentousness, and all too often its mysteries are only the trivial mystifications of cant and code. To crack the code is to realize that the poetry comes, not from a vast otherness, but from a perfectly intelligible literary ideology.

If one looks for the kind of coherence that is generated by the arrangement of a particular poem, rather than a coherence existing prior to the poem, one is likely to find the new poetry rough going indeed. Here, for instance, is W. S. Merwin's poem "The Night of the Shirts," from *The Carrier of Ladders* (1970):

Oh pile of white shirts who is coming
to breathe in your shapes to carry your numbers
to appear
what hearts
are moving toward their garments here
their days
what troubles beating between arms

you look upward through
each other saying nothing has happened
and it has gone away and is sleeping
having told the same story
and we exist from within
eyes of the gods

you lie on your backs
and the wounds are not made
the blood has not heard
the boat has not turned to stone
and the dark wires to the bulb
are full of the voices of the unborn

And here is James Atlas, an intelligent poet and critic, trying to
make sense of the poem:

> What is the purpose of asking all these questions?
> Is the line "to appear" essential, or just a repetition
> of the previous line? What motivates the metony-
> mous "hearts"? Where is "here"? What is "the
> same story"? What are "the wounds," what "the
> blood?" Where does "the boat" enter in, to what
> does it refer? What suggests that it should have
> "turned to stone"? The poem has no meaning, not
> even a style; it sounds like a poor translation.

Although I cannot answer all of Atlas's questions, I can answer
most of them. But I can do so only by reading "The Night of the
Shirts" in the context of other poems like it, as an example of a
shared rhetoric.

   The first question that needs to be answered is: Where is "here"?
It is a mistake to imagine the poet in a literal situation — at the
laundry, for instance, picking up his shirts and looking at all the
other shirts awaiting their owners' return. "Here" is an interior
place, and the poem refers to shirts in the mind's eye, not shirts on

the hanger. We are inside the psyche, in some mysterious place where recurring images like "the boat" appear and undergo strange transformations — as, for example, into stone. This interior space is magical, sacred, and so it is that "we exist from within / eyes of the gods." These gods are the sacred presences within the self, and what truly exists in us comes from them; we are most truly alive when we live in the inner self. The poem is about the descent from the quotidian world into the depths of the psyche. The "it" that has gone away is the "nothing" of the previous line; the nothing that has happened disappears and becomes less than nothing. In a world where nothing happens we are left with "the same story," the descent into the self, as the only possible event.

But Merwin's poetry, unlike that of the more optimistic Bly, Wright, and Simic, is a poetry of tantalizing, failed transcendence. If we could really get far enough down in the psyche, the blood would hear and the boat would turn to stone; but the journey fails, and the poet is doomed to repeat it again and again, as indeed he has done. The shirts (apostrophized throughout the poem) represent the external life, the socialized self. They lie on their backs, but cannot fall deeply enough asleep, are not filled with the flesh and blood of the inner, unconscious life; the external world fails to become the dream. Merwin's poem becomes more intelligible, though not necessarily better, when one understands its convention of poetry as a voyage inward, a quest for union with the unconscious. That convention is the single most important rule in the new poetics, and from it all the smaller rules are generated.

Often poems in the new style offer fairly explicit portraits of the inner depths, and the composite iconography that emerges is rather consistent. Journeys inward and downward do not end in a dense tangle of repressed memories, forbidden desires, and multiple associations, as Freudian theory might lead us to expect, but in the encounter with a mysterious presence, sacred and impersonal, inhabiting an interior space. Consider, for example, James Wright's well-known short poem, "The Jewel":

> There is this cave
> In the air behind my body
> That nobody is going to touch:
> A cloister, a silence
> Closing around a blossom of fire.
> When I stand upright in the wind,
> My bones turn to dark emeralds.

Clearly, this poem describes a sacred space within the self. The vocabulary insists on enclosure and interiority, sharp demarcation from the external world. The word "cloister," of course, points to a religious content, but equally decisive is the language of synesthesia and paradox, which invites and then frustrates visualization and leaves us at last with the contemplation of a mystery. One cannot envision a "silence / Closing around a blossom of fire." The "blossom of fire," like the fire and the rose in T. S. Eliot's "Little Gidding," is an image of mystical reconciliation between living form and inchoate energy. The title, "The Jewel," applies to the sacred mental space but also to the emerald bones of the last line. This interior sacredness extends to the body as well as to the mind, transforming even the bones. Conspicuously absent from Wright's poem is any evocation of a struggle to arrive at or establish this sacred space, or any hint of its relation to the ordinary reality outside it. The imagery is completely divorced from any profane content, or any reference to time and change. In this it parts company with "Little Gidding," and its complete isolation from the external life — guarded, as it were, by the chip-on-the-shoulder third line — gives the poem a disturbingly defensive, solipsistic quality. The transcendence does not overcome any resistance, and therefore seems unreal.

Other portraits of the inner mystery have a similar ambience. Here, for example, is a passage from Charles Simic's "Knife":

We go down
An inner staircase.
We walk under the earth.
The knife lights the way.

Through bones of animals,
Water, beard of a wild boar —
We go through stones, embers,
We are after a scent.

As with Wright, we are once again inside a cave. The stones, bones, and embers suggest that it was once inhabited by primitive man; by going "through" the "bones of animals," we reenter a state more primitive still, early in our evolution. The revelations of the "inner staircase" are impersonal and archaeological, connecting the psyche to some mysterious ancient presence that is tangible but vague, like a "scent."

Much the same atmosphere informs Robert Bly's poem "Turning Inward at Last":

The dying bull is bleeding on the mountain!

But inside the mountain, untouched
By the blood,
There are antlers, bits of oak bark,
Fire, herbs are thrown down.

When the smoke touches the roof of the cave,
The green leaves burst into flame,
The air of night changes to dark water,
The mountains alter and become the sea.

Again, the poet imagines the psyche as a cave in which man has built his fires; and again this place is sacred, impersonal, and primitive. In this case it is magical as well, changing air to water and mountains to sea.

These poems have nothing to do with the Freudian unconscious, but a great deal to do with the collective theogonic unconscious proposed by Jung, who broke with Freud over the question of whether the unconscious was the abode of banished desires or the wellspring of religious revelation. Even the dream that led Jung to postulate a collective unconscious employs a rhetoric startlingly similar to that of the poetry quoted above. In that dream, recounted in *Memories, Dreams, Reflections,* Jung descends from the second story of a house to the ground floor and then into the basement. As he proceeds downward, the furnishings become progressively older. Beneath the basement lies the oldest and deepest region of all:

> I looked more closely at the floor. It was of stone slabs, and in one of these I discovered a ring. When I pulled it, the stone slab lifted, and again I saw a stairway of narrow stone steps leading down into the depths. These, too, I descended, and entered a low cave cut into the rock. Thick dust lay on the floor, and in the dust were scattered bones and broken pottery, like remains of a primitive culture. I discovered two human skulls, obviously very old and half disintegrated. Then I woke up.

For Jung, the psyche is like the house in the dream, and its deepest recesses are the cave beneath the basement. The unconscious of Freud, which contains repressed wishes and memories of early traumatic events, is but an upper story; beneath it lies a collective, impersonal unconscious, which preserves, under the modern rational personality, an "archaic" self. In the collective unconscious, religion, magic, and myth continue to live for us as they do for primitive peoples, through the production of archetypal images in dreams, fantasies, and works of art.

The status of a symbol is not the same for Jung as it is for Freud, and the difference is important in understanding the essentially Jungian poetry of the current style. Freud insisted that even a dream, the most nearly direct expression of the unconscious, was "a thought like any other," which had been repressed. The strangeness of dreams comes not from the unconscious idea — which, once understood, is perfectly intelligible — but from the elaborate disguises the unconscious idea must assume in order to escape the censorship of the ego. The images of the manifest dream are usually quite remote from the latent meaning. In order to arrive at the meaning, one must work backward through a chain of substitutions; a word or image in the manifest dream will suggest still others. Gradually some common theme emerges in all these associations, and this common theme is the clue to unconscious meaning. Freud, in a metaphor he used more than once, compared the manifest dream to the facade of an Italian church, which reveals little or nothing of the internal design. Jung, in his essay "Dream Analysis in Its Practical Application," alludes explicitly to this metaphor in contradicting Freud:

> Perhaps we may call the dream a facade, but we must remember that the fronts of most houses by no means trick or deceive us, but on the contrary, follow the plan of the building and often betray its inner arrangement. The "manifest" dream-picture is the dream itself, and contains the "latent" meaning.

Proceeding on his assumption that the dream is an autonomous structure rather than an oblique commentary on the experience of the dreamer, Jung constructed a set of fixed categories, or archetypes, to explain the meaning of symbols in dream, myth, and art. Such a system pays little attention to the historical context in which those symbols were produced, but treats them as representatives of universal categories. In Freudian interpretation, we recover part of our self-knowledge, part of our response to the external world, which we had disowned and feared; in Jungian interpretation, we must give ourselves over to the unconscious as to a god whose scripture is the dream. Jung, to his credit, was aware of the solipsistic tendency of his own psychology, and warned that a process of "individuation," connecting the collective unconscious to one's own particular situation, was necessary to prevent the unconscious from engulfing the entire self. But this part of his theory seems to have got lost in popularization and has little counterpart in the new poetry.

Although Robert Bly has made explicit use of Jungian archetypes in his poetry and in his essays on poetry, the case is rarely so simple as that. Indeed, there is no evidence that all or even most of the poets in question are avowed Jungians. But the reader will already have remarked the curious self-referentiality of symbols in the poetry I have quoted. When Bly says, "The dying bull is bleeding on the mountain," we don't know where the mountain is or why it has a dying bull on it, and we never do find out. It seems that by merely uttering the words "bull," "bleeding," and "mountain," the poet expects to awaken powerful resonances in us. Certain words, as Marvin Bell and Robert Pinsky have noticed, come up in this poetry over and over again, carrying a heavy burden of portentousness in each instance. Editing the lists of Bell and Pinsky, and adding a few candidates of my own, I come up with the following lexicon: wings, jewels, stones, silence, breath, snow, blood, eats, water, light, bones, roots, glass, absence, sleep, and darkness. Pinsky calls this vocabulary a "literary diction," and he is right, but the issue goes further than the calcification of conventions into clichés. The nouns on this list have roughly the same status in discourse as Jungian archetypes: their significance is innate and prior to context. The point is not only the predictability of the diction, but also the way in which the key words are used, as if they came to the individual poem already charged with significance.

The diction, if not quite reducible to formula, is predictable enough. If space allowed, I could present scores of examples containing two or more words from my list. Here is one from Robert Bly's "Unrest":

now the darkness is falling
In which we sleep and awake — a darkness in which
Thieves shudder, and the insane have a hunger for snow,
In which bankers dream of being buried by black stones . . . .

Here is the beginning of "She Who Was Gone," an example obtained by a "Sortes Merwinianae" in *The Moving Target*:

Passage of lights without hands
Passage of hands without lights
This water between

I take in my arms

My love whose names I cannot say
Not knowing them and having a tongue
Of dust

My love with light flowing on her like tears. . . .

Even this poem, chosen at random, does not fail us: here are "water" and "light," and the fifth through seventh lines are a sort of cadential trill on the concept of silence. Consider also these lines from Charles Simic's poem "Sleep":

My blood runs
Past dark inner cities on fire.
I climb into deep wells,
Rock bottoms and bone bottoms. . . .

Here are two passages, the first from Mark Strand's "The Stone" and the second from Gregory Orr's "A Final Aubade," which might almost be taken for parts of the same poem:

The stone lives on.
The followers of the man with the glass face
walk around it
with their glass legs
and their glass arms.   (Strand)

Behind it [the "deeper darkness"] a river flows over stones
shaped like hands. The dead with their glass legs
walk by the river. The river
seems to pass through them.   (Orr)

Or there is Galway Kinnell, in *The Book of Nightmares,* asking us

to touch
the almost imaginary bones
under the face, to hear under the laughter
the wind crying across the black stones.

But enough. A reader familiar with contemporary poetry will have encountered many passages like these.

Reading poetry that depends so much on a revealed symbolism, rather than a symbolism created by the arrangement of the poem or the exploration of a recognizable subject, one begins to wonder what consequences, if any, this interior revelation may have for life as a whole. To judge from the nature of the key words, we are being asked to dismiss the quotidian world and take refuge in the collective unconscious. Some of these words — darkness, silence, absence — tell us how inscrutable, how inaccessible to sight or hearing the inner mystery is. The more concrete nouns rarely combine to form an exact image of something in the world, but remain, in Pinsky's phrase, the names of "blank, simple substances." The diction is impersonal, animistic, primitive: all things finally come down to bone and blood, water and stone. Above these elemental realities, personality, history, and culture weave their intellectualizing and fraudulent patterns, unregarded by the enlightened poet. What motive lies behind this extreme antihumanism and this extreme preoccupation with the unconscious?

If we can withdraw our rapt gaze from the vast otherness and the old buffalo wallows, and look under our own collective nose, the motive becomes fairly obvious. The new poetry was born in the early 1960s, at the same time as the white middle-class popular radicalism usually known as the New Left. The political theory most important to that movement — the work of Herbert Marcuse, Paul Goodman, N. O. Brown, and R. D. Laing — was *psycho*-political in emphasis. These thinkers, and those who made use of them, believed that in the apparently free society of a Western democracy, political oppression occurs primarily through psychological conditioning rather than coercive force. Through socialization we are led to accept a false self, intimidated and acquiescent, while repressing our own legitimate desires. Brown and Marcuse argued that repression was not, as Freud thought, the inevitable price of life within civilization, but an unnecessary burden imposed on the individual by an unjust society and a fear-driven culture. The recovery of the repressed through the exploration of one's own psyche was inextricably bound up with any real political change.

Certainly we should be grateful to the New Left for its tireless opposition to the war in Vietnam, but in dealing with issues beyond the war it was less than successful. In retrospect much of its political thinking was mere posturing; too often, its rhetoric confused revolution with therapy. Motives are rarely pure, and for many 1960s radicals the movement offered a welcome escape from cultural guilt. The sentimental reasoning behind this self-exculpation went something like this: White Americans and western Europeans, from whom I am descended, have imposed their will on other peoples in terrible ways. What they have done to others is analogous to what they have done to their own instincts, justifying such oppression and repression by appeals to reason and law. It is the ego that has done this; away with it, therefore, and with reason and law, which are its instruments. If I side with the instincts and the unconscious, I declass myself, and my guilt falls away. In such a view, all culture, all social and political institutions, and all attempts to govern human affairs according to reason are nothing but shams, designed to aid the despotic ego in its work of repression. This caricature of New Left thinking has survived into the 1970s.

The confessional poetry that preceded the new poetry also made use of New Left psycho-politics, and sometimes did so sentimentally. But in the best work of Robert Lowell, Sylvia Plath, and Allen Ginsberg, the psyche remains in the world. When the poetry is psycho-political, it includes both parts of that hyphenated term. Its psychology is essentially Freudian — that is to say, contextual, secular, and historical. And in the heyday of the New Left this was the poetry that seemed representative. It was around the time when the New Left began to collapse that confessional poetry went out of fashion and the new poetry came in. I do not believe that this was a coincidence. The ascendancy of the new poetry represents a giving up on the outside world, a retreat from psycho-politics into a solipsistic religion of the unconscious.

This attempt to recover innocence and faith at any cost, even the abolition of social reality and the conscious self, explains the ubiquity of the most popular key word in the new poetry: "stone." Galway Kinnell, early in *The Book of Nightmares,* writes:

> I sit a moment
> by the fire, in the rain, speak
> a few words into its warmth —
> *stone   saint   smooth stone. . . .*

Simic's devotions to Saint Stone include a book title, *Somewhere Among Us a Stone Is Taking Notes,* and a poem called "Stone," beginning "Go inside a stone / That would be my way . . . I am happy to be a stone." Orr has a sequence titled "The Adventures of the Stone"; Wright begins a poem with the line, "Hiding in the church of an abandoned stone . . ."; Merwin uses the word dozens of times per volume; I have already quoted from Mark Strand's "The Stone." And there are large outcroppings elsewhere, even among poets only tangentially related to the style — like Tom Clark, who wants to be "open to the stones / really open to them." A young poet, James Richardson, has recently trumped everybody with a long poem in sixty-odd sections called "The Encyclopedia of the Stones: A Pastoral," speculating on the mental and social life of stones.

Perhaps the pastoral charm of stones is that they are the furthest things from the human — the least conscious, the simplest, the most innocent. They have never discriminated against blacks or destroyed Vietnamese villages, never deceived themselves with a clever argument or capitulated to social convention. In their modest way, stones are perfect. But there is a positive, mystical implication behind the obsession with stones, as well as a merely negative desire to be rid of cultural guilt. For this meaning we may turn again to Jung, who found, in the turbulence of his youth, that it was

> strangely reassuring and calming to sit on my stone. Somehow it would free me of all my doubts. Whenever I thought that I was the stone, the conflict ceased. "The stone has no uncertainties, no urge to communicate, and is eternally the same for thousands of years," I would think, "while I am only a passing phenomenon which bursts into all kinds of emotions, like a flame that flares up quickly and then goes out." I was but the sum of my emotions, and the Other in me was the timeless, imperishable stone.

Galway Kinnell expresses much the same idea in an interview:

> If you could go even deeper, you'd not be a person, you'd be an animal; and if you went deeper still, you'd be a blade of grass, eventually a stone. If a stone could speak, your poem would be its words.

Stone, then, is the sacred Other within — the collective, impersonal unconscious. It is our immortal part, but its immortality, like that of the lovers on the Grecian urn, is purchased at the cost of being dead: if you are not alive in the first place, you cannot die, and so become "immortal." If Keats's urn is a "cold pastoral," then the stone is the pastoral of absolute zero.

But perhaps one can go further still. In their darker moods, Merwin, Strand, Tate, and Kinnell suspect that the authentic self is not even a stone but an absence; indeed, Tate calls one of his books *Absences*. Mark Strand begins his poem "Keeping Things Whole" by saying:

In a field
I am the absence of field.
This is always the case.
Wherever I am,
I am what is missing.

And yet the concept of absence takes on a religious meaning; it means purity, abandonment of the false strivings of the ego. As James Tate puts it,

I who have no home have no distination either,
one bone against the other,
I carve what I carve
to be rid of myself by morning
by deep dreams disintegrated.

Merwin, in a tentative statement of faith sharply hedged by the opening "Maybe," shows us how nearly interchangeable with "presence" this religious absence can become:

Maybe he does not even have to exist
to exist in departures
then the first darkness falls
even there a shining is flowing from all the stones
though the eye is not yet made that can see it
saying Blessèd
are ye

Here the absence of the divinity is hypostatized into a more rarefied form of presence; the "departures" somehow become a guarantee of the existence.

It is not surprising that the attempt to graft this dismal psychology onto the psycho-political thinking of the 1960s should produce a pretty dismal sort of political poem. Even a relatively successful piece like James Wright's poem on Eisenhower and Franco suffers from a pervasive sentimentality:

Eisenhower's Visit to Franco, 1959

. . . we die of cold, and not of darkness. — Unamuno

The American hero must triumph over
The forces of darkness.
He has flown through the very light of heaven
And come down in the slow dusk
Of Spain.

Franco stands in a shining circle of police.
His arms open in welcome.
He promises all dark things
Will be hunted down.

State police yawn in the prisons.
Antonio Machado follows the moon
Down a road of white dust,
To a cave of silent children
Under the Pyrenees.
Wine darkens in stone jars in villages.
Wine sleeps in the mouths of old men, it is a
   dark red color.

Smiles glitter in Madrid.
Eisenhower has touched hands with Franco, embracing
In a glare of photographers.
Clean new bombers from America muffle their engines
And glide down now.
Their wings shine in the searchlights
Of bare fields,
In Spain.

The poem is done almost entirely in short, simple sentences, thus assuring us that the speaker is not merely a clever manipulator of language, but a sincere votary of darkness and silence. The rhetoric simply inverts the moral symbolism of cowboy movies: the bad guys are wearing the light images; the good guys are wearing the dark. The world is divided into sinister "heroes" like Eisenhower and Franco (I'm no fan of Eisenhower's, but there *is* a difference) and the heroes' victims, such as the poor in the villages of Spain, the "cave of silent children / Under the Pyrenees," and "old men" who have the "dark red color" of wine "sleeping" in their mouths. The wine is stored — where else? — in *stone* jars. The defenseless children and the enfeebled old men, the poor and the weak, are in touch with darkness, silence, and the unconscious — just like poets, just like Antonio Machado, who is invoked as their witness. The poem tacitly assumes the helplessness of the poor and the poet's identification with them. Both assumptions are sentimental and, taken together, self-exculpating: the poor are helpless victims, like poets; I'm a poet, so don't blame me. In Robert Bly's "Romans Angry About the Inner World," political struggle is similarly reduced to psychic melodrama. Life is a mental war between "the executives," who know nothing of the lives of children or of floating "joyfully on the dark places," and the representatives of "the other world," which

> is like a thorn
> In the ear of a tiny beast!
> The fingers of the executives are too thick
> To pull it out!
> It is like a jagged stone
> Flying toward them out of the darkness.

Here, once more, is the stone, come to take its notes and judge the quick and the dead.

The new poetry, to sum up, is a desperate attempt to cure the discontents of civilization by radical surgery. By removing the part of the psyche that has been tainted with the arrogance, guilt, and skepticism of the culture we live in, we may regain our innocence and our capacity for belief. But can the psyche survive such an operation, even if it were possible? And would civilization really be any better for it? The offending part is nothing less than the entire ego, which is by definition the part of the psyche that has dealings with the outer world. Without the mediation of the ego, the unconscious has no access to people and things outside the self, except, in the Jungian version, through the shadow-community of the archetypes. One can say of the currently fashionable poetics what Philip Rieff, in *The Triumph of the Therapeutic,* said of Jungian psychology: "Inside his private myth, the individual can safely claim his discharge of catholic obligations. In the ritual of dream and fantasy he gains membership in the invisible church of common meanings. A socially and politically inconsequential symbolic universe is thus constituted."

But even Jung knew better than the Jungian poets when he wrote: "If anyone should set out to replace his conscious outlook by the dictates of the unconscious . . . he would only succeed in repressing the former, and it would reappear as an unconscious compensation. The unconscious would thus have changed its face and completely reversed its position. It would have become timidly reasonable, in striking contrast to its former tone." The unconscious has become so timidly reasonable that it consents to communicate in a thoroughly predictable literary diction.

What can be done to overcome this pervasive solipsistic ideology? For one thing, critics of contemporary poetry will have to stop talking the same cant as the poets — a circular demand, for the critic of contemporary poetry is, more often than not, a poet as well. The priestly incantations of Richard Howard, et al., must give way to a dry-eyed, attentive examination of new poetry. One must begin with an accurate description of the poems one is trying to evaluate, and take it from there. One does not want to discourage poetry about the mysterious and wonderful, but a genuinely mysterious subject should be regarded as a special challenge to the poet's gifts of intellect, feeling, and language, not as a convenient excuse for trotting out one's *misterioso* vocabulary. And a truly mysterious and wonderful poem, in turn, poses exactly the same kind of challenge to the critic.

Some of the poets mired in the common style have unquestioned talent. Merwin has an exquisite ear; Kinnell an intermittent gift for daring metaphor and the explosive line; Wright, when he is not worshipping stones and bones, is often a sympathetic observer of other people, or of the midwestern landscape. It would be mean spirited not to acknowledge that they have given us some very good poetry in spite of themselves. It is pointless to speculate on what they might have done had they not followed the zeitgeist down a blind alley. The point is that we need not rush into the alley after them. It ought to be clear by this time that the unconscious is not a god, but only a part of ourselves, and one that is knowable only indirectly, through its influence on our perception of people, places, and things. It does not need a cloister or a silence that nobody is going to touch.

Charles Simic

Negative Capability and its Children

. . . . that is, when a man is capable of being in uncertainties, mysteries, doubts, without any irritable reaching after face and reason.

John Keats

Today what Keats said could be made even more specific. In place of "uncertainties," "mysteries" and "doubts," we could substitute a long list of intellectual and aesthetic events which question, revise and contradict one another on all fundamental issues. We could also bring in recent political history: all the wars, all the concentration camps and other assorted modern sufferings, and then return to Keats and ask how, in this context, are we capable of being in anything *but* uncertainties? Or, since we are thinking about poetry, ask how do we render this now overwhelming consciousness of uncertainty, mystery and doubt in our poems?

To be "capable of being in uncertainties" is to be literally in the midst. The poet is in the midst. The poem, too, is in the midst, a kind of magnet for complex historical, literary and psychological forces, as well as a way of maintaining oneself in the face of that multiplicity.

There are serious consequences to being in the midst. For instance, one is subject to influences. One experiences crises of identity. One suffers from self-consciousness. One longs for self-knowledge while realizing at the same time that under the circumstances self-knowledge can never be complete. When it comes to poetry, one has to confront the difficult question: Who or what vouches for the authenticity of the act? After more than a century of increasing and finally all-embracing suspicions regarding traditional descriptions of reality and self, the question of authenticity ceases to be merely an intellectual problem and becomes a practical one which confronts the poet daily as he or she sits down to write a poem. What words can I trust? How can I *know* that I trust them?

There are a number of replies, as we'll see, but in an age of uncertainties there has to be a particular kind of answer. It includes, for example, the notion of experiment, .that concept borrowed from science and which already appears in Wordsworth's *Advertisement to Lyrical Ballads* (1798) and implies a test, a trial, any action or process undertaken to demonstrate something not yet known, or (and this is important) to demonstrate something known and forgotten. I was simply quoting Webster's definition and he reminded me that "experimental" means based on experience rather than on theory or authority. Empiricism, yes, but with a difference. In experimental poetry it will have to be an empiricism of imagination and consciousness.

Back to the notion of being in the midst. "Given the imperfect correspondence between mind and objective reality" (Hegel), given the fact that this "imperfect correspondence" is the product of a critique of language which since the Romantics has undermined the old unity of word and object, of concept and image, then modern poetics is nothing more than the dramatization of the epistemological consequences of that disruption. Certainly, to call it "dramatic" is to suggest contending voices. My purpose here is to identify some of them and establish, as it were, their order of appearance.

We can proceed with our "translation" of Keats. We can speak of Chance in place of his "uncertainty." Is it with Keats that Chance, that major preoccupation of modern experimental poetics, enters aesthetics?

One aspect of that history is clear. Dada and then surrealism made Chance famous, made it ontological. They turned it into a weapon. Cause and effect as the archenemies. Nietzsche had already claimed that "the alleged instinct for causality is nothing more than the fear of the unusual." Fear, of course, and its offspring, habit, which is there, presumably, to minimize that fear. But isn't poetry too a habit, a convention with specific expectations of content and form which have their own causal relationship? Certainly — and this I believe was understood by these poets. So the project became one of using Chance to break the spell of our habitual literary expectations and to approach the condition of what has been called "free imagination."

There's more to it, however. There's a story, almost a parable, of how Marcel Duchamp suspended a book of Euclidian geometry by a string outside his window for several months and in all kinds of weather, and then presented the result to his sister as a birthday present, and of course as an art object. A lovely idea. Almost a philosophical gesture, a kind of ironic critique of Euclid by the elements. Even more, this example and others like it offer a fundamental revision of what we mean by creativity. In that view, the poet is not a *maker,* but someone able to detect the presence of poetry in the accidental.

This is a curious discovery, that there should be poetry at all in the accidental, that there should even be lyricism. The implications are troubling. If we say "lyricism," we imply an assertion of a human presence and will, but how do we locate even a hint of human presence in operations that have no conscious intent and are left to Chance? Is it because there's a kind of significance (meaning) which is not the function of causality? In any case, you don't achieve anonymity when you submit yourself to the law of accident. "Chance," as Antonin Artaud said, "is myself." This is a magnificent insight. It humanizes the abstraction (Chance) and shifts the problem into an entirely different area.

Pound, Olson, and that whole other tradition we are heirs to, with its theory of "Energy," perhaps provides the next step. That theory, it seems to me, accounts for this astonishing discovery that the text is always here, that the content precedes us, that the labor of the poet is to become an instrument of discovery of what has always been with us, inconspicuous in its familiarity.

Olson says "a poem is energy transferred from where the poet got it . . . by the way of the poem itself to, all the way over to, the reader." Pound called it "Vortex." Both of them were pointing to the experience of one's own existence and its dynamics as the original condition which the poet aims to repossess. And for Olson, "there's only one thing you can do about kinetic, re-enact it."

That's the key term: re-enactment. Their definitions are concerned with locating the agent that fuels the poetic act. Their hope, above all, is to give us a taste of that original preconscious complexity and unselected-ness. The problem next is how to accomplish it? And the question remains. What does Chance re-enact?

Suppose what we call Chance is simply a submission to a message from the unconscious. The random then becomes a matter of obedience to inwardness and calls for an appropriate technique.

The surrealists, as we know, took it over from professional mediums and renamed it "automatic writing." In any case, it's still an interior dictation they are after, a trance, an altered state of consciousness. Breton gives the prescription: "A monologue that flows as rapidly as possible, on which critical spirit of the subject brings no judgment to bear, which is therefore unmarred by any reticence, and which will reproduce as exactly as possible spoken thought."

Now anyone can cut up words from a newspaper and arrange them at random, while only a few have a gift of speaking in tongues, so the technique of automatic writing is problematic and in practice obviously less "automatic" than one would like. The hope that runs through Breton's writings is visionary. He was after the angelic orders. In his pronouncements there's an element of faith which in turn simplifies the actual experience.

On the surface of it, what the other modern tradition proposes has some similarity. Creeley, for example, quotes William Burroughs to describe his own technique: "There is only one thing a writer can write about: *What is in front of his senses in the moment of writing.*" Olson is even more categorical: "The objects which occur at every given moment of composition (of recognition, we can call it) are, can be, must be treated exactly as they occur therein, and not by any ideas or preconceptions from outside the poem." There's a difference, of course. The faculty implied and cultivated here, and conspicuously missing from automatic writing, is attention. Consequently, the emphasis in this kind of poetry is on clarity, precision, conciseness, although still without any attempt at interpretation. The object of attention is set down without a further comment. The aim is that "precise instant when a thing outward and objective transforms itself, or darts into the inward, the subjective." The cutting edge.

In both cases, however, the emphasis is on immediacy, and the purpose is an exchange of a particular kind of energy. In both instances, the ambition is identical: To discover an authentic ground where poetry has its being and on that spot build a new ontology.

Unfortunately, there's always the problem of language, the problem of conveying experience. It's in their respective views of language and what it does, that surrealism and imagism part company.

Surrealism suspects language and its representational powers. In its view, there's no intimacy between language and the world; the old equation, word equals object, is simply a function of habit. In addition, there's the problem of simultaneity of experience versus the linear requirements of grammar. Grammar moves in time. Only figurative language can hope to grasp the simultaneity of experience. Therefore, it's the connotative and not the denotative aspect of language that is of interest, the spark that sets off the figurative chain reaction and transcends the tyranny of the particular.

But Pound, Williams, Olson and Creeley are in turn suspicious of figures of speech. The figurative drains attention. It tends to take us elsewhere, to absent us from what is at hand. Furthermore, there's a strong commitment in their poetry to living speech. "Nothing," as Ford Madox Ford advised Pound, "that you couldn't in some circumstances, in the stress of some emotion *actually* say." As for grammar, we have their related ideas of prosody, form, and poetic line, which are nothing more than attempts to create a grammar of poetic utterance which would pay heed to the simultaneity of experience.

I think what emerges out of these apposite views is a new definition of content. The content of the poem is determined by the attitude we have toward language. Both the attentive act and the figurative act are profoundly prejudiced by the poet's subjectivity. (Heisenberg's discovery that observation alters the phenomena observed applies here.) The content is that *prejudice,* at the expense of the full range of language. This is a constant in modern poetics regardless of whether we conceive of language as the expression of a moment of attention or, as in the case of surrealism, as the imaginative flight out of that privileged moment.

Nevertheless, we find both traditions speaking of *the image,* and insisting on its importance. And yet, the contexts are very different and carry incompatible views of the nature of our common reality.

For surrealism, the characteristic of a strong image is that it derives from the spontaneous association of two very distinct realities whose relationship is grasped solely by the mind. Breton says, "the most effective image is the one that has the highest degree of arbitrariness." For the imagists, an image is "an intellectual and emotional complex in an instant of time," but a complex (we might add) derived from a perception of an existing thing. Imagism names what is there. Surrealism, on the other hand, endlessly renames what is there, as if by renaming it it could get closer to the thing itself. The goal in surrealism as in symbolism is a texture of greatest possible suggestiveness, a profusion of images whose meaning is unknown and unparaphrasable through a prior system of signification. The surrealist poet offers the imaginary as the new definition of reality, or more accurately, he equates the imaginary with a truth of a psychological order. Here, the separation between intuition and what is real is abolished. Everything is arbitrary except metaphor, which detects the essential kinship of all things.

For imagism, that "necessary angel" of Stevens's, that reality out there with its pressures and complexities is unavoidable. Imagism accepts our usual description of that reality. The image for Pound is a moment of lucidity when the world and its presence is re-enacted by consciousness in language. He calls for sincerity, care for detail, wonder, faith to the actual. Zukofsky compared what was attempted to a photo lens "free or independent of personal feelings, opinions . . . detached, unbiased." In this context, attention and imagination mean almost the same thing, a power which brings the world into focus.

The surprising outcome of many surrealist operations is that they uncover the archetypal — those great images that have mythical resonance. Perhaps we can say that the imagination (surrealist) could be best described as "mythical," providing we understand what that implies. The characteristic of that mode is that it doesn't admit dualism. It is decidedly anthropomorphic. It intuits a link between the freedom of the imagination and the world. Owen Barfield has observed that already "the Romantic image was an idol-smashing weapon meant to return men to their original participation in the phenomena." Rimbaud, too, as we know, wanted to bridge that gap. However, the vision of the romantics and symbolists was essentially tragic, while that of the surrealists is comic. The surrealist myth-maker is a comic persona in a world which is the product of a language-act, and an age in which these language-acts have proliferated.

When Arp writes of a "bladeless knife from which a handle is missing," when Norge speaks of a "time when the onion used to make people laugh," we have images, configurations, which employ archetypal elements but are not properly speaking archetypes. Instead, we have the emergence of entities which only by the force of utterance and the upheaval they cause in the imagination and thought acquire existence and even reality. These "useless objects" have a strange authority. Even as visionary acts, they consist of particulars and thus curiously provide us with a semblance of an actual experience.

For as the imagists would say, "knowledge is in particulars." Nothing is in the intellect that was not before in the senses, or Williams's well-known "no ideas but in things." At issue here is an attempt to recreate experience which preceded thought and to uncover its phenomenological ground. To allow phenomena to speak for itself. "To let that which shows itself be seen from itself in the very way in which it shows itself from itself" (Heidegger). There's a kind of responsibility here, care toward the actual, the sheer wonder of dailiness, the manner of our *being* in the world. Authenticity in imagism is primarily this confrontation with the sensuous for the sake of recreating its intensities.

The great ambition in each case is *thought.* How to think without recourse to abstractions, logic and categorical postulates? How to sensitize thought and involve it with the ambiguity of existence? Poems, in the words of the Russian formalistic critic Potebnia are a "method of simplifying the thinking process." The surrealist Benjamin Peret goes further. He says simply that "thought is one and indivisible." Eluard says somewhere that "images think for him." Breton, as we have seen, defines psychic automatism as "the actual functioning of thought." Not far is Pound with his poetry as "inspired mathematics," or Duncan's saying that a poem is "the drama of truth." These are outrageous claims, but only so if we equate thought with "reason" and its prerogatives. To say that Chance thinks wouldn't make much sense, but to admit that Chance causes thought would be closer to what these statements intend. Again Olson raises an interesting question: "The degree to which projective (that is, the kind of poem I've been calling here imagist) involves a stance toward reality outside a poem as well as a new stance towards the reality of the poem itself." This is the whole point. Obviously, the rigorous phenomenological analysis of imagination and perception that surrealists and imagists have done has opened a whole new range of unknowns which address themselves to thought, and in the process alter the premises of the poems being written and the way in which they conceive of meaning.

Current criticism has unfortunately tended to simplify that historical predicament. It has seen the developments in recent poetry only within one or another literary movement, even when the strategies of these poetries have partaken of multiple sources. One can say with some confidence that the poet writing today can no longer be bound to any one standpoint, that he no longer has the option of being a surrealist or an imagist fifty years after and to the exclusion of everything else that has been understood since. Their questioning has involved us with large and fundamental issues. Their poetics have to do with the nature of perception, with being, with psyche, with time and consciousness. Not to subject oneself to their dialectics and uncertainties is truly not to experience the age we have inherited.

The aim of every new poetics is to evolve its own concept of meaning, its own idea of what is authentic. In our case, it is the principle of uncertainty. Uncertainty is the description of that gap which consciousness proclaims: Actuality versus contingency. A new and unofficial view of our human condition. The best poetry being written today is the utterance and record of that condition and its contradictions.

Brendan Galvin

The Mumblings of Young Werther

To make a clam play an accordion is to invent not to discover
—Wallace Stevens

There's a type of poem very much among us which means to sound compassionate and which tries to tell the reader how he ought to feel about the nonspecific predicament of an often unspecified person. Here, for instance, is Peter Cooley in Avon's *The American Poetry Anthology:*

> Here, someone is lining the trees up
> row to row, a theater of echoes,
> moss the ants parade or now crickets
> his limbs, their strings in this air
> an architecture offstage
> amazing to even the stones.
>
> Later there will be rain
> peeling the night back through his faces,
> graftings, while the birds come down
> to plant the small black fruit of his eyes.
> (from "Vanishing Point")

Or again, from Michael Waters' "Leaves & Ashes" in *The Ardis Anthology of New American Poetry:*

59

Sometimes,
when the bars close,
the streets seem to whisper in rain
like women mistaken for mother.

Her skin waves on a clothesline.
Her crotch bleeds over Chinatown.
The three graces of city life
moon in a doorway:

One is called *spare change.*
One is named *fire-in-the-trashcan.*
One resembles *death on a menu.*

Maybe the dark one
hauls you to her breast
like a blind lover on wedding night.

You would like to disappear.
You imagine dawn
opening your heart like a room.
Anyone could live there.

The effect of such stanzas — and they can be found in nearly every contemporary anthology and in many poetry collections and magazines — is like overhearing a drunken stranger talking to himself in a bar mirror late at night, and about someone we have never met. We aren't admitted to these poems because we are never told what has happened in the lives of "he" and "you." No particulars of their experience are given in a coherent way that might make us assent, "Yes, it is tragic that this has happened to a human being, and we are caught up in this tragedy because we are human, and this could happen to us."

Instead, the situations of these people are mumbled over, covered with a blanket of impersonal neo-surrealist cliches like "an architecture offstage / amazing to even the stones" and "the small black fruit of his eyes," or "the streets seem to whisper in rain / like women mistaken for mother." Familiar equipment (stones, blindness, dismemberment) is manipulated. Who can take even the dismantling of these characters seriously, particularly when it involves that inexplicable and unintentionally hilarious crotch bleeding over poor Chinatown? And is "You would like to disappear" how far we've come from Rilke's "You must change your life"? As if these poets wrestled the Angel of Death each time they picked up a pen, this kind of poem is regularly defended as being "close to the bone" or "risk-ready."

While compassion tops any list of decent human feelings, it may well be the single most-overworked word in contemporary American poetry. It appears regularly on book jackets to endorse the poet's content and sincerity, and the implicit charge against readers who aren't moved by these "compassionate" poems, and against poets who don't write them in the approved tone and style, is that they lack empathy with their fellow men. Actually, poets who employ this tone (and its similarity in poet after poet obscures whatever minor differences there may be) while appropriating someone else's predicament without taking the trouble to reveal it, are being self-indulgent.

While it is more accomplished than many of its genre, David St. John's "Gin" (from *Hush,* Houghton Mifflin) is a manual of such mannerisms.

> There's a mystery
> By the river, in one of the cabins
> Shuttered with planks, its lock
> Twisted; a bunch of magazines flipped open,
> A body. A blanket stuffed with leaves
> Or lengths of rope, an empty gin bottle.
> Put down your newspaper. Look out
> Beyond the bluffs, a coal barge is passing,
> Its deck nearly
> Level with the water, where it comes back riding
> High. You start talking about nothing,
> Or that famous party, where you went dressed
> As a river. They listen,
> The man beside you touching his odd face
> In the counter top, the woman stirring tonic
> In your glass. Down the bar the talk's divorce,
> The docks, the nets
> Filling with branches and sour fish. Listen,
> I knew a woman who'd poke a hole in an egg, suck
> It clean and fill the shell with gin,
> Then walk around all day disgusting people
> Until she was so drunk
> The globe of gin broke in her hand. She'd stay
> Alone at night on the boat, come back
> Looking for another egg. That appeals to you, rocking
> For hours carving at a hollow stone. Or finding
> A trail by accident, walking the bluff's

Face. You know, your friends complain. They say
You give up only the vaguest news, and give a bakery
As your phone. Even your stories
Have no point, just lots of detail: The room
Was long and bright, small and close, angering Gaston;
They turned away to embrace him; She wore
The color out of season,
She wore hardly anything at all; Nobody died; Saturday.
These disguises of omission. Like forgetting
To say obtuse when you talk about the sun, leaving
Off the buttons as you're sewing up the coat. So,
People take the little
They know to make a marvelous stew;
Sometimes, it even resembles you. It's not so much
You cover your tracks, as that they bloom
In such false directions. This way friends who awaken
At night, beside you, awaken alone.

Portentousness is introduced immediately in the "mystery" of the first line, but by poem's end one is hard put to say just what the mystery is about. The protagonist hasn't even been identified to the point where one can say with certainty what sex he or she is. Should we take "that famous party, where you went dressed / As a river" literally? Is there anything inevitable to the poem about being dressed as a river, or is it just a clever image shoved into its slot at that juncture? Might the person just as well have gone dressed as a barge, for instance? Since the person carves a hollow stone and apparently writes pointless stories, is he/she an artist? Does the reader agree that "obtuse" is a necessary word when talking about the sun? What about the inaccuracy of giving "a bakery / As your phone"? "Gin" blooms in such false directions itself that the reader will want to ask his own questions about its sequence of weakly-related tropes, which seem to have been created to cover the lack of mystery, the absence of a "you" who might exist outside the claustrophobic atmosphere of the poem.

In such poems, the protagonist is nearly always a Young Werther whose choices are suicide or death-in-life, and the message is that we are all psychic cripples. "Infirmity truly has, under Surrealism, become a kind of horticultural verbal blight threatening 'firmess at the core'," Marianne Moore said over twenty-five years ago, and the *angst* by blueprint and near-catatonic rhythms of the poems above prove her correct. Like that monotonous patois called psychobabble, which substitute platitudes for thought, the

Mumbling Poem substitues odd imagery for direct statement, and a maundering tone for real feeling, and — yes — it patronizes the reader by *telling* him how to feel rather than *showing* him coherent particulars and letting him judge for himself.

We are in the midst of a conformity of technique different from, but as cohesive as, that in the two Hall, Pack, Simpson *New Poets of England and America* anthologies of the late '50's, and perhaps Robert Frost's shrewd introduction to the first of those is pertinent here:

> [The reader] is given his chance to see if he can tell all by himself without critical instruction the difference between the poets who wrote because they thought it would be a good idea to write and those who couldn't help writing out of a strong weakness for the muse, as for an elopement with her. There should be some way to tell that just as there is to tell the excitement of the morning from the auto-intoxication of midnight.

In other words, is there a feeling of inevitability about the poems, or are they merely arranged to *resemble* necessary statements about experience? A new form of Academicism is at work here. Written by academically-trained writers who teach in writing programs where presumably they seek tenure and promotion as other professors do, these are as much "publications" as they are poems. One sure way to publish is to imitate what is already trendy, rather than taking the time, with attendant risks, to strike off in search of one's own voice.

Horror stories of editors getting letters from young poets begging acceptance so they can get teaching jobs are common, as are stories of writers psyching out the biases of particular magazines and writing toward those biases; some creative writing students fill notebooks with bizarre, unattached images which they will later tuck into the poems they will write. There are poets who publish their pieces by the hundreds each year, without regard for quality, as if all one has to do is get his name before readers often enough, as in other types of advertising. In the face of such work, one longs for the reticence of a Larkin or Tranströmer.

The Australian poet A. D. Hope predicted this situation some years ago in an essay called "Literature versus the Universities":

> The poet trained in a school of creative writing by academic critics and taking a job in the same

atmosphere is more and more tempted . . . to produce work which, more or less unconsciously, is
written in illustration of current critical theories;
and thus reversing the proper order of nature in
which the critical theories arise to deal with the
independent raw material of the creative imagination . . . What is really disturbing is when the
young lover has the professor in bed with him and
knows his performance is being graded as a first or
second class honours, pass or fail. Writing is, or
should be, a single-minded process.

(in The Cave and the Spring: Essays on Poetry,
University of Chicago Press)

Even *Time,* in a recent review of Anne Sexton's letters, appears
to know that "a poem is a one-of-a-kind, heart-made object," but
reading those above one might think that a poem is a school neck-
tie. It's possible to tell not only who the authors admire to the
point of imitation, but which poets they studied with, and at
which universities. A good percentage of these poems are dedicated
to those who write in the same way, and many are about the
process of writing itself, surely an index of self-consciousness, if
not a symptom of terminal disease.

Curiously, or maybe predictably, few of these poets write out
of a sense of place, a location, a concrete set of external circumstances which might tempt concentration on something other
than their own cerebrations. There is no eye close on the subject,
because external objects are appropriated merely as glosses for the
mind, and rarely does the reader feel the rhythms of experience as
one does in Lawrence's animal poems or in Frost's poems about
physical work, for instance. A poet has to know **where** he succeeds
and where he fails, and the reasons why. If there is no anchor in
reality, he can't go back again to the events that generated the
poem; if a poem's genesis is internal, it can hardly be subject to
external corroboration.

The true risk is still in presenting felt expressions of the way
things are, statements that move the inner life of the hearer because they offer him a truth deeper than one he previously knew.
Perhaps as an antidote to "Gin," I want to close with a poem that
is plain-spoken and proves to me that clarity is still the deepest
mystery of all; and that real *frisson* doesn't come from hyperbole,
but from understatement; that Godzilla is a comic figure when set
beside the likes of Peter Quint. The poem is "Stove," from Philip
Booth's collection, *Available Light* (Viking).

I wake up in the bed my grandmother died in.
November rain. The whole house is cold.
Long stairs, two rooms through to the kitchen:
walls that haven't been painted
in sixty years. They must have shone then:
pale sun, new pumpkin, old pine.

Nothing shines now but the nickel trim
on the grandmother stove, an iron invention
the whole room leans to surround; even
when it is dead the dogs sleep close behind it.
Now they bark out, but let rain return them;
they can smell how the stove is going to be lit.

Small chips of pine from the woodshed. Then
hardwood kindling. I build it all into the firebox,
on top of loose wads of last June's *Bangor News*.
Under the grate, my first match
catches. Flames congregate, the dogs watch,
the stove begins to attend old wisdom.

After the first noisy moments, I listen for Lora;
she cooked all the mornings my grandmother died,
she ruled the whole kitchen the year I was seven:
I can see Boyd Varnum, a post outside the side door;
he's waiting for Lora, up in the front of the house,
to get right change for his winter squash. Lora says

Boyd's got the best winter squash in the village.
When Boyd gets paid, she ties her apron back on
and lets in the eggman. He has a green wagon.
Lora tells him how last night her husband hit her;
she shows him the marks. All her bruised arms
adjust dampers and vents; under the plates where turnips

are coming to boil, she shifts both pies in the oven.
The dogs feel warmer now. I bank on thick coal.
The panes steam up as sure as November: rain,
school, a talkative stove to come home to at noon;
and Lora sets my red mittens to dry on the nickel shelves
next to the stovepipe. Lora knitted my mittens.

I can still smell the litter of spaniels
whelped between the stove and the wall; there's

venison cooking, there's milktoast being warmed on
the furthest back plate, milktoast to send upstairs
to my dead mother's mother. Because, Lora says,
she is sick. Lora says she is awful sick. When Lora goes up

to my grandmother's bed, I play with the puppies
under the stove; after they suckle and go back to sleep,
because I am in second grade and am seven, I practice
reading the black iron letters raised on the black oven door;
even though I don't know who Queen Clarion was,
I'm proud I can read what the oven door says: it says
                    Queen Clarion
                    Wood & Bishop
                    Bangor, Maine
                    1911

Galway Kinnell

Poetry, Personality, and Death

In this little poem by Stephen Crane, I find an image which stands as the portrait of us all:

> In the desert
> I saw a creature, naked, bestial,
> Who squatting upon the ground,
> Held his heart in his hands,
> And ate of it.
> I said, "Is it good, friend?"
> "It is bitter — bitter," he answered;
> "But I like it
> Because it is bitter,
> And because it is my heart."

The poetry of this century is marked by extreme self-absorption. So we have been a "school" of self-dissection, the so-called confessional poets, who sometimes strike me as being interested in their own experience to the exclusion of everyone else's. Even Robert Lowell, in *Life Studies* — that rich, lively book which remains more fascinating than all but a few of the books of its time — puts me off somewhat by the strange pride — possibly the pride by which the book lives — that he takes in his own suffering.

I was on a bus some years ago, when a man suddenly spoke up in a loud, pained voice: "You don't know how I suffer! No one on this bus suffers the way I do!" Somebody in the back called out,

To the desert, to the parched places, to the landscape of zeros;
And I shall give myself away to the father of righteousness,
The stones of cheerfulness, the steel of money, the father of
    rocks.

The individual lines are strong; yet the poem as a whole leaves
me unsatisfied, as do all poems which divide men into two kinds.
Someone less unwilling to reveal himself might have reversed the
positives and negatives. But if Bly had said, "To the mother of
solitude will I give myself / Away, to the mother of love . . .,"
then he would, perhaps, have been obliged, in the second stanza,
to say, "And yet I give myself, also, to the father of righteousness . . . ." Speaking in his own voice, the voice of a complicated
individual, he would have been forced to be lucid regarding his
own ambiguous allegiances. Bly stumbles as if through fear into
setting up this simplified *persona,* the "busy man."

A *persona* has its uses, and also its dangers. In theory, it would
be a way to get past the self, to dissolve the barrier between poet
and reader. Writing in the voice of another, the poet would open
himself to that person. All that would be required would be for
the reader to make the same act of sympathetic identification, and,
in the *persona,* poet and reader would meet as one. Of course, for
the poem to be interesting, the *persona* would have to represent a
central facet of the poet's self; the kind of thing Browning's
dramatic monologues do very well, prose fiction does much better.

In the voice of J. Alfred Prufrock, Eliot expressed his own
sense of futility and his own wish to die. Without the use of the
persona Eliot might not have been able to express this at all, for
isn't it embarrassing for a young man to admit to feeling so old?
The *persona* makes it OK. For the same reason, it is an evasion. As
he develops his character, even Eliot forgets that this sense of
futility and this wish to die are his own, as well as Prufrock's. The
persona makes it unnecessary for him to confront the sources of
these feelings or to explore their consequences in himself. It functions like the Freudian dream, fictionalizing what one does not
want to know is real.

The problem is similar in James Dickey's "The Firebombing,"
the most famous *persona* poem of recent years. In his attack on
the poem — an attack almost as famous as the poem — Robert Bly
says:

> If the anguish in this poem were real, we would
> feel terrible remorse as we read, we would stop
> what we were doing, we would break the television

set with an axe, we would throw ourselves on the
ground sobbing.

Oddly enough, Dickey, in the poem, accuses his *persona* of just
that indecent coldness of which Bly accused Dickey, and in much
the same terms:

> My hat should crawl on my head
> in streetcars, thinking of it,
> the fat on my body should pale.

Over and over in the poem, Dickey makes clear the moral limits of
his *persona,* that exfirebomber whose aesthetic relish in his exploits
was a function of his lack of imagination, his inability to conceive
of the persons he killed, and who lives ever after in confusion and
unresolved guilt.

The poem is not about the pleasure of war, but about the
failures of character which make war, or mechanized war, possible.
And yet, Bly's criticism is not irrelevant. I, too, find something in
this poem which makes me uneasy, something which has to do, I
think, with the evasions permitted by the use of the *persona.*

In an essay James Dickey wrote on the *persona* in poetry, he
says,

> A true poet can write with utter convincingness
> about "his" career as a sex murderer, and then in
> the next poem with equal conviction about tender-
> ness and children and self-sacrifice.

This is true. Even a poet who does not write "dramatic" poetry,
who writes only about himself, must experience all manner of
human emotions, since he uses the words which express these
emotions. As Whitman says,

> Latent in a great user of words, must be all passions,
> crimes, trades, animals, stars, God, sex, the past,
> might, space, metals, and the like — because these
> are the words, and he who is not these, plays with
> a foreign tongue, turning helplessly to dictionaries
> and authorities.

I admire James Dickey for exposing the firebomber within himself
— particularly since the firebomber does appear to be a central
facet of Dickey's makeup. It is a courageous act. Few poets would

"Rent a hall!" Someone else said, "Do you want to borrow my crutches?" and actually produced a pair of crutches and offered them across the aisle. The man tapped his knee and looked out the window with an exasperated expression, as if to say, "I wish there weren't so many nuts riding the buses." What I would like to find in poetry, as on that bus, is one who could express the pain of everyone.

Robert Bly's poems often seem liberated from this self-absorbed, closed ego. In his first two books Bly avoids specific autobiographical detail almost entirely. Though he speaks in the first person about intimate feelings, the self has somehow been erased. The "I" is not any particular person, a man like the rest of us, who has sweated, cursed, loathed himself, hated, envied, been cold-hearted, mean, frightened, unforgiving, ambitious, and so on. Rather it is a person of total mental health, an ideal "I" who has more in common with ancient Chinese poets than with anyone alive in the United States today. This would be a blessing for all of us if Bly had really succeeded in "transcending" personality in his poetry. But I think he has not. He simply has not dealt with it. He has been vehement about getting rid of old poeticisms, and this he has done: his poetry is, indeed, contemporary; it is his role as poet he has borrowed out of old literature.

This borrowed self, this disguise, may be deliberate, the consequence of a theory of impersonality. It seems to spring, too, from a compulsive need for secrecy, from the poet's reluctance to reveal himself in his poems. Consider this poem, "The Busy Man Speaks":

> Not to the mother of solitude will I give myself
> Away, not to the mother of love, nor to the mother of
>   conversation,
> Nor to the mother of art, not the mother
> Of tears, not the mother of the ocean;
> Not to the mother of sorrow, not the mother
> Of the downcast face, nor the mother of the suffering of
>   death;
> Not to the mother of the night full of crickets,
> Nor the mother of the open fields, nor the mother of Christ.
>
> But I will give myself to the father of righteousness, the father
> Of cheerfulness, who is also the father of rocks,
> Who is also the father of perfect gestures;
> From the Chase National Bank
> An arm of flame has come, and I am drawn

be as willing to reveal their inner sickness, and we can be sure that many poets seem healthier than Dickey only because they tell us less about themselves.

Yet revelation alone is not sufficient. In the same essay on the *persona*, Dickey has this curious sentence — curious for what it fails to say:

> The activity [of poetry] gives the poet a chance to confront and dramatize parts of himself that otherwise would not have surfaced.

Between "confront" and "dramatize," aren't certain crucial verbs missing? If Dickey does feel as close to his *persona* as he seems to, if he feels within himself a deadness of imagination regarding those whom he hurts, if he himself even vicariously takes aesthetic pleasure in killing, can't we expect him, as a poet, to explore this region of himself — not merely to dramatize it as though it belonged to another? We don't ask that he suppress the firebomber within; on the contrary, we want him to try to find out what it means in his own life. Thoreau said, "Be it life or death, we crave only reality." Dickey does not accept the risk of this search, the risk that in finding reality we may find only death; that we may find no sources of transfiguration, only regret and pain. Instead, he uses a *persona* as a way out, in much the same way Eliot does.

In *Earth House Hold,* Gary Snyder points out that

> The archaic and primitive ritual dramas, which acknowledged all sides of human nature, including the destructive, demonic, and ambivalent, were liberating and harmonizing.

Neither liberation nor harmony can result from "The Firebombing," for the drama it enacts has no protagonist: now it is the poet, now it is someone else invented to bear the onus the poet does not care to take on himself. As a result, this poem trying to clarify the sources of war adds to our confusion.

We can't understand this phenomenon in poetry — this closed, unshared "I" — unless we look at its source, the closed ego of modern man, the neurotic burden which to some degree cripples us all. I mean that ego which separates us from the life of the planet, which keeps us apart from one another, which makes us feel self-conscious, inadequate, lonely, suspicious, possessive, jealous, awkward, fearful, and hostile; which thwarts our deepest desire, which is to be one with all creation. We moderns, who like to see ourselves as victims of life — victims of the so-called absurd condition — are in truth its frustrated conquerors. Our alienation is in proportion to our success in subjugating it. The more we conquer nature, the more nature becomes our enemy, and since we are, like it or not, creatures of nature, the more we make an enemy of the very life within us.

Alchemy, the search for the philosopher's stone, was, on the surface, an attempt to master nature, to change base metals into gold; secretly, however, it was a symbolic science, and its occult aim was to propitiate the sexual, creative forces in nature, and to transfigure the inner life. When a chemistry finally overthrew alchemy, in the seventeenth century, it was a decisive moment, among all the other decisive moments of that century. Overtly a quest for pure knowledge, chemistry derives its enormous energy from the desire to subdue and harness.

This is the case, of course, with the whole scientific and technological enterprise. The fatal moment was when the human mind learned the knack of detaching itself from what it studied, even when what it studied was itself. The mind became pure will: immaterial, unattached, free of the traumas of birth and death. Turned on any natural thing, the eye trained to scientific objectivity and glowing with the impersonal spirit of conquest becomes a deathray. What it kills is the creative relationship between man and thing. In the science fiction stories that scientists sometimes write on the side, they often reveal the fantasies of cosmic hostility which lurk unobserved in their learned treatises.

Not long ago it was commonly supposed that the scientific spirit would solve our social ills. We heard talk of a "cultural lag," according to which we had gained control over nature but not yet over ourselves. Science was to cure that. We now know that science is the trouble. I cannot forget how, in those days when our involvement in Vietnam was just beginning, so many social scientists blithely stepped forward to defend our madness. They were not bloodthirsty men; for the most part they were polite, mild, and well-meaning. But they saw Vietnam in geopolitical terms, as an objective, technological problem, to be dealt with by technological and social-scientific means. The United States undertook this most stupid of wars, during which so many have died, die, and will die for nothing, in exactly the same spirit in which it undertakes the exploration of space — as a challenge to our technology: *Can we do it!* Did I say, "die for nothing?" That is not quite it. They died for science.

One might have thought the Americans would be more likely to die for material gain. But no, America is not a materialist country. Perhaps there has never existed a people who cared less for material. We despise it. The effort of our technology is to turn us into nearly immaterial beings who live in a nearly immaterial world. Our most pervasive invention, plastic, is an antimaterial; it puts up no resistance, it never had its own form, it is totally subject to our will, and relative to organic materials, which return to the life cycle, it is immortal. We spend billions of dollars trying to render our bodies acceptable to our alienated condition: as odorless, hairless, sanitary and neutral as plastic. Americans who are white feel that the black man with his greater physical grace, spontaneity, and "soul" resides closer to nature, and therefore regard him as a traitor to mankind, and fear him.

This attempt to transcend materiality is, of course, a worldwide phenomenon, involving all countries and all races. It is only that the white American has taken the lead. He is the one marked and transfigured by the technological age — and I mean "transfigured" literally. What else can one make of the changes that have come over the European face after it migrated to technological America? Contrast the ancestral faces one still sees in Europe, contrast the faces in old paintings and photographs. Is it just in my imagination that the American chin has thickened, its very bones swollen, as if to repel what lies ahead? And those broad, smooth, curving, translucent eyelids, that gave such mystery to the eyes — is it my private delusion that they have disappeared, permanently rolled themselves up, turning the eyes into windows without curtains, not to be taken by surprise again? And that the nose, the feature unique to man, the part of him which moves first into the unknown, has become on our faces a small, neat bump? Maybe only healthily large teeth cause the lips to protrude, giving the all-American mouth its odd, simian pucker.

That the human face has changed at all is, of course, a question. I have perceptive friends who assure me the American face differs in no way from its European sources. These things are all guesses, and guessing itself can make it so. But Max Picard so loved the human face, so carefully meditated on it, that I have to believe something of his sense of its fall. He writes — and I choose a passage from *The Human Face* almost at random:

> In our day, it seems sometimes that were eternity but to touch it, the face of a man must fall apart, even as a ghost collapses at the touch of holy reality . . . .

> In such a face there is a fear that it may be the last. It is timorous, lest from it be taken, and it cowers

within itself, it holds itself tightly, it becomes sharp and shiny. Such a face is like polished metal. It is like a metallic model: cold. It is fashioned to endure, but not based upon eternity as were the faces of olden days. Such a face watches constantly over itself. It even fears to rest at night, so mistrustful is it of its very own sleep.

I spent a year not long ago in Southern California. There I saw men with these changed faces willing to do anything — pollute, bulldoze, ravage, lay waste — as long as it made money. That seemed in character. What surprised me was that they were willing to do it even if it didn't make money. California matters because it represents the future of the rest of us; it is a huge mirror set up on the western shore of what we shall become, just as the United States mirrors the future of the world. The Asians, too, appear to adore our technology — some of them doubtless worshiping it even while it burns them to death.

Yet one sees signs around us of the efforts to reintegrate ourselves with life. One sees it in poetry, perhaps particularly in poetry. For poetry has taken on itself the task of breaking out of the closed ego. To quote from Gary Snyder again:

> Of all the streams of civilized tradition with roots in the paleolithic, poetry is one of the few that can realistically claim an unchanged function and a relevance which will outlast most of the activities that surround us today. Poets, as few others, must live close to the world that primitive men are in: the world, in its nakedness, which is fundamental for all of us — birth, love, death; the sheer fact of being alive.

The first important poem of this new undertaking is Allen Ginsberg's "Howl." It is the first modern poem fully to break out, fully to open itself. It is a poem which *consists* of autobiography, just as confessional poetry does; yet at the same time it transcends autobiography and speaks on behalf of everyone. "Howl" has become the most famous poem of its time less by its "style" or "subject matter" than by this inner generosity.

"Howl" suffers the self, it does not step around it. It gets beyond personality by going through it. This is true of much of the interesting poetry of today. It is one reason that Robert Bly's prose poems are so moving. For the first time in his poetry, Bly in

The Morning Glory speaks to us — and for us — in his own voice. As one reads, the "I" in the poem becomes oneself.

I am in a cliff-hollow, surrounded by fossils and furry shells. The sea breathes and breathes under the new moon. Suddenly it rises, hurrying into the long crevices in the rock shelves, it rises like a woman's belly as if nine months has passed in a second; rising like milk to the tiny veins, it overflows like a snake going over a low wall.

I have the sensation that half an inch under my skin there are nomad bands, stringy-legged men with firesticks and wide-eyed babies. The rocks with their backs turned to me have something spiritual in them. On these rocks I am not afraid of death; death is like the sound of the motor in an airplane as we fly, the sound so steady and comforting. And I Still haven't found the woman I loved in some former life — how could I, when I loved only once on this rock, though twice in the moon, and three times in the rising water. Two spirit-children leap toward me, shouting, arms in the air. A bird with long wings comes flying toward me in the dusk, pumping just over the darkening waves. He has flown around the whole planet, it has taken him centuries. He returns to me the lean-legged runner laughing as he runs through the stringy grasses, and gives back to me my buttons, and the soft sleeves of my sweater.

The poem is personal yet common, open yet mysterious. For the moment of the poem, I, too, have loved "only once on this rock, though twice in the moon, and three times in the rising water."

We move toward a poetry in which the poet seeks an inner liberation by going so deeply into himself — into the worst of himself as well as the best — that he suddenly finds he is everyone. In James Wright's "The Life," whatever is autobiographical — and the reference in the first stanza must have its origin in something very personal and particular in Wright's life — is transmuted, opens out as the inner autobiography of us all:

Murdered, I went, risen,
Where the murderers are,
That black ditch
Of river.

And if I come back to my only country
With a white rose on my shoulder,

What is that to you?
It is the grave
In blossom.

It is the trillium of darkness,
It is hell, it is the beginning of winter,
It is a ghost town of Etruscans who have no names
Any more.

It is the old loneliness.
It is.
And it is
The last time.

That poem, and the following passage from John Logan's poem, "Spring of the Thief," are among the great, self-transcending moments of contemporary poetry.

Ekelof said there is a freshness
nothing can destroy in us —
not even we ourselves.
Perhaps that
Freshness is the changed name of God.
Where all the monsters also hide
I bear him in the ocean of my blood
and in the pulp of my enormous head.
He lives beneath the unkempt potter's grass
of my belly and chest.
I feel his terrible, aged
heart
moving under mine . . . can see the shadows
of the gorgeous light
that plays at the edges of his giant eye . . .
or tell the faint press and hum
of his eternal pool of sperm.
Like sandalwood! *Like sandalwood!*
the righteous man
perfumes the axe that falls on him.

The selflessness in these passages is the result of entering the self, entering one's own pain and coming out on the other side, no longer only James Wright or John Logan, but all men. The voice is a particular recognizable voice; at the same time it mysteriously sheds personality and becomes simply the voice of a creature on earth speaking.

If we take seriously Thoreau's dictum, "Be it life or death, we crave only reality," if we are willing to face the worst in ourselves, we also have to accept the risk I have mentioned, that probing into one's own wretchedness one may just dig up more wretchedness. What justifies the risk is the hope that in the end the search may open and transfigure us. Many people feel one shouldn't poke under the surface — that one shouldn't tempt the gods or invite trouble, that one should be content to live with his taboos unchallenged, with his repressions and politenesses unquestioned; that just as the highest virtue in the state is law and order, so the highest virtue of poetry is formality and morality — or if immorality, then in the voice of a *persona* — and on the whole cheerful, or at least ironic, good humor. In Tacoma, Washington, once, after a reading in which I read certain poems that exposed my own wretchedness, a woman came up and handed me a poem she had written during the reading. There was a little hieroglyph for the signature. Under it, it said, "If you want me, ask." The poem went like this:

> Galway Kinnel
> Why
> Are you in love with blood?
> What
> Dark part of your soul
> Glories so
> To wallow in gore?
> Deep in your mind there lies
> Despair, disgust, disease.
> When
> Did the beauty of life
> Go from your desolate soul?
> How
> Can life be sweet to you
> Who hold a wondrous gift
> And use it for
> Depravity?
> Your voice too is false
> Your comments cruel
> As the depths of your heart
> Exalt in ugliness
> And dwell
> In death
> Here

In the midst of life
You
Are a sickness.

I laughed later that night, when I read it. But the laughter died quickly. For a long time I kept the poem pinned to the wall above my desk, as a *memento mori.* It *is* a risk: it is possible we will go on to the end feeding, with less and less relish, on the bitter flesh of our heart. The worst is that we ourselves may be the last to know that this is how we spent our life.

If much stands to be lost, however, it is true that everything stands to be gained. What do we want more than that oneness which bestows — which *is* — life? We want only to be more alive, not less. And the standard of what it is to be alive is very high. It was set in our infancy. Not yet divided into mind and body, our mind still a function of our senses, we laughed, we felt joyous connection with the things around us. In adult life don't we often feel half-dead, as if we were just brains walking around in corpses? The only sense we still respect is eyesight, probably because it is so closely attached to the brain. Go into any American house at random, you will find something — a plastic flower, false tiles, some imitation paneling — *something* which can be appreciated as material only if apprehended by eyesight alone. Don't we go sightseeing in cars, thinking we can experience a landscape by looking at it through glass? A baby takes pleasure in seeing a thing, yes, but seeing is first act. For fulfillment the baby must reach out, grasp it, put it in his mouth, suck it, savor it, taste it, manipulate it, smell it, physically be one with it. From here comes our notion of heaven itself. Every experience of happiness in later life is a stirring of that ineradicable memory of once belonging wholly to the life of the planet.

Somehow it happened that the "mind" got separated from the rest of us. It got specified as the self. In reality, the mind is only a denser place in the flesh. Might we not just as well locate our center in the genitals, or in the solar plexus? Or even in that little shadow which Hesse describes, that goes from the shoulder to the breast? We have to learn anew to take delight in the physical life.

If I worship one thing more than another it shall
    be the spread of my own body, or any part of it,
Translucent mould of me it shall be you!
Shaded ledges and rests it shall be you!
Firm masculine colter it shall be you!
Whatever goes to the tilth of me it shall be you!

You my rich blood! your milky stream pale strippings
    of my life!
Breast that presses against other breasts it shall
    be you!
My brain it shall be your occult convolutions!
Root of wash'd sweet-flag! timorous pond-snipe! nest
    of guarded duplicate eggs! it shall be you!
Mix'd tussled hay of head, beard, brawn, it shall be you!
Trickling sap of maple, fibre of manly wheat, it shall
    be you!
Sun so generous it shall be you!
Vapors lighting and shading my face it shall be you!
You sweaty brooks and dews it shall be you!
Winds whose soft-tickling genitals rub against me it
    shall be you!
Broad muscular fields, branches of live oak, loving
    lounger in my winding paths, it shall be you!
Hands I have taken, face I have kiss'd, mortal I have
    ever touch'd, it shall be you.

I dote on myself, there is that lot of me and all
    so luscious . . .

The great thing about Whitman is that he knew *all* of our being must be loved, if we are to love any of it. I have often thought there should be a book called *Shit,* telling us that what comes out of the body is no less a part of reality, no less sacred, than what goes into it; only a little less nourishing. It's a matter of its moment in the life cycle: food eaten is on the cross, at its moment of sacrifice, while food eliminated is at its moment of ascension. There is a divine madness, remember; and if you dismiss the exuberance of self-love, you may be left with an impeccable reasonableness, but a dead body.

In the tale of Dr. Jekyll and Mr. Hyde, the vicious, animal half of the man escapes the control of the civilized, rational half and destroys it. The story is a Victorian fantasy which plays out the dread of nature; it is also a true myth of repression and its consequences. I wonder if the tale shouldn't be rewritten, with a happy ending? How would it be if, in his nightly cruising, Mr. Hyde should discover the possibility of tender love? What would happen if he came back to the fearful, overly mental, puritan, self-enclosed Dr. Jekyll and converted him, so that they went out cruising together; or else, if he came back and seduced him? This conjectural version of the story would assume that the blame for their disharmony lay more with Dr. Jekyll than with Mr. Hyde, and it would look primarily to Mr. Hyde for their salvation.

Many ancient stories tell of the mating of man and animal — the Dr. Jekyll and Mr. Hyde of nature. It seems always to be a female human and a male animal who mate, never the reverse. Of course, around farms men have always copulated with animals, and it would be difficult to render this act into an instructive myth, since the men use the animals, if not rape them. In Colin Wilson's *Encyclopedia of Murder,* he records the case of a man who preliminary to killing someone would fuck a goose, or after fucking a goose would kill someone, however you like to look at it — the basic pathology is clear. But the basic reason is that women — at least in the imagination of men — reside closer to nature, feel less threatened by it, are more willing to give themselves up to it. Leda undoubtedly knows terror as she lies under the swan — for in matings between beings so alien there must be an element of rape — but she also knows exaltation, as she gives herself to the natural life. Therefore men always depict the Muse as female; and in this sense the poet knows himself to be of a more feminine disposition than the banker.

> Muses resemble women who creep out at night to give themselves to unknown sailors and return to talk of Chinese porcelain — porcelain is best made, a Japanese critic has said, where the conditions of life are hard — or of the Ninth Symphony — virginity renews itself like the moon — except that the Muses sometimes form in those low haunts their most lasting attachments.

So wrote Yeats. If one chooses, one can think of the muse in less fanciful terms, as Gary Snyder does:

> Widely speaking, the muse is anything other that touches you and moves you. Be it a mountain range, a band of people, the morning star, or a diesel generator. Breaks through the ego-barrier. But this touching-deep is as a mirror, and man in his sexual nature has found the clearest mirror to be his human lover.

Let me turn for a moment, then, to that widely used — or perhaps not so widely used — sentence, "I love you." Who is the "I?" Who is the "you?" Everyone except people who make scientific studies of love admits that love is a force of a kind which transcends person and personality. Wasn't Gatsby's most devastating put-down of the love between Tom and Daisy to say that it was "only personal?" Plato was eloquent in persuading us that love is a transcendent force, but in his dream, the loved person, and indeed the whole realm in which love takes place, turn into rubble. For the Christians, too, love transcended person and personality; it was not the man or woman, but the image of God in the person, that one loved. The Christians, unfortunately, were unable to permit this love to include sexual love, for it was too much for them to conceive of God as having sexual intercourse with himself through the instrumentality of his images.

D. H. Lawrence wrote an odd little poem on the subject:

I wish I knew a woman
who was like a red fire on the hearth
glowing after the day's restless draughts.
So that one could draw near her
in the red stillness of the dusk
and really take delight in her
without having to make the polite effort of loving her
or the mental effort of making her acquaintance.
Without having to take a chill, talking to her.

It isn't always easy to know when Lawrence is serious and when he is joking. As a rule of thumb, probably serious. But this union deeper than personality, as Lawrence of course knew, is not to be had that way. As with poetry, so with love: it is necessary to go through the personality to reach beyond it. Short of a swan descending from heaven, the great moments of sexual love are not between strangers, but between those who know and care for each other, and who then pass beyond each other, becoming nameless creatures enacting the primal sexuality of all life.

It is curious that sexual love, which is the only sacred experience of most lives on this earth, is a religion without a Book. Even the *Kama Sutra* is too much like a sex manual. It is a religion that has many poems, though, and I would like to quote two of them, the first D. H. Lawrence's "River Roses," a matchless account of the casting off of selves:

By the Isar, in the twilight
We were wandering and singing,
By the Isar, in the evening
We climbed the huntsman's ladder and sat swinging

In the fir-tree overlooking the marshes,
While the river met with river, and the ringing
Of their pale-green glacier water filled the evening.

By the Isar, in the twilight
We found the dark wild roses
Hanging red at the river; and simmering
Frogs were singing, and over the river closes
Was savour of ice and of roses; and glimmering
Fear was abroad. We whispered: "No one knows us.
Let it be as the snake disposes
Here in this simmering marsh."

The separate egos vanish; the wand of cosmic sexuality rules.

The following poem, section 5 from "Song of Myself," though not ostensibly a love poem, obviously has its source in a love experience. It is the kind of poem Dr. Jekyll would write, after his seduction by Mr. Hyde.

Loafe with me on the grass, loose the stop from your
    throat,
Not words, not music or rhyme I want, not custom or
    lecture, not even the best,
Only the lull I like, the hum of your valved voice.

I mind how once we lay such a transparent summer
    morning,
How you settled your head athwart my hips and gently
    turn'd over upon me,
And parted the shirt from my bosom-bone, and plunged
    your tongue to my bare-stript heart,
And reach'd till you felt my beard, and reach'd till
    you held my feet.

Swiftly arose and spread around me the peace and knowledge
    that pass all the argument of the earth,
And I know that the hand of God is the promise of my
    own,
And I know that the spirit of God is the brother of my
    own,
And that all the men ever born are also my brothers, and
    the women my sisters and lovers,
And that a kelson of the creation is love,
And limitless are leaves stiff or drooping in the fields,

And brown ants in the little wells beneath them,
And mossy scabs of the worm fence, heap'd stones, elder,
    mullein and poke-weed.

The death of the self I seek, in poetry and out of poetry, is not a drying up or withering. It is a death, yes, but a death out of which one might hope to be reborn more giving, more alive, more open, more related to the natural life. I have never felt the appeal of that death of self certain kinds of Buddhism describe — that death which purges us of desire, which removes us from our loves. For myself, I would like a death that would give me more loves, not fewer. And greater desire, not less. Isn't it possible that to desire a thing, to truly desire it, is a form of having it? I suppose nothing is stronger than fate — if fate is that amount of vital energy allotted each of us — but if anything were stronger, it would not be acquiescence, the coming to want only what one already has, it would be desire, desire which rises from the roots of one's life and transfigures it.

This Navajo night-chant, which is no more than an expression of desire, gives whoever says it with his whole being, at least for the moment of saying it, and who knows, perhaps forever, everything he asks.

Tse'gihi.
House made of dawn.
House made of evening light.
House made of the dark cloud.
House made of male rain.
House made of dark mist.
House made of female rain.
House made of pollen.
House made of grasshoppers.
Dark cloud is at the door.
The trail out of it is dark cloud.
The zigzag lightning stands high upon it.
Male deity!
Your offering I make.
I have prepared a smoke for you.
Restore my feet for me.
Restore my legs for me.
Restore my body for me.
Restore my mind for me.
This very day take out your spell for me.
Your spell remove for me.

You have taken it away for me.
Far off it has gone.
Happily I recover.
Happily my interior becomes cool.
Happily I go forth.
My interior feeling cool, may I walk.
No longer sore, may I walk.
Impervious to pain, may I walk.
With lively feelings may I walk.
As it used to be long ago, may I walk.
Happily may I walk.
Happily, with abundant dark clouds, may I walk.
Happily, with abundant showers, may I walk.
Happily, with abundant plants, may I walk.
Happily, on the trail of pollen, may I walk.
Happily may I walk.
Being as it used to be long ago, may I walk.
May it be beautiful before me.
May it be beautiful behind me.
May it be beautiful below me.
May it be beautiful above me.
May it be beautiful all around me.
In beauty it is finished.

Tess Gallagher

The Poem as a Reservoir for Grief

As more and more of contemporary life is forced into the present moment, or NOW moment, there seem to be fewer mechanisms which allow the past to be fully absorbed and lived once it has "happened." It has become harder to experience grief since it is a retroactive emotion which requires subsequent returns to the loss over a period of time. For only through such returns may one hope for the very real gain of transforming losses of various kinds into meaningful contributions to our own becoming.

It is not simply release from sufferings we need, but understanding of loss and, beyond understanding, the need to feel, as in the word "mourning," the ongoing accumulation of bodily and psychic communication which loss initiates in us. Here I am not only speaking of the loss one experiences in the death of a loved one, but of those diminishments of being which become known gradually too, as when child or parent or lover discovers piecemeal the signs of neglect and lost trust. Poems have long been a place where one could count on being allowed to feel in a bodily sense our connection to loss. I say *bodily* to emphasize the way poems act not only upon the mind and spirit, but upon the emotions which then release the bodily signs of feeling — so that we weep, laugh, are brought to anger, feel loneliness or the comfort of companionship.

What often happens early on with a death or other calculable loss, is that one has a feeling of shock which brings about an absence of feeling. We are cut off from our bodily entrance to the loss. We stand outside the loss and are pulled along into new experiences before we have had the chance to ask "what can this mean?" We may feel a kind of guilt because *we have not felt enough.* This can cause even more avoidance of the grieving process, so that the integrative steps that might be taken to bring the loss into some meaningful consequence in our lives are never attempted.

We have too, in this time of mass communication, the opposite cause of an inability to grieve — that one is asked to feel too much: we are asked to witness disasters claiming thousands of lives, numerous political atrocities, domestic brutalities, massacres in distant countries, and the rape around the corner. It is no wonder that a certain emotional unavailability has become a part of the modern temperament.

In such a world, poems allow a strictly private access to the grief-handling process, or, on another level, poems may bring one's loss into communion with other deaths and mythic elements which enlarge the view of the solitary death. It is as if the poem acted as a live-in church, and one might open the book of poems in order, through experiencing loss, to arrive at an approach to one's particular grief and thereby transform that grief.

The failure of professional counselling, including psychiatry, to provide a lasting solace and a spiritual resource for those who need to grieve, are failures of American societal attitudes in general. America, is, perhaps, a country *almost* ready for grief, for the serious considerations and admissions, recognitions and healings of grief. I see the public and private reassessments of the Vietnam War as one of the recent signs of this new willingness and capacity. The building of the Vietnam War memorial restored, in a symbolic way, the memory of those Americans who died in that war. Presently, there is the growing awareness of the possibility of nuclear holocaust, so that whole days are viciously intersected by fears of such proportion that we have few ways of addressing them. It is as if we have been propelled into a kind of before-the-fact mourning for the earth and live in general because our fears are so stupifying. It is a productive mourning, however, in that it has provided the energy to motivate many sectors of the country to take action against this threat.

In my own considerations of grieving I have begun to wonder if the ramifications of an entire society's inability to grieve might be more central to our problems than we have yet been able to recognize. For instance, one might consider the high divorce rate and its possible relationship to various kinds of unexpressed grief. Then too, the rise in other violences, especially those against women and children, should be mentioned.

The divorce rate relates perhaps more particularly to the grieving of an entire sex, the grieving of women, who have come to value themselves in new ways, and who, in many cases, must eschew entire lives lived in the dominions of choices made by others.

As a stop-gap measure for these ruptures in domestic matters, counselling and being counselled has become practically a national pasttime, a place for assessment and change-making. But it has not answered this deeper need of the individual to grieve because its motives are too future-oriented in the short term sense.

I am reminded of my own disappointment with marriage counselling at the time when my second marriage was in a state of collapse. The counsellor was sympathetic when I cried in the first session, but when I cried in the second and third sessions, she reverted to a very businesslike disapproval. I was not making "progress." I was not "forgetting" the attachments of the relationship quickly enough. I should have been able, within the space of three weeks, to leave grief behind and plunge ahead into My Own Life. But my life had been so intricately defined in terms of the "other" that the grieving could not be accelerated as she would have liked. Counselling may often be aimed at the practical — getting one to function *as though* the loss has been accommodated. And, of course, we do this . . . we act *as if we could* move on, and we do. But counselling or other "self-help" methods for grief-handling often belong to what J. T. Fraser in *Of Passion, Time and Knowledge* has aptly named "the business present."

The business present, he says, "pays only lip service to past and future; its essence is the removal of tension associated with future and past, in sharp contrast to the tragic present with its wealth of temporal conflicts." [1] Fraser explains that the Tragic Present "involves continuities and hidden necessities," while "the business present is informed only of discontinuities, that is, of chance." [2] When things happen to us only by chance we are not encouraged to search for meaning. Chance is its own meaning.

Self-help books exist to help the seeker package the problem and thereby allow a quick solution. They are the hamburger stands of the soul. We are all familiar with the questions, warnings and promises of their titles: "Who Do You Think You Are?", "The Hazards of Being Male", "How to Win Over Depression" and "How Not to Make Love"!

Mass communication, unlike poetry, is aimed at the shrinking attention span. Its messages, according to Fraser, are engineered "to make the material digestible with minimal effort and with no effect other, or deeper, than the one desired by the financial sponsor." [3] This describes how the business present wants to act upon language and consequently upon our lives. It wants to drive out the ambiguity of language which is the life blood of grief-feeling and of poem-making and reading.

"A green parrot is also a green salad *and* a green parrot.
He who makes it only a parrot diminishes its reality."
—Picasso

So a diminishment of reality takes place when our experience is negotiated without ambiguity. What most often allows ambiguity to operate is an access to our past in a way that re-lives it in some fullness, so that it is not lost or left behind as dross, but is incorporated into the present.

What the business present encourages, as Fraser sees so acutely, is "the flight of the masses from the terror and *responsibility* of knowing time." [4] (My italics.) When we are told to scttlc a loss account quickly, efficiently, this often involves placing the experience in the old business file. We do this by relegating that experience to the past — the dead past. It was briefly relevant, but we must move on like good soldiers.

Poems, through ambiguity and the enrichments of images and metaphor, invite our returns. Poems partake of the tragic and re-created present, while the business present continues to focus entirely on the NOW. But the time of the poem is multi-directional. It reaches richly into the past and forms linkages with the present and with other isolated pasts. The poem searches into the future. It reminds us of longings.

Poems restore our need to *become*, a capacity the modern self is in danger of losing. Fraser recognizes the tragic poet as "the free, time-roaming ambassador" [5] who assists in our becoming. The poem does not package, or like a trained seal, deliver the message. Its knowledge evolves. Its very ambiguities point to the individualistic character of the artistic expression itself. This ambiguity permits the spectator to insert details of his/her own, niches of perception left undermined or open by the artist.

Poems often remake the grief-causing experience in terms of myth or analogy so that the unconscious and the conscious experiences of the speaker and the reader are enabled to meet. Myth mediates between the conscious and the unconscious minds. It moves from ego release to psychic and spiritual embrace.

There are many poems one might turn to as examples of what I've been talking about — the elegies of Milton, Gray, Thomas, Yeats, Dickinson, Auden, the entire work of Rainer Maria Rilke, poems by Akhmatova and Tsvetayeva and countless contemporary

American women — some whose voices are almost entirely elegaic in tone: Bogan, Plath, Glück and Gregg. With so much to choose from, I don't introduce the poems I've selected with any sense of them as definitive except in their appeal to me at this writing for their particular ways of handling grief.

The first poem by Galway Kinnell typifies the power of many poets to move through the separations of grief into a state of embrace. His poem "Goodbye" begins with the death of his mother. Kinnell told me a fact outside the knowledge which the poem gives that might be useful. This was that he could not be at his mother's death bed, much to his sorrow. The poem was written in order to absorb regret: "I swallow down the goodbyes I won't get to use . . . ." There is also the suggestion that there was unresolved anguish between mother and son in the line . . . "whatever we are, she and I, **we're nearly cured**" - as though the mother's death were some closing of that case. The act of writing the goodbye is perhaps what will afford the speaker the wholeness of cure.

Goodbye

1
My mother, poor woman, lies tonight
in her last bed. It's snowing, for her, in her darkness.
I swallow down the goodbyes I won't get to use,
tasteless, with wretched mouth-water;
whatever we are, she and I, we're nearly cured.

The night years ago when I walked away
from that final class of junior high school students
in Pittsburgh, the youngest of them ran
after me down the dark street. "Goodbye!" she called,
snow swirling across her face, tears falling.
2
Tears have kept on falling. History
has taught them its slanted understanding
of the human face. At each last embrace the dying give,
the snow brings down its disintegrating curtain.
The mind shreds the present, once the past is over.

In the Derry graveyard where only her longings sleep
and armfuls of flowers go out in the drizzle
the bodies not yet risen must lie **nearly forever** . . .
"Sprouting good Irish grass," the graveskeeper blarneys,
he can't help it, "a sprig of **shamrock**, if they were young."

3
In Pittsburgh tonight, those who were young
will be less young, those who were old, more old, or more likely
no more; and the streets where Syllest,
fleetest of my darlings, caught up with me
and hugged me and said goodbye, will be empty. Well,

one day the streets all over the world will be empty —
already in heaven, listen, the golden cobblestones have fallen
                              still —
everyone's arms will be empty, everyone's mouth, the Derry
                              earth.
It is written in our hearts, the emptiness is all.
That is how we have learned, the embrace is all.

The time-sense of the poem is actively making an arena to re-
examine the loss of the mother. In the second stanza the poem
suddenly shifts to "years ago" and the impulsive act of a student
who runs after the poet in order to simply call out a furtive "goodbye." Her weeping and her calling after him enact the speaker's
own wish for himself as regards his dying mother — that he could
rush after, or to her, to say goodbye. The impassioned necessity
and simple beauty of that act is impressed upon us through the
superimposition of the past moment onto the present.

Part Two of the poem moves the voice out of the personal
realm into "history." The mother becomes "the dying." The snow
in the poem is a secret emblem of separation, of "disintegrating" in
the poem, of loss of connection. But paradoxically, goodbye in
the poem is given *in order to restore* the connection. The mind is
seen to *need* the past, to wish to continue and complete it until
the present is no longer needed. The present exists not for itself,
as we often assume, but as the place to resolve the past. This
means that the currency of the present is not as powerful as we
often assume. It exists merely to facilitate the re-living of the past
and, as Kinnell indicates, is "shredded" once the past is "over" or
resolved. The present undergoes a reversal of importance here
according to contemporary life modes which recommend the killing of the past in order to live in the NOW. But ironically, once
this killing happens, the NOW suffers a loss of consequence and is
not fulfilled.

As Kinnell approaches in imagination the Derry graveyard
where his mother is buried, it is her longings he addresses first,
linking her to a future embodied as "armfuls of flowers" that "go
out in the drizzle," as if they were candles whose light had been

extinguished by the gradual and natural element of the weather — not downpour, but "drizzle" so we almost hear the hiss as the flames go out, each with its little radius of silence. The mother's body lies with "the bodies not yet risen," so the act of the poem is the raising of the mother (her death) into the human embrace. Her body is seen to return to the elements, in the grave keeper's words — "sprouting good Irish grass." This physical actuality co-exists with the "nearly forever" which brings together the temporal and atemporal at this point.

Then we return with the speaker to Pittsburgh, the scene of the young student's goodbye. But now the time span, the aging of the speaker and the student and those in the world at large are acknowledged: "those who were young / will be less young, those who were old, more old, or more likely / no more." The absence of that one caller who is now named tenderly "Syllest, fleetest of my darlings" is experienced as streets which "will be" empty. It's an imaginative living of those streets since the speaker is not there except as he recalls the moment of Syllest's catching up to him in streets where she no longer appears, as he also does not appear. Now the poet brings us physically closer to Syllest by allowing her to hug the speaker. We are moving closer to the longing for total embrace which impells the poem forward. Next, the speaker leaps from the emptying of particular and remembered streets to future streets: "one day the streets all over the world will be empty." The word "empty" moves us from the streets to the emptiness of arms, and now "everyone" begins to include the speaker of the past *and* the present. "Everyone's arms will be empty, everyone's mouth, the Derry earth." So at last, even the earth *will be* empty. The future exists as longing, but takes on a new palpability in the verbalization of it in the poem.

The end of the poem carries us into "our hearts" which includes the reader, uniting the word "emptiness" with the word "all" so the loss becomes enlarged. "All" has become the hinge which brings emptiness and embrace into conjuction. The last lines embrace but also release. Emptiness has somehow been carried into a fullness which *allows* release by virtue of the embrace.

It is written in our hearts, the emptiness is all.
That is how we have learned, the embrace is all.

This completion is the speaker's acknowledgement of the loss, having been able to bring together emptiness and embrace. Had Kinnell ended the poem on "the emptiness is all" we would have had an entirely different feeling at the end. But we are gathered back *into* the all, enclosed. The necessity of the embrace has been reinstated. This perhaps allows the speaker to return that embrace Syllest gives him in the past, and enables him to give the ungiven embrace to his dying mother, and finally to the "everyone" the poem admits at its close.

So it is the past which nourishes the present, allows the resolution, the grieving for the death the speaker could not attend. There is an undercurrent too in the poem of the speaker's own self-embrace. It's as though he also has had to say goodbye to that part of himself which died with his mother. He enters the "all" which is the union with others and with the earth and the spirit of the lost one the poem has been seeking. A symbolic accompanying of the mother's death does then finally occur.

William Heyen's poem, "The Berries", moves not toward embrace so much as toward loss experienced as a joy let go. Heyen brings grief to the point of joy through the sacramental acts of the speaker who carries the gift of a jar of jam to a friend whose father has died of cancer.

The Berries

My wife already there to comfort,
I walked over icy roads
to our neighbor who had lost her father.
The hard winter starlight glittered, by breath
formed ascending souls that disappeared,
as he had, the eighty-year-old man
who died of cancer.

In my left coat pocket, a jar
of raspberry jam . . . . I remembered
stepping into the drooping canes, the ripe
raspberry odor. I remembered bending over,
or kneeling, to get down under the leaves
to hidden clusters . . . .

Then, and on my walk, and now, the summer berries
made/make a redness in my mind. The jar
presses light against my hip, weight
to hand to the grieving woman. This gift
to her, to me — being able to bear
the summer's berry light like that, like this,
over the ice . . .

When I was a boy, the Lord I talked to
knew me. Where is He now? I seem to have
lost Him, except for something
in that winter air, something insisting on being
there, and here — that summer's berries, that mind's
light against my hip, myself kneeling again
under the raspberry canes.

By the fourth line of the poem we're made aware of the vast spatial dimensions of the universe: "The hard winter starlight glittered . . ." Then the speaker's own breath becomes the breath of "ascending souls" as though breath made them visible for that moment. This image is then connected with the particular death of the friend's father.

The picking of the raspberries which the speaker is carrying as jam to comfort the surviving friend, comes back to the speaker in very rich, sensual terms. The berries "made/make a redness in my mind", and this enables them to continue as memory even as "The jar presses light against my hip." The gift-giving becomes a gift to the self as well, in that the speaker is carrying, is the bearer of the summer's *light,* and so in this act unites summer and winter. Earlier in the poem, the act of kneeling and the secret, hidden nature of the harvesting (which refers also to the death of the eighty-year-old father) has connected the natural act of harvesting with the painful loss of the loved one. These co-exist in a new proximity in the poem, thereby transferring to the death the idea of ripeness, of readiness for harvest.

The union of summer and winter has been moved, in the last stanza, toward the recognition of distance between a childhood closeness to "the Lord" and the adult loss of this spiritual closeness. So the loss of the friend has evolved into recognition of a loss of touch with God. But the winter air and the memory of summer light in the berries restores an ambiguous closeness to the Divine. The poem closes with the act of kneeling, thereby suggesting a humbling of the speaker to the gift of the berries — and the death. The death of the friend has now been transformed, through an act of memory, into a richness that includes gift and childhood and harvest, as well as spiritual questioning. The emotional alchemy of this poem is a restoration of order, the sense of naturalness and rightness, of childlike simplicity before those absent presences of ripening berries, of one's God, and of a recently lost loved one.

In a last example, Michael Burkard's much less linear and narrative movement in the poem, "Islands of Feeling", enacts the disconnective effects of loss in its very method. When, under the pressures of business-time we are seen to *endure* rather than to *become,* time seems cut off from its temporality, its ongoing arrival. "It no longer passes," Fraser has observed. "It no longer completes anything."6 As in Beckett's *Waiting for Godot* we are marooned in a stagnant present. Having come forward without memory, we are simply prolonged. Similarly, in Burkard's poem, we experience time cut off from its healing possibilities. The time unit of the poem is "the moment" as in business-time. We are made to feel the ways in which one moment is cut off irrevocably from other moments until each becomes "an island of feeling."

Islands of Feeling

Here are a few branches of
those condescensions you never wanted
me to speak of or mention,
a few examples
of how and when winter
spoke with such heart that I alone
fell. For a moment
no one else knew it. No one knew
this one example that keeps you

at a door in my mind, speaking
these feelings, these slight sharp blades
which accompany
speaking. O as you say:
I do not want to hear of that.

Even though as another, my friend
left me as he died and I walked
toward a winter door today, sharply,
then told myself to go back
and walk again. Any given call
that makes me walk has still
this lonely return to my friend.

I love you as no other, I would fall
asleep for you, as a few branches did,
as any act sharpens
a simple town,
a simple place lighted, left on for you.
Would I love as my friend

stepped through a few doors?
I would. These islands

condescend, come back to me — nothing
except their heart
and daily isolation
speaks for me. With your visitation
once I wanted
every answer, the kind an island
makes for me, a white reflection
of smoke off some ledge, some
view, which takes me by the hand,
walks down. Another moment

would sharpen, slapping at
such mind or deed. You bring to me
an island
of feeling. For that I cannot follow
I love.

In the third stanza the "you" avoids reception: "O as you say /
I do not want to hear of that." The death of the friend (whether
actual or emotional) is represented as "another." Is this the death
of yet another loved one? or does this mean that the speaker himself has been changed by the death *into* another? This is left
ambiguous, but does not, I think, injure our reception of the line
intuitionally. We know there is a "dying" of some sort taking
place, the dying of a friend, and that the speaker is developing an
attitude toward that dying, that loss. The poem does not encour-
age the reader to "connect" images too surely and rather, rushes
the syntax so as to dislocate that impulse to relieve tension with
sequential assurances.

The poem begins to open up in the fourth stanza with an admission of love which is given in spite of "those condescensions
you never wanted me to speak of or mention." The speaker seems
to volunteer the self more fully here, and this becomes one of
those "islands of feeling" the reader clings to because it allows
emotional access to events not comprehended in a narrative and
factual sense, events which the writer does not "condescend" to
offer because to do so would invite an understanding more palpable than the true isolations of "feelings."

As the speaker concludes, he brings the reader to an island of
feeling he calls love. The poem releases its grief into the word
"love" only when it acknowledges that the speaker can not *follow*

the loved one, the friend, the you. Love then, seems to grow out of our *inability* to bridge one event, one feeling with another. So loving develops as a result of our island status, and not, as we normally assume, out of our coincidences with those we love or our accompaniments of them.

For Burkard, the moment keeps revising experience — "slapping at such mind or deed." This means that one may connect or follow only secretly, through acts of the heart, the mind: that which keeps the loss "at a door in my mind, speaking / these feelings, these sharp blades which accompany speaking." *Speaking* is what joins the words in time and space, words so sharp in their time-slicing power they are represented as blades.

The ending of the poem gives one a sense of the loneliness of the word "love," its isolations, but also its generosity, as though love happens as a result of loss rather than in a reciprocation of feelings: *i.e.,* I love *instead* of following because that is what is possible. Love becomes the only following the speaker can accomplish. Because of the completeness we associate with the word "love" it seems that love becomes almost *more* than following as the poem ends, so that the island affords a feeling which transcends the moment, the isolation of one person from another, or of the living from the dead, or of the speaker from the friend who makes a "visitation."

There is a mixture of regret and longing at the end of the poem, as if love takes on what cannot be lived in the impossibility of "following." Love paradoxically occurs in the absence of the loved one — "a lonely return."

I began this consideration of poems as aids to our grief-handling by pointing out that poems allow imaginative returns to the causes, the emblems of loss — returns which do often involve regret and longing toward a hoped-for embrace. The poem may also transform grief by placing it in relation to rituals or natural cycles such as harvesting, or the return the poem makes may simply lead to a more complete experiencing of the disintegrating aspects of loss, its refusals.

By concluding with Burkard's view of our island status, I wish to return to the solitary and most often lonely act that the reading and writing of poems involves. It demands such huge leaps of faith and audacity as a writer to ask that one be followed, be understood, felt — especially in the poetry of grief, because each loss is ultimately singular, an "only."

Poems engage our imaginations and emotions in a way that is particularly needed now, if we are, in our national and personal identities, to move from a state of being *almost* ready for the serious work of grieving to a true state of readiness. For it is the experiencing of grief which allows us to value fully those events, those people who are irreplaceable, so that, as Burkard says, we "love them as no other."

It is important that the inner nature of our beings be strengthened by the wisdoms of our grievings. The scientists may tinker, the politicians may instruct us in the various ploys of unconsciousness, the physicians may delay death awhile with yet another cure, but, until each individual maintains a responsible relationship to their own losses and changes, there will be no such thing as a hopeful future. For, like the Taoist description of the wheel in terms of the strong, empty spaces *between* the spokes, one's future depends not only on the visible spokes of the present, but also on those invisible elements from the past — those things we are missing, are grieving for and which we have forgotten and left behind in order to recover them again as new meaning, new feeling.

It seems important that grieving not be separated from other aspects of one's work toward a wholeness of being. It belongs there within the fabric of psychic, spiritual, intellectual, emotional and intuitional perceptions through which we move. Because poems, like no other way way in which we use language, are able to carry the density of such a complex synthesis, they are the best and oldest forms we have for attending and absolving grief, for bringing it into a useful relationship to those things we are about to do towards a future.

Footnotes

1   J.T. Fraser, *Of Time, Passion and Knowledge*, George Braziller, 1975, p. 416.

2   Ibid. p. 416.

3   Ibid. p. 426.

4   Ibid. p. 426.

5   Ibid. p. 420.

6   Ibid. p. 419.

Sandra Gilbert

My Name is Darkness: The Poetry of Self-Definition

"Something hangs in back of me," wrote Denise Levertov in "The Wings," a poem published in the middle sixties. "I can't see it, can't move it. // I know it's black, a hump on my back....black / a hump on my back .... black // inimical power." A few years later, in 1972, Anne Sexton published a poem called "The Ambition Bird" that made a similar point:

> I would like a simple life
> yet all night I am laying
> poems away in a long box ...
>
> All night dark wings
> flopping in my heart.
> Each an ambition bird.

Both poets, whether consciously or not, seem to have been echoing the terrified and yet triumphantly self-defining metaphors of Sylvia Plath's "Stings":

> I stand in a column
>
> Of winged, unmiraculous women, ...
>
> ... but I
> Have a self to recover, a queen.

Is she dead, is she sleeping?
Where has she been,
With her lion-red body, her wings of glass?

Now she is flying
More terrible than she ever was . . . .

And all three women — Plath, Levertov, Sexton — are writing in a vein of self-definition that has also been worked by other recent women poets as diverse as Adrienne Rich, Diane Wakoski, Muriel Rukeyser, Ruth Stone, Gwendolyn Brooks, Erica Jong, and Margaret Atwood. In fact, I'd like to speculate here that the self-defining confessional genre, with its persistent assertions of identity and its emphasis on a central mythology of the self, may be (at least for our own time) a distinctively female poetic mode.

"Confessional" poetry has, of course, been generally associated with a number of contemporary male poets, most notably Berryman, Lowell, and Snodgrass. A tradition of such writing, moreover, can easily be traced back through such male mythologists of the self as Whitman and Yeats to Wordsworth and Byron, those romantic patriarchs whose self-examinations and self-dramatizations probably fathered not only the poetry of what Keats called the egotistical sublime but also the more recent ironic mode we might call the egotistical ridiculous. Most male poets, however, have been able to move beyond the self-deprecations and self-assertions of confessional writing to larger, more objectively formulated appraisals of God, humanity, society. Writers like Bly and Snyder, though they, too, are descendants of Whitman and Wordsworth, cannot by any stretch of the vocabulary be called confessional. Such obviously confessional male poets as Lowell and Berryman write verse in which (as M. L. Rosenthal's definition of confessional poetry puts it) "the private life of the poet himself . . . often becomes a major theme." Yet they manage to be "at once private and public, lyrical and rhetorical" (as Rosenthal also notes) because the personal crisis of the male poet "is felt at the same time as a symbolic embodiment of national and cultural crisis." Thus, just as the growth of Wordsworth's mind stands for the growth of all self-fulfilling human minds, so "the 'myth' that Lowell creates is that of an America . . . whose history and present predicament are embodied in those of his own family and epitomized in his own psychological experience."

The male confessional poet, in other words, even while romantically exploring his own psyche, observes himself as a representative specimen with a sort of scientific exactitude. Alienated, he's nevertheless an ironic sociologist of his own alienation because he considers his analytic perspective on himself a civilized, normative point of view. Lowell, describing his own mental illness with desperate intensity, is still able to note with detachment the "hackneyed speech" and "homicidal eye" of "the kingdom of the mad," and, recalling an impassioned past, to describe his younger self with surgical precision as "boiled and shy / and poker-faced." Like other modern male *poètes maudits,* in short, he has a cool faith in his own ability to classify his own exemplary sufferings, a curious, calm confidence that even in madness he is in some sense at the intellectual center of things. Can it be (at least in part) that because he's a man, he can readily picture himself as Everyman?

Certainly, by contrast, the female confessional poet seems to feel no such paradoxical ease with her own anxieties. Even when she observes herself with amused irony, as Plath does in "Lady Lazarus" ("What a trash / To annihilate each decade . . . . It's the theatrical // Comeback in broad day . . . . That knocks me out"), she enacts as well as dissects her suffering, her rage, her anxiety:

> Herr God, Herr Lucifer
> Beware
> Beware.
>
> Out of the ash
> I rise with my red hair
> And I eat men like air.

The detached irony of a Lowell or a Berryman — the irony possible for a self-assured, normative sensibility — is largely unavailable to her, unavailable because even at her most objective she feels eccentric, not representative; peripheral, not central. More, she struggles with her suffering, grapples with it in bewilderment, writing what Plath (who is again paradigmatic here) called "sweating, heaving poems," because she cannot easily classify either herself or her problem. To define her suffering would be to define her identity, and such self-definition is her goal, rather than her starting point.

The male confessional poet — Lowell, Berryman, Yeats — writes in the certainty that he is the inheritor of major traditions, the grandson of history, whose very anxieties, as Harold Bloom has noted, are defined by the ambiguities of the past that has shaped him as it shaped his fathers. The female poet, however, even when she is not consciously confessional like Plath or Sexton, writes in the hope of discovering or defining a self, a certainty, a tradition. Striving for self-knowledge, she experiments with different propositions about her own nature, never cool or comfortable enough to be (like her male counterparts) an ironic sociologist; always, instead, a desperate Galileo, a passionate empiricist who sees herself founding a new science rather than extending the techniques and discoveries of an old one. It is for this reason, I believe, that otherwise radically different poets like Plath, Sexton, Rich, Wakoski, and Levertov all write verse characterized by such recurrent self-defining statements — hypotheses, really — as the following:

"I am your opus / I am your valuable."
"I am a nun now . . . ."
"I am not a nurse . . . . I am not a smile."
"I am dark-suited and still, a member of the party."
"I am the arrow, / The dew that flies / Suicidal . . . ."
"I am a miner."
"I am a letter in this slot . . . ."
"I / Am a pure acetylene / Virgin."
"I think I may well be a Jew."
"I am not a Caesar."
"I am the magician's girl."
"I am no source of honey."
"I am no drudge . . . ."
"O God, I am not like you . . . ."

Sylvia Plath, *Ariel*

"I am a tree gypsy: you can't shake me out of your branches."
"Here I am . . . . a strange combination of images."
"I am like the guerrilla fighter / who must sleep with one eye / open for attack."
"I am blue, / I am blue as a blues singer, / I am blue in the face . . . ."
"My body dries out / and becomes a bone sceptre . . . ."
"I am the sword with / the starry hilt . . . ."
"I am ringless, ringless . . . ."
"I am a blackbird."
"I am / also a ruler of the sun, I am / the woman / whose hair lights up a dark room, whose words are matches . . . ."
"I am solitary, / like the owls I never see . . . ."

Diane Wakoski, *Inside the Blood Factor* and *Dancing on the Grave of a Son of a Bitch*

"I'm . . . a naked man fleeing / across the roofs . . . ."
"I am a galactic cloud . . . / I am an instrument in the shape of
    a woman . . . ."
"I am a woman in the prime of life, with certain powers . . . ."
"I am the androgyne / I am the living mind you fail to de-
    scribe . . . ."
"I am she: I am he / Whose drowned face sleeps with open
    eyes . . . ."
"I am an American woman, / my body a hollow ship . . . . / I
    am not the wheatfield / nor the virgin forest."

Adrienne Rich, *Poems: Selected and
New, 1950–1974*

"Everyone in me is a bird, / I am beating all my wings."
"I am no different from Emily Goering."
"I am a watercolor. / I wash off."
"I'm Ethan Frome's wife. I'll move when I'm able."
"I am no longer the suicide / with her raft and paddle."
"I am not an idler, / am I?"
"Yes! I am still the criminal . . . ."
"I have become a tree, / I have become a vase . . . ."
"I am an ocean-going vessel . . . ."
"I am a small handful . . . ."
"I am not immortal. Faustus and I are the also-ran."

Anne Sexton, *Love Poems, The Book
of Folly,* and *The Death Notebook*

"The moon is a sow / . . . . and I a pig and a poet."
"Am I a pier, / half-in, half-out of the water?"
"I am faithful to / ebb and flow . . . / I hold steady / in the
    black sky . . . . / There is no savor / more sweet, more
    salt / than to be glad to be / what, woman, / and who,
    myself / I am, a shadow / that grows longer as the sun /
    moves, drawn out / on a thread of wonder."

Denise Levertov, *O Taste and See*
and *The Sorrow Dance*

Though they were taken out of context, you probably recognized many of these lines. They might all have been by one,
anxiously experimental, modern Everywoman, so strikingly similar
are they in structure and intention. Considering and discarding
different metaphors, different propositions of identity, each of
these five writers seems to be straining to formulate an ontology

of selfhood, some irreducible and essential truth about her own nature. While the male poet, even at his most wretched and alienated, can at least solace himself with his open or secret creativity, his mythmaking power, the female poet must come to terms with the fact that as a female she is that which is mythologized, the incarnation of otherness (to use de Beauvior's terminology) and hence the object of anthologies full of male metaphors. Many of her hypotheses about herself are therefore in one way or another replies to prevalent definitions of her femininity, replies expressing either her distress at the disparity between male myths about her and her own sense of herself, or else her triumphant repudiation of those myths. Men tell her that she is a muse. Yet she knows that she is not a muse, she *has* a muse (and what is its sex?). Men tell her she is the "angel in the house," yet she doesn't *feel* angelic, and wonders, therefore, if she is a devil, a witch, an animal, a criminal. Men tell her that she is Molly Bloom, Mother Earth, Ishtar, a fertility goddess, a *thing* whose periodicity expresses the divine order (or is it the *dis*order?) of seasons, skies, stars. They tell her, echoing Archibald MacLeish's definition of a poem, that she should not mean but be. Yet meanings delight her, along with seemings, games, plays, costumes, and ideas of order, as they delight male poets. But perhaps, she speculates, her rage for order is mistaken, presumptuous?

"Alas!" complained Anne Finch, Countess of Winchilsea, in the late seventeenth century,

> a woman that attempts the pen,
> Such an intruder on the rights of men,
> Such a presumptuous Creature, is esteem'd,
> The fault, can by no vertue be redeem'd.
> They tell us we mistake our sex and way;
> Good breeding, fassion, dancing, dressing, play
> Are the accomplishments we shou'd desire;
> To write, or read, or think, or to enquire
> Wou'd cloud our beauty, and exaust our time,
> And interrupt the Conquests of our prime;
> Whilst the dull mannage, of a servile house
> Is held by some, our outmost aft, and use.

"The Introduction"

Given these disadvantages, she admonished herself to "Be caution'd then . . . and still retir'd . . . / Conscious of wants, still with contracted wing, / To some few freinds [*sic*], and to thy sorrows sing . . . ." Nevertheless, this modest poetess of "Spleen" and sorrow, contending against a sense of her own contracted wing, pioneered a poetic mode for other women, a mode of reticence conquered by assertion and self-examination, a mode of self-definition *within* and *against* the context of prevailing male definitions of women.

Today, doubting her likeness to crops and fields, the woman poet asks herself, with Adrienne Rich, "Has Nature shown / her household books to you, daughter-in-law, / that her sons never saw?" ("Snapshots of a Daughter-in-Law"), and, refusing to be "a woman in the shape of a monster," she defines herself instead as "an instrument in the shape / of a woman trying to translate pulsations / into images for the relief of the body / and the reconstruction of the mind" ("Planetarium"). With Esther Greenwood in *The Bell Jar* she denies that she is the passive "place an arrow shoots off from" and proposes, rather, to "shoot off in all directions" herself, to be as active and full of intentions as "the colored arrows from a Fourth of July rocket." Yet all the while, limited and defined by others, enclosed in cells of history, she perceives that she is supposed to be living quietly in her kitchen, adhering, as Plath wrathfully wrote, "to rules, to rules, to rules" ("A Birthday Present"). And so she wonders if she is, after all, a monster like Spenser's Duessa. "A thinking woman sleeps with monsters," notes Adrienne Rich. "The beak that grips her, she becomes" ("Snapshots"). And Plath asks, "What am I / That these late mouths" — the dissenting mouths of her mind — "cry open . . . .?" ("Poppies in October").

What am I? Who am I? What shall I call myself? Another aspect of the woman poet's struggle toward self-definition is her search for a name. Significantly, the problems and possibilities of naming recur throughout the poetry of such writers as Plath, Rich, Sexton, Levertov, and Wakoski. Perhaps even more significantly, however, where the male confessional poet uses the real names of real people to authenticate his ironic sociology, the self-defining female poet uses names as symbolic motifs, as mythic ideas. Robert Lowell, for instance, entitles one of his books *For Lizzie and Harriet,* and confesses that "hand of glass / and heart in mouth [I] / outdrank the Rahvs in the heat / of Greenwich Village . . . , " while Dewitt Snodgrass sardonically insists that "Snodgrass is walking through the universe." But Levertov gives herself a generic name, reconciling herself with deep serenity to "what, woman, / and who, myself, / I am." And Plath, trapped in the identity crisis Levertov appears to have transcended, relinquishes her name, symbolic of a mistaken identity, with intense relief: "I am nobody; I have nothing to do with explosions. / I have given my name and my day-clothes up to the nurses . . ." ("Tulips").

Even Sexton, who seems at first to be playing with her name as Snodgrass toys with his, invents an imaginary Christopher to go with the reality of Anne and sets the two names in the context of a series of psalms outlining a private myth of origins: "For Anne and Christopher were born in my head as I howled at the grave of the roses . . . ." Adrienne Rich goes further still, defining herself as a participant in a mysterious universal reality — "The Stranger," "the androgyne" — and noting, therefore, that "the letters of my name are written under the lids / of the newborn child." Finally, Diane Wakoski, perhaps the most obsessed with names of all these poets, mythologizes one aspect of herself by emphasizing the various implications of her name: "If you know my name, / you know Diane comes across diamond in the word book," she writes in "The Diamond Merchant," "crossing my life . . . leaving me incomplete . . . ." Elsewhere she adds: "There is / an ancient priestess / whose tears make the spider-lilies grow. / She knows my name is darkness" ("The Mirror of a Day Chiming Marigold"). And she reveals a crucial tension between her name and her real identity: "Feeling the loneliness / of my cold name, / I live in a secret place, / behind a carved door. / My house is a diamond and my life / is unspoken" ("In the Secret Room, East of the Sun, West of the Moon").

This tension between the woman's name and the reality that it may not after all represent suggests, however, a central problem that shadows all the attempts at self-definition made by the female poets discussed here. For as she struggles to define herself, to reconcile male myths about her with her own sense of herself, to find some connection between the name the world has given her and the secret name she has given herself, the woman poet inevitably postulates that perhaps she has not one but two (or more) selves, making her task of self-definition bewilderingly complex. The first of these selves is usually public and social, defined by circumstance and by the names the world calls her — daughter, wife, mother, Miss, Mrs., Mademoiselle — a self that seems, in the context of the poet's cultural conditioning, to be her natural personality (in the sense of being both physiologically inevitable and morally proper or appropriate). The female poet's second self, however, is associated with her secret name, her rebellious longings, her rage against imposed definitions, her creative passions, her anxiety, and — yes — her art. And it is this *Doppelgänger* of a second self which, generating the woman's uneasiness with male myths of femininity, gives energy as well as complexity to her struggle toward self-definition.

For if the first self is public, rational, social, and therefore seems somehow "natural," this dark, other, second self is private, irrational, antisocial, and therefore — in the best romantic tradition — associated with the supernatural. Denise Levertov's poem "In Mind" outlines the dichotomy between the two selves better than any prose analysis could. Noting that the poet's mind contains two radically opposite (but implicitly complementary) selves, Levertov describes the first of these as "a woman / of innocence," a woman who is "unadorned" but sweet-smelling and "fair-featured." She wears

> a utopian smock or shift, her hair
> is light brown and smooth, and she
>
> is kind and very clean without
> ostentation —
>   but she has
> no imagination.

Shadowing this kindly public woman, however, the poet imagines a

> turbulent moon-ridden girl
> or old woman, or both,
> dressed in opals and rags, feathers
>
> and torn taffeta,
> who knows strange songs —
>
> but she is not kind.

Innumerable male writers have also, of course, spoken in ways similar to this of doubles and otherness, imagining second supernatural selves ranging from good wizards like Superman to bad alter egos like Mr. Hyde. But the exploration of inner alterity is only one of many modes of self-analysis available to the modern male confessional poet, whereas all the women whose poetry has been discussed here seem to share a real obsession with the second, supernatural self. "The Other" and "Again and Again and Again" are just two of many poems by Sexton that deal with this phenomenon of otherness. In the first, interestingly, she describes her supernatural self — her "other" — as masculine, an early avatar, I suppose, of Christopher, the imaginary twin she associates (in *The Death Notebooks*) with the mad eighteenth-century poet Christopher Smart:

Under my bowels, yellow with smoke,
it waits.
Under my eyes, those milk bunnies,
it waits.
It is waiting.
It is waiting
Mr. Doppelgänger. My brother. My spouse.
Mr. Doppelgänger. My enemy. My lover.

Like Levertov's second self, Sexton's is unkind and therefore unfeminine, aggressive, masculine. My "other," she writes, "swallows Lysol."

When the child is soothed and resting on the breast . . . .

My other beats in a tin drum in my heart . . . .

It cries and cries and cries
until I put on a painted mask
and leer at Jesus in His passion.

Then it giggles.
It is a thumbscrew.
Its hatred makes it clairvoyant.
I can only sign over everything,
the house, the dog, the ladders, the jewels,
the soul, the family tree, the mailbox.

Then I can sleep.

Maybe.

Inhabited by such rage, it is no wonder that the woman poet often struggles, with a kind of feverish panic, to define herself, frantically clearing away the debris of alternative selves like "old whore petticoats" — to quote Sylvia Plath — in the hope of re-attaining the blazing chastity, the unviolated singleness, of a "pure acetylene / Virgin" ("Fever 103° "). For, inhabiting her, the second self is a cry that keeps her awake — to go on quoting Plath — flapping out nightly and "looking, with its hooks, for something to love." Yet she can define it no more precisely, can define instead only her own pain, her fear of its otherness. "I am terrified by this dark thing / That sleeps in me . . . ," Plath continues in "Elm." "All day I feel its soft, feathery turnings, its malignity." In

"Again and Again and Again" Sexton notes: "I have a black look I do not / like. It is a mask I try on. / . . . its frog / sits on my lips and defecates." Even Adrienne Rich, usually affirmative in her definition of a second, supernatural self, acknowledges the awful anxiety associated with such experiences of interior otherness; "A pair of eyes imprisoned for years inside my skull / is burning its way outward, the headaches are terrible" ("Ghazals: Homage to Ghalib"). Diane Wakoski, who writes of wanting "to smash through the fortified walls of myself / with a sledge," describes, in heavily sexual terms, "the anger of my own hair, / which is long / and wants to tie knots, / strangle, avenge this face of mine . . ." ("This King: The Tombed Egyptian One," and "Water Shapes"). Inhabited by this cry of fury, these self-assertive, witch-dark wings that flap inside so many women poets, she feels a sort of supernatural electricity "dripping" from her "like cream" and perceives the whole world as transformed, seething with magical dangerous blue phenomena: "blue trains rush by in my sleep. / Blue herons fly overhead . . . . / Blue liquid pours down my poisoned throat and blue veins / rip open my breast. Blue daggers tip / and are juggled in my palms. / Blue death lives in my fingernails" ("Blue Monday"). "The Eye altering alters all," as Blake observed so long ago, and the woman poet who defines herself as possessor of (or possessed by) a deadly second self inevitably begins to imagine that she's lost in a universe of death.

Where is the way out of such a universe? What kind of self-definition is possible to someone who feels herself imprisoned there, her back humped with black inimical power, black wings flapping in her heart? — to go back to the poems with which I began these speculations. One answer, the one Sylvia Plath most often chooses, is for the woman poet to completely reject the "natural" self — the public, outer self of roles and names — and instead to identify entirely with her supernatural self. "Mrs. Hughes," for instance, is clearly one of Plath's old whore petticoats, as are "Otto Plath's daughter" and "the Guest Managing Editor of *Mademoiselle*." Her real self, she insists, is "no drudge" but a queen, unleashed and flying, more terrible than she ever was. Yet here the terror is not a cause of anxiety but a sign of life and triumph. Become celestial like Rich's woman-as-galactic-cloud, healing the wounds of self-division, Plath's supernatural self appears at last as a "red / Scar in the sky, red comet," flying "Over the engine that killed her — / The mausoleum, the wax house" of the dying "natural" self ("Stings").

Denise Levertov, on the other hand, opts in "The Wings" for a very different solution to the problem of her black inimical power, speculating that she may have *two* wings, two second selves, both equally supernatural but "one / feathered in soot, the other // . . . pale / flare-pinions." "Well —" she asks, repudiating the rage of Plath's terrible flying scar, "Could I go / on one wing, // the white one?" Perhaps, she implies, the second self is not witch, devil, animal, but in the best, Blakean sense, goddess, angel, spirit.

But, of course, to go on only one wing is a compromise, an admission of defeat and fragmentation akin to Anne Finch's sorrowful presentation of her "contracted wing." And Adrienne Rich, determined "to save the skein" of "this trailing knitted thing, this cloth of darkness, / this woman's garment" of enigmatic selfhood, refuses to compromise ("When We Dead Awaken"). Like both Plath and Levertov, however, she identifies primarily with a supernatural self, a self flying "lonely and level as a plane . . . / on its radio beam, aiming / across the Rockies" ("Song"). But unlike Plath in "Stings" or Levertov in "The Wings," she's untroubled by questions about the morality of this second self. Neither black nor white, neither terrible nor blessed, it exists, Rich suggests, because it has to, for the sake of the survival of all women. Thus, the second pair of eyes, which gave the poet headaches in the 1968 "Ghazals," reappears later in "From the Prison House" as a single, healthy, visionary, third eye that is impervious to pain, pure, objective, an instrument of accurate perception:

Underneath my lids another eye has opened
it looks nakedly
at the light

that soaks in from the world of pain
even when I sleep . . .

This eye
is not for weeping
its vision must be unblurred
though tears are on my face

its intent is clarity
it must forget
nothing.

Despite this affirmation of the justice and inevitability of her visionary anger, it's plain that Rich, too, sees herself as fragmented. Displacing her poetic vision onto a supernatural third eye and leaving the eyes of her outer, natural self merely for weeping, she implicitly concedes — at least in this poem — the difficulty of achieving a wholeness, a single, entirely adequate self-definition. And to be honest, very few women poets, from Anne Finch to the present, have in fact managed a definitive statement of self-assertion, a complete self-definition. Yet I hope that these preliminary speculations have at least partly recorded what I think women poets themselves have fully recorded: a difficult process of self-discovery that is in full progress, moving all women continually forward toward what D. H. Lawrence (for whom the problem was considerably simpler) called "self-accomplishment."

Like Lawrence, W. B. Yeats was an heir of the romantic movement's egotistical sublime, so it was natural for him to imagine a woman singing, " 'I am I, am I; / The greater grows my light / The further that I fly,' " and to note, "All creation shivers / With that sweet cry." But soon, perhaps, such self-assertive imaginings will be equally natural for women poets. Already Muriel Rukeyser, in one of her most famous passages, has envisioned a radiant union of inner and outer selves, a first jubilant joining of the fragments into a true creative whole: "No more masks! No more mythologies! / Now, for the first time, the god lifts his hand, / the fragments join in me with their own music." And Denise Levertov, transcending her divided self of black and white wings, has proclaimed: "There is no savor / more sweet, more salt / than to be glad to be / what, woman, / and who, myself, / I am . . . ." As for the hump of black inimical power on her back, the burden of her wings, that other self can be assimilated, she suggests in "Stepping Westward," into a force that nourishes her wholeness:

If I bear burdens
they begin to be remembered
as gifts, goods, a basket

of bread that hurts
my shoulders but closes me

in fragrance. I can
eat as I go.

Alicia Ostriker

In Mind: The Divided Self in Womens' Poetry

"The Nerves of a Midwife" is a first take; "In Mind" is a blowup of one section. In 1977 I had been reading women poets intensively for a year or so, and wrote to make sense of what I was finding — in the poetry and in myself. I am still trying to do that. The later essay is an expansion, part of a work-in-progress which will, I hope, more fully define the chorale of the women's poetry movement today: we are all hearing it, we feel in our bones how exciting, challenging, disturbing it is; something is happening for the first time, but what is it? That is what I am trying to figure out.

The Nerves of a Midwife

I am obnoxious to each carping tongue
Who says my hand a needle better fits.

Thus briskly wrote the pilgrim mother Anne Bradstreet in a "Prologue" to her book of poems, first published in 1650, and thus meekly two stanzas later the first woman poet in America apologized:

Men have precedency and still excel . . .
Men can do best and women know it well.

Preeminence in each and all is yours;
Yet grant some small acknowledgment of ours.

A fraction over three centuries later, Erica Jong observed in "Bitter Pills for the Dark Ladies" (1968) just how small the acknowledgment could be:

If they let you out it's as Supermansaint
& the ultimate praise is always a question of nots:
     viz. not like a woman
     viz. "certainly not another poetess"
meanin'
  she got a cunt but she don't talk funny
  & he's a nigger but he don't smell funny
& the only good poetess is a dead.

The "certainly not another poetess" remark was Robert Lowell's at the advent of Sylvia Plath's *Ariel,* and Plath, who certainly did not want to be another poetess, might well have been pleased by it. But Plath and Jong have in fact both contributed to an extraordinary tide of poetry by American women poets since the late 1950s which shows no sign of abating. An increasing proportion of this work is explicitly female in the sense that the writer has consciously chosen not to "write like a man" but to explore experiences central to her sex, to find the style necessary to express such experiences, and therefore, at least at first, often to invite the scorn of conventional literary critics, editors, and male poets.

In the 1970s, dozens of little magazines and presses have sprung up which print only women's poetry. Universities across the country run series of women's poetry readings, as do, on a more modest level, coffeehouses; conferences of women poets occur and recur. The audience upon which these activities depend takes its poetry avidly and personally. One young woman poet I know calls the work of other women "survival tools." Another writes me:

> About women poets. I like them and read them because I think they're writing more exciting poetry than most men. Their poetry is about discovery and breaking new ground and it feels more like life to me . . . like work that comes to grips with what I feel is essential in all arts — what are we doing in our lives? Why do we do it? How

do we see each other? How can we change what
we have into what we want?

Among commercial and university presses, good women poets are
widely published and recognized for their individual voices. Their
books on the whole receive thoughtful reviews, written with clearer understanding and less condescension every year.

Anthologies of women's poetry fare differently from books of
poems by individual women. I read *Parnassus* for enlightened,
stimulating criticism of poetry and poetics, and am seldom disappointed. But in the Spring/Summer 1975 *Parnassus* I find a review
which spends six lines on Segnitz and Rainey's *Psyche: An Anthology of Modern American Women Poets* and calls it "petite" (it is
256 pages, or about the same size as Donald Hall's *Contemporary
American Poetry,* which for years was a standard volume). "The
twenty poets are good," says the reviewer, but does not name one,
or quote one line; and then proceeds to six encomiastic pages on
Rothenberg and Quasha's *America A Prophecy,* finding it "a big
anthology." That is rather extreme old-school. Yet the Fall/Winter
issue of the same year contains a review of two other women's
anthologies, in which the reviewer, though far more conscientious
and detailed in analysis — he distinguishes intelligently between
the two volumes, argues soundly against the editorial polemic of
one of them while allowing the justice of its essential points, and
appreciates excellence in the poems of both — nevertheless confesses discomfort with the existence of such anthologies. He praises
Levertov for "triumphing on tiptoe over biology and destiny,"
Rich for "the emotional distance that enables her to perfect aesthetic form," and gives his opinion that many of the poets "would
prefer to be read as women second, as poets first." What causes
him, I wonder, to think so? Must we prefer one of those terms to
the other?

True, instead of "certainly not another poetess," the highest
praise in some circles is "certainly not another feminist," but even
this is changing.

What has not changed is that most critics and professors of
literature, including modern literature, deny that "women's
poetry," as distinct from poetry by individual women, exists.
Many women writers agree. Some will not permit their work to
appear in women's anthologies.

The superficial plausibility of this position rests on the undeniable fact that women writers are a diverse lot, adhering to no
single set of beliefs, doctrines, styles, or subjects. Yet would anyone deny the usefulness of the term "American poetry" (or

"French poetry" or "Brazilian poetry") on the grounds that American (or French, or Brazilian) poets are diverse? Should we call Whitman, Frost, Pound, and Stevens "poets" but not "American poets"? Did T. S. Eliot's rejection of America make him any less quintessentially an American poet? In all these cases, the poet's nationality is central to his work; we might even argue that the more deeply an artist represents a nation, the more likely that artist is to represent humanity. Shakespeare was thoroughly English, Dante thoroughly Italian, and so on.

Because of the critical assumption that poetry has no gender, we have not learned to see women poets generically, or to discuss the ideas, apart from the temporary ideologies, that the flowering of their poetry generates. In what follows, I make the assumption that "women's poetry" exists in much the same sense that "American poetry" exists, and that from it we should discover not only more of what it means to be a woman but also more of what it means to be human. Although we may not be able to guess just which poems or poets from the present lively moment will in the long run endure, we can reasonably expect that whatever is shallow will evaporate by itself, and that whatever is profound and strong will ultimately enrich the mainstream of letters. Here I would like to touch, speculatively, on four elements in women's poetry which seem to me original, important, and organically connected with one another. These are the quest for autonomous self-definition; the intimate treatment of the body; the release of anger; and what I call, for want of a better name, the contact imperative. Each of these themes appears in the work of many more writers than I will be able to quote, and some of those I quote will be familiar names while some will not, precisely because the ideas, the feelings, are not merely the property of individuals. I will also say a few hesitating words about stylistic and formal considerations in women's poetry, and how they may correlate with certain emotional requirements.

First of all, then, it appears that to define oneself as authentically as possible from within has become the major female enterprise in poetry. "No more masks!" is a line from Muriel Rukeyser and the title of an anthology. Not what our fathers and mothers told us, not what our teachers expected, not what our lovers suppose, nor necessarily what literature and mythology, however beautiful and compelling, tell us: what are we then? As soon as the question is asked, certain typical rifts appear. Denise Levertov in the poem "In Mind" discovers two incompatible selves: one a woman

of innocence, unadorned but
fair-featured, and smelling of
apples or grass. She wears
a utopian smock . . .
                    And there's a
turbulent moon-ridden girl
or old woman, or both,
dresses in opals and rags, feathers
and torn taffeta . . .

The first "is kind" but lacks imagination. The second "knows strange songs" but is not kind. A self approved by others, modest, decorous, and humanistically valuable (it has written, I think, Levertov's poems of social and political compassion), stands against a darker, more mysterious and dangerous self. Both are natural — it is not a question of one being real, one hypocritical — although the latter might perhaps better be called preternatural. Levertov, perhaps the sweetest and most life-celebratory of poets writing today, nevertheless writes of a "coldness to life," an inner-directedness which seems "unwomanly" because insufficiently nurturing of others. Or she writes of cherishing a "madness . . . blue poison, green pain in the mind's veins" though she has always been the sanest of her friends, the one they came to for comfort. The split is a central one in Levertov, and many young women warm to her work because it expresses both clearly and gently a dilemma they find in themselves. More flamboyantly, Diane Wakoski in "Beauty" parades a self something like Levertov's moon-ridden girl, asking:

and if I cut off my long hair,
if I stopped speaking,
if I stopped dreaming for other people about parts of the car,
stopped handing them tall creamy flowered silks,
and loosing the magnificent hawks to fly in their direction . . .
if I stopped crying for the salvation of the tea ceremony,
stopped rushing in excitedly with a spikey bird-of-Paradise,
and never let them see how accurate my pistol-shooting is,
who would I be?

The dilemma in Wakoski, and again it is a common one, is a sense of overpowering pride, vitality, and imaginative energy crossed by a self-destructive dependence on others for its confirmation. "Where is the real me I want them all to love," she asks self-mockingly, as she swings from one father-lover figure to another —

George Washington whom she excoriates at one end of her pendulum, Beethoven to whom she clings at the other, and the easy riders whom she invites to make her life hard in between.

Not only roles and temperaments may come into question, but sexual identity itself, as it does in Adrienne Rich:

> I do not know
> if sex is an illusion
>
> I do not know
> who I was when I did those things
> or who I said I was
> or whether I willed to feel
> what I had read about
> or who in fact was there with me
> or whether I knew, even then
> that there was doubt about these things
>
> "Dialogue"
>
> If I am flesh sunning on rock
> if I am brain burning in fluorescent light
>
> if I am dream like a wire with fire
> throbbing along it
>
> if I am death to man
> I have to know it
>
> "August"

I have to know it. That is the unspoken theme behind the self-regard which dominates many women's work, whether the work is a delicate blend of feeling, sensation, and thought like Levertov's, passionately exhibitionistic like Wakoski's, or essentially intellectual like Rich's. The fact that the question of identity is a real one, for which the thinking woman may have as yet no satisfactory answer, may turn her resolutely inward. It may also make her poetry urgent and emotional, insofar as feelings initially inhibited, whether from within or without, have permission to erupt into the poem — and she will not know who she is until she lets them. In such work, academic distinctions between art and life, or between the self and what we in the classroom call the speaker or the persona of a poem (persona, recall, means "mask"), move to the vanishing point.

A good deal of the confusion felt by some readers confronted with women's poetry may be a simple matter of fashion. Our present critical milieu expects and rewards the maintenance of low profiles in poetry: "reticence," for example, is the term Richard Howard employs to recommend Ammons's *Sphere,* and Ashbery's *Self-Portrait in a Convex Mirror* enjoys a *succès d'estime* for implying that a distorting lens tells us all we know and all we need to know about the self. "Control" and "distance" make good buzz-words on any book-jacket, while the phrase "confessional poetry" has become equivalent to wrinkling up one's nose as at a nasty odor, something vulgar. But when a woman poet says "I" she is likely to mean the actual "I" as intensely as her verbal skills permit, much as Wordsworth or Keats did — or Blake, or Milton, or John Donne of the *Holy Sonnets,* before Eliot's "extinction of personality" became the mandatory twentieth-century initiation ritual for young American poets.

Another problem is that the woman poet who seeks herself puts trivial material, that is, the material of her own daily life and feelings, into poems. "Some women marry houses," begins Anne Sexton's terse and deadpan "Housewife":

It's another kind of skin; it has a heart,
a mouth, a liver and bowel movements.
The walls are permanent and pink.
See how she sits on her knees all day,
faithfully washing herself down.
Men enter by force, drawn back like Jonah
into their fleshy mothers.
A woman *is* her mother.
That's the main thing.

Or, again, "They say women are too personal. We are not personal enough," begins Penelope Schott, in a poem which speaks of insufficient empathy with other women, who push baby carriages she has grown free of. She remembers how it felt to push the baby carriages, laden with groceries, down curbstones. She remembers that her mother lied to her about growing pubic hair, and about the pain of childbirth, and that "I have already lied to my daughter." To tell the truth to our daughters requires that we acknowledge it ourselves. The poem becomes the tribunal where a persona will not suffice; it is oneself who will be found innocent or guilty.

As the two poems just quoted already indicate, one subject that all women have in common to tell the truth about is anatomy; not, perhaps, as destiny but as priority, especially since in a world where perhaps not much is to be trusted, "the body does not lie."

Tota mulier in utero, says the Latin, although until recently anatomy was not a subject for women's pens. While Lawrence, Joyce, and Henry Miller wrote and let censorship be damned, Virginia Woolf in a lecture on "Professions for Women" recalled her impulse, when young, to describe "something about the body . . . which it was unfitting for her as a woman to say. Men, her reason told her, would be shocked . . . . For though men sensibly allow themselves great freedom in these respects, I doubt that they realize or control the extreme severity with which they condemn such freedom in women." In the 1970s, descriptions of bodily experiences have become the most common sign of female identification in poetry. Tactility and orality abound — Sexton and Jong are particularly oral, for example, their poems filled with images of food, eating, sucking, licking. Sex receives graphic treatment hot and cold — Lynn Lifshin is probably the silkiest siren among the Wife of Bath's daughters, Elizabeth Sargent and Alta the lustiest. Looking at and touching oneself, dressing and adorning oneself, menstruation, pregnancy and birth, abortion, rape, the surgeon's knife, the process of aging, the handling of children — because women have traditionally been defined by and confined to the secret gardens of their physical selves, while being forbidden to talk in mixed company about them, they now have much to say. The abundance and variety of body images in women's poetry presently outweighs that of men's, as does the non-airbrushed intimacy of focus.

The range of attitudes women take toward the body is also startling. At one extreme, which would be medieval were it not so modern, Sylvia Plath perceives the flesh as infinitely and fascinatingly vulnerable. "I am red meat," she realizes in "Death & Co.," and her poems form a *totentanz* of the body's subjection to laceration, mutilation, disease, paralysis, rendered in chillingly vivid images of passivity and pain:

> They have propped my head between the pillow and the sheet-cuff
> Like an eye between two white lids that will not shut.
> Stupid pupil, it has to take everything in . . .
> My husband and child smiling out of the family photo;
> Their smiles catch onto my skin, little smiling hooks.

The world of Plath's imagination is bounded by the brutal destruction of flesh in the Nazi holocaust and the everyday brutality of "The butcher's guillotine that whispers 'How's this, how's this?' " More recently, the young poet Ai depicts a rural Southwest in which men and women alike exist at a level of ruthless bodily hungers. When a man beats a runaway woman:

> The corner of your mouth bleeds
> and your tongue slips out, slips in.
> You don't fight me, you never do.

When a midwife does her job:

> A scraggy, red child comes out of her into my hands
> like warehouse ice sliding down the chute.

The bondage of a female body takes another form in poems which deal with the ambivalence of beauty. To cosmetize or not to cosmetize? This is a subgenre in itself, opening a rich vein of comic possibilities. Carolyn Kizer in *Pro Femina* remarks on "Our masks, always in peril of smearing or cracking," attention to which keeps a woman from serious work, neglect of which keeps her without a love life, catching up on her reading. Honor Moore's "My Mother's Mustache" gives the pros and cons of depilatories. Karen Swenson worries about a bosom less ample than Monroe's. "It's a sex object if you're pretty / love and no sex if you're fat," observes Nikki Giovanni. Jong writes a hilarious poem on "Aging," with a surprise happy ending. These poems are as undignified as they are funny — we are off the pedestal — and of course, like all good clowning, work of this sort spins from a painful core. Raised up to be narcissists, which is a game every woman ultimately loses, we must laugh that we may not weep.

Also among the poems just beginning to be written are some which treat the female body as a power rather than a liability. In Sharon Barba's "A Cycle of Women," the poet evokes

> that dream world Anais speaks of
> that dark watery place
> where everything is female,

and imagines a new Venus emerging from it, "a woman big-hipped, beautiful and fierce." Sexton writes "In Celebration of my Uterus," comparing "the central creature and its delight" to a singing schoolgirl, a spirit, a cup, "soil of the fields . . . roots," and hyperbolically declares:

> Each cell has a life.
> There is enough here to feed a nation . . .
> Any person, any commonwealth would say of it,

"It is good this year that we may plant again
and think forward to a harvest."

Robin Morgan's long "Network of the Imaginary Mother" recounts
the poet's conversion from loathing to loving her own body, pre-
cipitated by the baptismal experience of nursing her dying mother,
and defines her biological capacities in terms of goddess-figures
representing a triumphant will to love and nurture, opposed to the
killing abstractions of technology. Muriel Rukeyser has developed
a language similarly rooted in gender and ramifying into politics,
which envisions radical social change impelled by principles of
maternity. The power of the maternal drive to transform even the
most intimate grief and guilt into strength appears in Lucille Clif-
ton's "The Lost Baby Poem:"

> the time i dropped your almost body down
> to meet the waters under the city
> and run one with the sewage to the sea
> what did i know about waters rushing back
> what did i know about drowning
> or being drowned . . .
>
> if i am ever less than a mountain
> for your definite brothers and sisters
> let the rivers pour over my head
> let the sea take me for a spiller
> of seas let black men call me stranger
> always for your never named sake

And for Adrienne Rich, in the difficult yet triumphant close to
"The Mirror in Which Two Are Seen as One," it is ourselves to
whom we must heroically give birth:

> your mother dead and you unborn
> your two hands grasping your head
> drawing it down against the blade of life
> your nerves the nerves of a midwife
> learning her trade.

It will be interesting to see whether such female metaphors will
come to take their place alongside more conventional metaphors
for heroism. Meanwhile, whether engaged or not in ideology, it
would be difficult to find a woman poet writing today who does
not treat the facts of her and our physical experience as essential

material for poetry.

If we turn to sexual politics in the sense coined by Kate Millett, we find less pleasure, more anger, and a striking development of poems about violence, although (or because) neither violence nor anger has been a traditionally acceptable mode of expression for women. When women perceive themselves as victims, suppressed, confined, their strengths denied and their weaknesses encouraged under the collective and personal system feminists have come to call patriarchy, they write self-pity poems, mad-housewife poems, off-our-back poems, all of which are interesting at least symptomatically. The most interesting of them are those which generalize, or make generalization possible, by plunging to the principles which animate persons.

One recalls Plath's archetypically authoritarian male figure in "Lady Lazarus," the composite Doctor-Nazi-sideshow manager, "Herr God, Herr Lucifer." In the eyes of this figure the poet is, she knows, an object to be manipulated, a freak, "your jewel . . . your valuable." In Mona Van Duyn's complex and witty "Death by Aesthetics," the same unpleasant figure appears as a physician-lover, probably also psychoanalyst, an icy Doctor Feelgood:

> His fluoroscope hugs her. Soft the intemperate girl
> disordered. Willing she lies while he unfolds
> her disease, but a stem of glass protects his fingers
> from her heat, nor will he catch her cold . . .
>
> He hands her a paper. "Goodbye. Live quietly,
> make some new friends. I've seen these stubborn cases
> cured with time. My bill will arrive. Dear lady,
> it's been a most enjoyable diagnosis."

In vain the patient begs:

> meet me, feel the way my body feels,
> and in my bounty of dews, fluxes and seasons,
> orifices, in my wastes and smells
> see self.

He has already gone, saying "Don't touch me," and his prescription reads "Separateness."

The experimental playwright and poet Rochelle Owens, in the ironically titled "The Power of Love: He Wants Shih," has composed a sadistic fantasy for a practitioner of martial arts. The hero explains that a woman's love for him is his weapon, that as her feeling increases, his disappears:

> It's heaven's will, shua hsi!
> In my mind I smear the mucus
> from my nose on her breasts . . .
> & drop ants into her two mouths . . .
> I fill up all her orifices —
> I'm very generous . . .
> & she calls me the divinity
> of mountains & streams &
> I think of how it would be
> to piss on her!

May Swenson's "Bleeding" takes the form of a dialogue between a cut and a knife, the former apologetic, the latter angry about being made "messy with this blood." Similarly grim is the dialogue in Marge Piercy's "The Friend," in which a man across the table tells a woman to cut off her hands because they poke and might touch him, to burn her body because it is "not clean and smells like sex." She agrees and says she loves him. He says he likes to be loved and asks her if she has cut off her hands yet.

Such poems, it seems to me, probe deeply into the sources of male-female misery, directing one's horror almost equally against the hypocrite male's inaccessibility to emotion, and the female's compliance in her victimization. Men, in poems about male domination, are always authority figures associated with technology, abstract and analytical thinking instead of feeling, a will to exercise control, and a gluttonous demand for admiration. But the women are helpless petitioners: all they need is love, they make no demands, they will do anything and permit anything to be done to them, they are all too ready to obey. Nor is it an accident that the scenes of these poems are all intimately physical. The presumably male idea of the uncleanness of flesh, and of women's flesh in particular, which we inherit with the rest of our Judeo-Christian dreamlife baggage (e.g., Tertullian, "Woman is a temple over a sewer"), is one that perhaps few women themselves evade. Self-disgust is a strong drink, and to the passive woman an intoxicant: "Every woman adores a fascist / The boot in the face."

One need not believe that individual men necessarily fill the role which so many women's poems have men play, that of aggressive or impassive villain; or that women themselves are universally innocent of such vices. Some men mop the floor. Some women are bitches. One of the excellences of a poem like Swenson's is that it assigns no explicit gender to the cut and the knife — the masochistic cut in fact sounds very much like Shakespeare's Shylock. Such games can be played by persons of any sex, in any combination; compare Ginsberg's "Master" in *The Fall of America.* But this does not invalidate the individual suffering in the poems, or the generic applications implied by them. We know the bleeding cut feels feminine, we know the knife which wants to be hard and shiny feels masculine.

What follows, then, at any rate in a significant number of poems, is the fantasy of vengeance. Plath imagines a ritual slaying of the father she loves and hates in "Daddy," and a return from the grave to devour men in "Lady Lazarus." Rich in "The Phenomenology of Anger" dreams of becoming an acetylene torch, to burn away the lie of her enemy, the killer of babies at My Lai, the defoliator of fields. She desires, she says, to leave him a new man, yet one cannot escape the sense of her compulsion to punish. In her more down-to-earth manner, Diane Wakoski dedicates *The Motorcycle Betrayal Poems* "to all those men who betrayed me at one time or another, in hopes they will fall off their motorcycles and break their necks." In one of the poems of that volume, Wakoski imagines shooting a lover in the back with a Thompson Contender, and watching him topple over once for every man — from her father to the President — who has neglected her. In "They Eat Out," Margaret Atwood punctures, with a fork, a self-important gentleman friend. Grisliest of the lot, perhaps, is Cynthia Macdonald's "Objets d'Art." Having been told by a stranger in a railway station that she was "a real ball-cutter," she thinks it over, goes into the business, finds that freezing is the best method of preservation — and is interested, of course, only in volunteers:

> It is an art like hypnosis
> Which cannot be imposed on the unwilling victim,

which brings us full circle on the fine line between fear and need in human motivation.

But if the release of anger is a major element in women's poetry, so, to an even greater degree, is the release of a contrary passion, which in part explains the vehemence of women's rage. The superiority of male over female (or the mind over the body, or the impersonal over the personal) appears to be the more intolerable to many women poets because of intense cravings for unity, for a sense of relationship which escapes the vertical grid of dominance and submission altogether. Mutuality, continuity, connection, identification, touch: this theme in women's work is one which we might call the contact imperative, and it strongly affects the way women write about love, time, history, politics, and themselves.

In love poetry, the contact imperative means goodbye to the strong silent type. "I like my men / talky and / tender," says Carol Bergé, and in poem after poem describing gratified desire, those lovers and husbands are praised who are most gentle and warm; i.e., who release rather than suppress their "feminine" qualities. Conversely, the poets seem best satisfied with themselves when they quit passivity and take some form of initiative, like Nikki Giovanni in "The Seduction," forth-rightly undressing her man while he lectures on about the revolution. Domestically, women tend to envision love as something natural, normal, and shared, as in Lisel Mueller's "Love Like Salt." To explain ecstasy, women consistently seem to employ the idea of interpenetration between two lovers, the dissolving of boundaries between individual selves, and at especially blissful moments, the elimination of distinctions between human and nonhuman existence. A couple makes love in a bedroom, and then there is

> the hot joy spilling
> pudldes on the bed, the rug,
> the back yard, the earth
> happy with us, needing our joy.

"Anybody could write this poem," insists Alta in her title. "All you have to say is Yes." Again, in Maxine Kumin's "We Are," the lovingly developed metaphor for a pair of lovers is that of a pond, complete with frogs whose legs open like very small children's, skimmed by waterbugs, surrounded by blackberry bushes: "We teem, we overgrow." Still again, in Daniela Gioseffi's quasi-surrealistic, quasi-pornographic "Paradise Is Not a Place," the lovers sail the seas on their mattress, and ultimately fuse into a giant Mount Androgynous which becomes a permanent tourist attraction in the mid-Pacific. One would think of Donne's "The Canonization," except that for Gioseffi, as for women love poets in general, love does not signify transcendence of carnality or mortality, nor does it involve trials, tests, obstacles. The images are of relaxation and immanence rather than strenuousness. The motion of love is down, not up: down toward the earth, down into the flesh, easily.

The need for connection can also express itself in terms of exploring continuities between generations. Daughters write of parents or grandparents, mothers write of children. Women write of continuities from one writer to another (not, *pace* Harold Bloom, on the Oedipal model of killing and superseding, but on the Demeter-Kore model of returning and reviving), or the love-and-support relationships (sexual or not) generated and reinforced by the feminist movement.

Among politically radical writers such as Rich, Piercy, and Morgan, desire for personal affection assumes the status of a non-negotiable demand. Intimacies between friends and lovers become a model for the conduct of political life. What resists the self-surrender of love in the microcosm of private relationships is also what resists it in Vietnam, Biafra, Harlem, and these poets want to break that resistance, tear off the armor, and liberate the willing lover at the core of the unwilling enemy. Thus an embrace is a "guerrilla tactic" in Piercy's "Agitprop," and the woman who inflicts it on an unresponding man is sending his deeper self "promises . . . of interim relief / and ultimate victory."

These are also the writers who make poems for and from the lives of lost women, the insulted and injured of present and past history, and an occasional heroine. Working-class girls appear in several of Piercy's poems, and Piercy has done a fine lament for Janis Joplin. The lives of frontierwomen are celebrated and mourned in Rich's "From an Old House in America"; Rich has also written about Marie Curie and Caroline Herschel. Morgan's "Network of the Imaginary Mother" includes a recital of the names of witches executed, or tortured and executed, up until the eighteenth century. Susan Griffin writes equally of welfare mothers, her own middle-class alcoholic one, and Harriet Tubman. Judy Grahn writes a sequence of poems entitled "The Common Woman," concluding with Marilyn Monroe. One of the most powerful statements about the personal and social dimensions of women's love for women is Grahn's *A Woman Is Talking to Death*. To extract quotations from this work is to mutilate it, but Grahn should be better known. The following passage is from a mock interrogation:

What about kissing? Have you kissed any women?

I have kissed many women.

When was the first woman you kissed with serious feeling?

The first woman ever I kissed was Josie, who I had
loved at such a distance for months. Josie was not only
beautiful, she was tough and handsome too. Josie had
black hair and white teeth and strong brown muscles.
Then she dropped out of school unexplained. When
she came back she came back for one day only, to

finish the term, and there was a child in her. She was all shame, pain and defiance. Her eyes were dark as the water under a bridge and no one would talk to her, they laughed and threw things at her. In the afternoon I walked across the front of the class and looked deep into Josie's eyes and I picked up her chin with my hand, because I loved her, because nothing like her trouble would ever happen to me, because I hated it that she was pregnant and unhappy, and an outcast. We were thirteen.

You didn't kiss her?

How does it feel to be thirteen and having a baby?

You didn't actually kiss her? . . .

In a later section of the poem, Grahn is knocked down in a diner by a Spanish-speaking youth who calls her "queer." Counterman and police prove indifferent. Weeks later it occurs to her that this might be Josie's son. In a still later section, she and her "pervert" friends encounter a fifty-five-year-old Chinese woman who has been raped by a cabdriver and left bleeding in the snow. They kiss and try to reassure her, knowing it is not enough. Grahn burns with desire to rule the city with this woman, but she lets her go in the ambulance with the bored policemen, guiltily unable to enact her defiance, to "get the real loving done."

Within the symposium of the self, a number of women poets evidently wish to reverse Yeat's dictum that from the quarrel with ourselves we make poetry. They struggle rather to make poetry about coming to peace with ourselves by reconciling internal antimonies. Coleridge, Rimbaud, and Woolf are invoked for the idea of the androgynous being who combines both intellect and emotion, strength and gentleness. Rukeyser, in a poem on Kathe Kollwitz, quotes Kollwitz' testimony that her own work required a masculine element. Rich, in "Diving into the Wreck," discovers as she descends to the depths of personal and communal history, "I am he . . . I am she." Although Rich has since repudiated the ideal of androgyny, it remains attractive to others, and perhaps is responsible for the tough-but-tender style of a writer like Grahn.

I believe that it is the contact imperative which finally accounts for the confessional or diarist mode in women's writing, because of the intimacy this mode imposes on the audience. One cannot read, for example, a Wakoski or a Sexton poem with feeling that the ordinary objectivity of readership comes under severe attack, and the same is true, if to a less breathtaking degree, with many other women poets. "No more masks" means something for reader as well as writer. As the poet refuses to distance herself from her emotions, so she prevents us from distancing ourselves. We are obliged to witness, to experience the hot breath of the poem upon us. Or perhaps we want to wrestle loose. The poem is impolite, crude, it imposes too much. In either case, we have been obliged to some degree to relinquish our roles as readers, and to respond personally. That, evidently, has been the aim of the poet. In a sense beyond what Plath intended, these are disquieting muses.

Having said this much, I do not suppose I have exhausted the themes and modes of contemporary women's poetry, any more than I have mentioned all the "good" women writers. I suspect, for example, that the need to define presocial strata in female nature is producing a revival of mythology in poetry, much as the compulsion to explore nonrational human passions led Coleridge to the supernatural, Keats and Shelley to classical Greek myth, Blake to a self-invented mythology, Yeats to occultism, Eliot to *The Golden Bough.* I would not be surprised to find that certain traditional images and symbols reveal new facets for women artists. Water, in women's poetry, seems to function as an image not of chaos and danger, but of security and a potential for rebirth. Another instance is the symbol of the flower, which in women's poetry today repeatedly signifies vitality, power, sensuousness to an almost predatory degree, much as in the visual imagery of Georgia O'Keeffe or Judy Chicago. Still another is blood, which becomes in many poems an image for creativity.

Nor do I suppose that the issues I have been outlining are the exclusive property of women writers. Poets like Ginsberg, Duncan, and Bly work intensively on some of the same problems that beset women, and in fact each of these men has identified his concerns as symbolically female. Theodore Roethke's profound sensuousness and discomfort with abstractions had a feminine cast (although through most of his career his explicit self-identifications were emphatically with plants and animals, and his treatment of women thoroughly conventional). Paul Goodman's poetry shares many antiauthoritarian ideas with that of the radical feminist poets, including the idea of congruence between the body and the body politic. Galway Kinnell dives faithfully into his own wreck, and his essay on "Poetry, Personality, and Death" eloquently discusses the limitations of impersonality in poetry, pointing out that while a persona may enable a writer to dramatize otherwise hidden aspects of his own personality, it may also release him from the painfulness of a full examination. The poet, Kinnell remarks, "knows himself to be of a more feminine disposition than the banker." To a greater or lesser extent, such writers defy the dominant "modern" mode of weary irony which has characterized English and American poetry for fifty years, deviations from which have usually been antiacademic, grassroots movements of one sort or another. Yet at the present moment, the flying wedge of dissent and quest is composed mainly of women, who collectively are contributing an extraordinary intellectual, emotional, and moral exhilaration to American poetry, and who may be expected to have an impact on its future course.

In Mind: The Divided Self and Women's Poetry

To define oneself as authentically as possible from within has become the major female enterprise in poetry. "No More Masks!" is a phrase from Muriel Rukeyser and the title of a popular anthology. "If we don't name ourselves, we are nothing," says Audre Lorde. "If the world defines you, it will define you to your disadvantage." External authority is to be mistrusted, since it either gives us lessons in sweetly singing, sweetly speaking, as the poet Horace says, for someone else's benefit, or it assures us we are visible when we know we are not. (See Robin Morgan's "The Invisible Woman," a small-scale version of Ellison's *Invisible Man.*) Not what our fathers and mothers taught us a good girl was, not what our teachers expected, not what our lovers desire and suppose, nor even what literature and mythology, however beautiful and compelling, tell us: what are we then? Every woman is in Lear's lonely condition: Is there none can tell me what I am?

As soon as the question is asked, certain typical rifts appear. We arrive at a landscape illustrated by poet after poet, poem after poem, in works of such evident impact that to read them is plainly to hit a psychic bedrock. Consider, as examples of escalating extremity, the three well-known poets — in most respects quite different from each other — Denise Levertov, Diane Wakoski, and Sylvia Plath.

Levertov in the poem "In Mind" discovers two incompatible selves:

> one a woman
> of innocence, unadorned but
> fair-featured and smelling of

apples or grass. She wears
a utopian smock . . .
　　And there's a
turbulent moon-ridden girl
or old woman, or both,
dressed in opals and rags, feathers
and torn taffeta. . .

The first "is kind" but lacks imagination. The second "knows strange songs" but is not kind. A self approved by others, modest, decorous, and humanistically valuable (it has written, we may suppose, Levertov's poems of social and political idealism), stands against a darker, more mysterious and dangerous self. Both are natural — it is not a question of one being real, one hypocritical — although the latter might better be called preternatural. Levertov, the sweetest and most life-celebratory of poets, worries over her "coldness to life," an inner-directedness which seems "unwomanly" because insufficiently nurturing of others. Or she writes of cherishing a "madness . . . blue poison, green pain in the mind's veins" though she has always been the sanest of her friends, the one they came to for comfort.

This split between a tame and a wild self is a central one in Levertov as far back as the early "The Earthwoman and the Waterwoman." Her "Sunday Afternoon" describes how a Mexican coffee merchant's daughters, after taking First Communion and eating "the banquet of mangoes and bridal cake,"

　　　　　　lay down
for a long siesta, and their white dresses
lay beside them in their dreams as the flies buzzed.
But as the afternoon
burned to a close they rose
among the halfbuilt villas
alive, alive, kicking a basketball, wearing
other new dresses, of bloodred velvet.

It is delightful here to see domestic passivity alternating with recreational vigor, a meal including prophetic wedding cake followed by a basketball, innocent white leading without conflict to erotic red. The reason for the lack of conflict, of course, is that these females are pre-pubescent. Grown women enjoy less flexibility. Levertov's "Rose White and Rose Red" in "An Embroidery" are separate beings, as are the two figures of "The Woman," a later and a more astringent poem, where "the one in homespun / you

Daily to awaken and open her eyes, says Atwood, is to trigger an automatic closing of hydraulic doors "between the hands and some other time // that can't exist." A stanza break dividing the words "time" and "that can't exist" represents the instant of mental hesitation during which rational consciousness gathers itself to reject the deep knowledge of the sleeping self. "Can't exist" signifies cannot be conceived as existing, and must not be permitted to exist. Consciousness, a control panel, "whispers softly as a diamond cutting glass." To get up is to "extend the feet / into my body which is a metal spacesuit."

> I have armed myself, yes I am safe: safe:
> the grass can't hurt me.
> My senses swivel like guns in their fixed sockets:
> I am barriered from leaves and blood.

To fear what is natural, to fear the dreamlife and the unguarded subconscious, requires that one transform oneself into artifact, even to the extent of making organs of sensation, which in nature are organs of receptivity, into weapons. To fear what is natural is to become absurd, and it is to become symbolically male instead of symbolically female. "A Fortification" divides into two halves, with this stanza as pivot. Atwood's conclusion describes a tantalizing glimpse of another self, "the one that has real skin, real hair," at the moment of its diurnal disappearance "down the line of cells / back to the lost forest of being vulnerable."

All such poems, aligning themselves as they do around stated or implied dualities, at least one of which is the duality between vulnerable nature and invulnerable art, intersect illuminatingly with one of the most famous poems of the modern era, Yeat's "Sailing to Byzantium." Yeats in this poem rejects the sensual music of nature's cycle in which, as an old man, he can no longer participate except by dying. To the "dying generations" of fish, flesh and fowl, he prefers "Monuments of unageing intellect," and to the scarecrow rags of the body he prefers the soul. Leaving the country of life he sails to the holy city of art, where he longs to be gathered "Into the artifice of eternity" and to assume the form of a precious object:

> Once out of nature I shall never take
> My bodily form from any natural thing,
> But such a form as Grecian goldsmiths make
> Of hammered gold and gold enamelling.

hunger for / when you are lonesome" alternates with "the one in crazy feathers" who "wearies you." The poet remarks that she wearies herself, that the homespun one is weary too, and concludes:

> Alas,
> they are not two but one,
> pierce the flesh of one, the other
> halfway around the world, will shriek,
> her blood will run. Can you endure
> life with two brides, bridegroom?

We may attribute the violence in "The Woman," as well as its quiet hinting at generic male insensitivity, atypical for Levertov, with the fact that it was written during the Vietnam War, waged by her nation against a small Asian nation, which Levertov opposed. Rage at war tends to make misanthropists of the mildest women.

Levertov's version of the split self is a gentle one compared with Wakoski's and Plath's. In one of her typical demonstrations of simultaneous exhibitionism and self-depreciation, Diane Wakoski in "Beauty" parades a self something like Levertov's moon-ridden girl, asking:

> and if I cut off my long hair,
> if I stopped speaking,
> if I stopped dreaming for other people about parts of the car,
> stopped handing them tall creamy flowered silks,
> and loosing the magnificent hawks to fly in their direction . . .
> if I stopped crying for the salvation of the tea ceremony,
> stopped rushing in excitedly with a spiky bird-of-Paradise,
> and never let them see how accurate my pistol-shooting is,
> who would I be?

The dilemma in Wakoski is again a common one. On the one hand is the poet's pride, vitality, and flashing imaginative energy unconfined by gender stereotypes (note her typically spectacular repertoire including parts of the car and pistol-shooting adjacent to flowered silks and the tea ceremony). This vitality is crossed by a self-destructive dependence on others for its confirmation. "Where is the real me I want them all to love," she asks self-mockingly, as she swings from one father-lover figure to another — George Washington whom she excoriates at one end of her pendulum, Beethoven to whom she clings at the other, the King of Spain who would be Eros to her Psyche, and the easy riders whom she invites to make her life difficult in between.

131

The two most thoroughly elaborated personae in the myths Wakoski has elaborated about herself are the poet, master of her craft, "the eye of the world," a proud, controlling, even predatory force, whom she often describes in male pronouns, and the woman deserted in childhood by her father, desperately in need of love and doomed to be rejected by all her lovers. The first of these personae is fiercely strong, hard as a rock, poetically abundant, controlling a range of images as wide and wild as any surrealist's, possibly wider and wilder than any other American poet's. The other is pathetically needy, barren as a moonscape, wilted as the pink dress she cannot wear because it reminds her of a lover's betrayal. Wakoski's work vividly illustrates the All or Nothing syndrome in female romantic fantasies. The two sides of herself are appropriately also an all and a nothing, a strong and weak. When the poet speaks of their relationship she says that the poet comes into being as a compensation for the lonely self:

My poetry is about beauty and how it rescues us, if only through our fantasy lives, from what is mundane and dull . . .

The act of writing is an act of completion. If you get what you want, you don't write about it. You write about what you don't get.

We can see the iron link going the other way also, in a woman's version of the nineteenth century assumption that if you are going to write, you had better suffer. If strength, aggressiveness, independence, control are "masculine" qualities presumably if not necessarily repellent to male lovers, the woman who has such qualities in abundance can expect lengthy spells of uncoupled existence. She can expect to see herself as abnormal, unfeminine — and perhaps this is intolerable. The "feminine" personality clings to love, cannot exist without it. Consequently the strong woman who needs to deny/punish herself for her strength and to retain a feminine self-image might contrive to design an unhappy love life for herself; might believe that this destiny is due to powers beyond her control, like a father's desertion or a plain face; might anchor her power to her weakness. That she should succeed in both art and love might well seem to her, and to us, unthinkable.

As a number of commentators have observed, the most brilliant single split-self poem of our time is probably Sylvia Plath's "In Plaster," composed when the poet was in hospital with appendicitis. "In Plaster" posits not only a relationship between a self and a plaster cast, but a process, exfoliating in three stages, finely designed to seem psychologically inevitable. It is a classic Doppelganger poem in that the double is the depository of qualities the "I" is certain it lacks, and becomes a nemesis. Like Mr. Hyde, or the shadow-self in Dostoevsky, or Hawthorne's Chillingsworth to Reverend Dimmesdale, the double is a contrivance whereby a guilty, inadequate self accomplishes self-punishment.

First, the poem's two personae are described in detail. The "absolutely white person" is "certainly the superior one." "She doesn't need food, she is one of the real saints." She is "so cold." When the speaker hits her, "she held still, like a true pacifist." The speaker, on the contrary, is "the old yellow one . . . ugly and hairy." Far from the blank purity of the plaster saint, she writhes with passions, all of them negative, all of them directed against the uncomplaining double: "I hated her . . . I was scared . . . I couldn't sleep . . . I blamed her . . . I couldn't understand her stupid behavior . . . I hit her."

During the poem's second stage, the speaker announces that the relationship is developing advantageously. She decides that the other one wants love, and that the situation can be exploited:

Without me, she wouldn't exist, so of course she was grateful.
I gave her a soul; I bloomed out of her as a rose
Blooms out of a vase of not very valuable porcelain,
And it was I who attracted everybody's attention.

Now the hatred and fear modulate to condescension, as the plaster self appears to enjoy servitude. "You could tell almost at once she had a slave mentality." But as the self grows to admire and need the other's care, "our relationship grew more intense" and also unstable, and the poem moves into its final phase. The speaker decides that her saint is growing irritable and that the care is deteriorating. The saint, she concludes, wants to leave and is "resentful:"

Wasting her days waiting on a half-corpse!
And secretly she began to hope I'd die.

In this phase the plaster self seems to acquire some of the characteristics of the original self, such as a mind of her own, pride, resentment, hostility, or the speaker thinks she does. Dependence and passivity now reverse. "Without me she wouldn't exist" becomes

I wasn't in any position to get rid of her.

She'd supported me for so long I was quite limp —
I had even forgotten how to walk or sit.

In the poem's conclusion, the speaker is being craftily conciliatory. Though the relationship is "like living with my own coffin," she plots revenge:

One day I shall manage without her,
And she'll perish with emptiness then, and begin to miss me.

A conceivable meaning of the ending is that the speaker plans to return to wholeness and health so that she will not need her plaster cast. Another possibility, supported by the poem's opening exclamation "I shall never get out of this!" as well as by the physical decline of the speaker in the course of the poem and by the resemblance of her final declaration to a suicide threat, is that she will get her revenge by dying, an appropriate *dénouement* since she is the opposite of a saint, which is a sinner, and we know what the wages of sin is. "In Plaster" is a tour de force of extreme solipsism. Nothing and nobody exists inside the poem but "I" and "she;" "I" rejects both responsibility and dependence by insisting not "I need doctors and nurses" but "I am dependent only on an aspect of myself which is dependent of me," and her meanness throughout the poem illustrates the tight connection between passivity, dependence, solipsism, and self-loathing.

"In Plaster" is dated 18 March 1961. In the spring and summer of 1961 Plath was writing *The Bell Jar*, the autobiographical novel about her breakdown and suicide attempt in the summer of her eighteenth year. *The Bell Jar* is peopled with characters who are forms of plaster saint, successful and confident role-players on whom the heroine Esther depends and whom she dislikes. But the resentment is a private secret, never publicly expressed. Esther's good-student, prize-winning public personality is all compliance, designed to please and not offend her mother, her boyfriend's mother, her college teachers, the fluffy lady writer who has given her one scholarship, the staff of the fashion magazine which has given her another one, not to mention other girls, her boyfriend and other men — anyone, in short, whom she perceives as having power. Her public personality is, until her breakdown, the very image of plaster saint itself, and so is implicitly both necessary and despicable, despicable because necessary. "Why did I attract these weird old women? . . . they all wanted to adopt me in some way, and for the price of their care and influence, have me resemble them." But Esther herself attempts to imitate almost everyone influential she encounters, "through year after year of doubleness and smiles and compromise," as she sees her life while skiing recklessly downhill on the way to breaking her leg in two places. Hence, in part, the suicide attempt in *The Bell Jar*, and hence also the "ugly and hairy" self-image of "In Plaster," and its implied momentum toward self-destruction.

As with Wakoski but even more extremely, Plath's divided selves lock into place. There is a public self designed to please others, which is so perfect that it drives all antisocial "ugly" impulses back into secrecy, where they seethe and increase. Or, looking at it the other way, there is an "ugly" self so distressing that an unbreakable self of "whiteness and beauty" must be invented to mask it. Either way, division is self-perpetuating. The Sylvia Plath who played perfect daughter, schoolgirl, eager young woman of letters and hard-working wife, and wrote the painfully cheerful *Letters Home*, created and was created by the Sylvia Plath who hated obedient role-playing and wrote the angry and self-punishing *The Bell Jar* and *Ariel*.

Wild self and tame self in Levertov, strong rational poet and weak emotional woman in Wakoski, perfect external and ugly internal selves in Plath — never far from the surface in all this work is the sense that self-division is culturally prescribed, wholeness culturally forbidden, to the woman and the woman poet. "Will there never be a being to combine a man's mind and a woman's heart, and who yet finds life too rich to weep over? Never?" cried Margaret Fuller. The cleavage in the brain is inherited from Dickinson and other ancestresses. It appears conspicuously in Margaret Atwood, Anne Sexton, Adrienne Rich, and many lesser-known women poets. Moreover, a disguised form of the double self pervades women's poetry even when no split is explicitly mentioned.

For R. D. Laing, schizophrenia "is a special strategy that a person invents in order to live in an unlivable situation,"typically a situation of family tyranny disguised as love. Schizoid personalities suffer what he calls ontological insecurity, and what many women poets call nonexistence, invisibility and muteness: unable to feel their existence confirmed by others, they cannot affirm it for themselves. Such an individual, says Laing, may create a false self organized to comply with the expectations of others, while the true self remains a detached, hyperconscious, critical observer. This sort of temporary dissociation is normal as an escape reaction in threatening or disagreeable situations. To the shizophrenic, however, reality is permanently threatening and unpleasant, so that all activity seems "meaningless, futile and false" — void contrivance or performance — and dissociation becomes not only chronic but progressive. The false self, says Laing, "is compulsively compliant to the will of others," its excessive goodness being reinforced by the secret self's dread of being unmasked. The false self may not only obey but impersonate or caricature the hated, controlling person, whole the true self in its increasingly doomed search for security, baffled by fear of the "helplessness and bewilderment which would be the inevitable start to being oneself," may degenerate into fantasies of transparency, loss of the body, lethal magic powers. Consciousness becomes charged with hostility, fear, envy; ever more elaborate games of pretense and equivocation are played with others, while the inner self may subject itself to experiences of pain and terror in the elusive pursuit of convincing itself it is alive. To the outer world the psychotic "appears to be extremely narcissistic and exhibitionistic. In fact he hates himself and is terrified to reveal himself to others."

One key concept in Laing's analysis needs reformulating, if it is to be adequate to the poems I have been discussing, and to the many poems by women that resemble them — if not, indeed, to the clinical schizophrenic. The idea of "false self" and "true self" is a theorist's imposition — the terms do not occur in his patient's recorded fantasies — a residue, perhaps, of Aristotelian logic. To suppose that the mind, or the self, cannot truly encompass both X and Y is like supposing that a tree cannot truly encompass both roots and leaves. The split selves in women's poems are both true, both false — or rather their truth or falsity is not the issue. The issue is division: that the halves do not combine to a whole, as if a tree had roots and leaves but no trunk. The issue is that the left foot is cut off from the right, the right from the left, and that the division reflects and is reinforced by our culture's limited images of feminine personality.

Among Laing's most provocative images, derived from Wilhelm Reich's metaphor of character armor as the layer of an individual personality designed to protect the vulnerable interior, is the image of "petrification." The schizoid, Laing observes, may fear being turned to stone, or into a robot or automaton; or may believe he can turn others to stone. He is in fact often doing what he fears: mounting a rigid outer personality for himself while defensively depersonalizing others.

Of such a pattern, "In Plaster" is a particularly striking example, but images of self as stone, or armor, or metal, are extremely common in women's poems, whether or not they include explicit statements of self-division. Often the precise point is that the self was once soft but has become self-protectively hard. Often there is more than a hint that the self is imitating, exaggerating or caricaturing the hardness of an enemy who once controlled it and made it suffer. Thus the poem can be at once an embodiment of self-protection and an act of hostility. A poem in Judith Hemschemeyer's *I Remember the Room Was Filled With Light* begins:

> I used to have fur
> and dimensions
> and handles
> I got drunk at parties
> and let people in
> Now I know better

Presently she is an almost completed "sphere / made of plates / of vanadium poems. . . . your hands glance off me now . . . your words are filed / and worked on / and bolted into place." The change from organic to inorganic, irregularly shaped to smoothly spherical, spontaneous to calculating, is also explicitly a change from life to art, or at any rate artifact. The poet's new ability to resist and even exploit the hands and words of the invading "you" is punitive as well as defensive.

A set of poems by Louise Glück about a failed romance appropriately includes one poem entitled "The Fortress." The obvious anatomical locus for a woman's sense of the distinction between permeable and impermeable provides the metaphor in Glück's succinct "Aphrodite," which plays simultaneously with the Greek habit of personifying rocky headlands as goddesses, and with the Odysseus-Penelope story. The poem begins by announcing that "A woman exposed as rock / has this advantage: / she controls the harbor." To adventuring men, the story of life should terminate joyously in a harbor, where they expect after life's wanderings to find no drudge but a goddess. However,

> In time, the young wife
> naturally hardens . . .
> On a hill, the armless figure
> welcomes the delinquent boat,
> her thighs cemented shut, barring
> the fault in the rock.

Blood turns to lava and a body becomes "a black lace cliff fronting a deadpan sea" in Adrienne Rich's "Night in the Kitchen." Margaret Atwood's "A Fortification" raids science fiction for images of consciousness crystallized into a set of self-protection devices that are ultimately indistinguishable from aggression.

How beautiful this is, indeed how feminine, compared with the stony and metal voices of our women. To compare is apparently to apprehend a melancholy gap between the strongest yearnings of men and of women. For one thing it is not dying that the women object to and want to defend themselves against, but being hurt, wronged, violated. Second, when they see themselves as artifacts it is not beauty and preciousness that they envision. A plaster cast and a space suit are more functional, less pleasing, than a singing golden bird in a fantasy emperor's court. Finally, unlike Yeats, the women do not really want to be secure, hard, dispassionate objects. They hate it. The flat inflections of their voices say they hate it. They are angry, despising in themselves the necessity, or what they take to be the necessity, of their petrification. Of this split between a self that desires, and one that dreads, human contact, needing and hating the roles socially prescribed for it, needing and hating self-protection, we see little in contemporary men's poetry. Neither do we see the "elaborate game of pretence and equivocation" so firmly embedded in the poetic strategies of writers like Atwood, Plath, Wakoski, Glück: the nearest things to it, John Ashbery's elusive coyness, Mark Strand's evanescences, are quite without the desperation of the female. That women's poetry in our time is powerful rather than beautiful we have known for some time. A primary source of that power is women's struggle with and against a divided self, experienced at once as inescapable — "I shall never get out of this!" — and as intolerable.

Parts of a Grand Design

Howard Nemerov

Image and Metaphor

When you look back on what is called Modern Poetry in the light of the assumption that it is now over, its victories won for good and ill, its spirit accepted as the very ground of our thoughts and our feelings, the liberties from tradition it insisted on also accepted to the point of becoming matters of indifference, you discover a rather strange thing: you don't find it at all easy to remember what Modern Poetry was.

This is so, perhaps, because while something is visibly producing its manifestations all around you, so that you have no doubt of its existence, you incline to accept whatever fashionable name is commonly given, vaguely aware that the name contains contradictions that someone ought someday to resolve . . . but that is for the historians. Meanwhile you use the name and are confident of being understood; when the name 'Modern Poetry' comes up in a conversation devoted to examples of it, people rarely question the term itself, it is accepted in the way that people accept for convenience the name Time when they are asked What time is it? whereas when people ask themselves What is Time, the name itself is the first thing that comes into question.

There's this as well. If the name Modern Poetry is to become the historical shorthand label for a period of time, it will have to cover the poetry written during that period, which I should roughly limit as the poetry written during the first half of the present century, though I am aware that others would locate it more narrowly, 1910–1925 for instance, and that still others would say it was still going on. But one remembers that the term had its not inconsiderable liveliness in argument just because it distinguished itself from 'contemporary.' Robert Frost was contemporary with Eliot and Pound, but he was not for a long time admitted to be modern with them, though curiously the very same poems that looked merely contemporary in 1940 made Frost seem a modern poet in 1960. Perhaps that is merely the snobbery that is compelled at last to include in its canon whatever had made great reputation, even if that reputation had to be made outside and indeed against the judgment of professionals in the first place.

You can see this clearly if you look for a moment at what would seem to be the most obvious characteristic of work that called itself Modern, its insistence on freedom from conventional forms. The supposed simplicity and purity of this distinction dissolve in endless nigglings and redefinitions, the plain fact of the matter being that despite all the noise made on the subject it was possible for poets to be accepted as Modern Poets whether they wrote free verse or whether they wrote sonnets, or whether they wrote both at once or in turn. If you look chiefly at manifestos and statements of intention, the question of free verse as over against conventional measure and form appears to be thematic for the entire period; but if you look at the poems you see that as a means of telling you who is a Modern Poet and who is not, it is utterly confusing and indeterminate; it is rather like tracing the scatterings and involutions of typography in a poem by cummings only to find it is a sonnet.

There are, I think, thematic and recurrent questions raised in and by the poetry of the period, questions that are thematic for precisely the reason that they get answered in ever so many ways but never in such a way as to put the questions to rest; they come back. I make them out to be three in the main.

The first one centers on such questions as What is an image? When and how does it become a metaphor? Ought it to become a metaphor? At the extreme, some poets have tried to do without metaphor altogether, and some lines of critical thought have supplied, or attempted to supply, philosophical justification for this limitation, which seems to me a little like trying to walk on one foot; you might somehow justify it, for criticism can do much, but how can you do it? And other poets have tried to do without explicit or stated meaning.

The second theme has to do with the immense development of criticism, and especially interpretation, or instruction, during the century; so massive and energetic and programmatic a development as to suggest a shrewd definition of Modern Poetry: the poetry taught in universities.

My third theme is that of Myth, or — though it is best to say this in a low voice — Religion. I mean the often-heard-of obligation upon the Modern Poet to invent, or revise, or somehow inherit all over again for the present century, an account of the creation in which poor old Modern Man — that allegorical invention who has forgotten what he is an allegory of — can invest the immense capital of his idle belief; to find him a god he will be able to pay lip service to.

I shall not here address each of these three themes. In this essay I shall simply try to show that the relation of image and meaning is both defining and difficult for Modern Poetry, to say something about the nature of the difficulties, and, with the help of some examples from William Carlos Williams, to indicate a few different ways of resolving those difficulties.

Poetry and Meaning

The simplest relation of image and meaning is assertive: Look at x, says the poet. I will describe it clearly, and then I will tell you what it means, at any rate what it is going to mean while it is in *my* poem. This is like the relation of photograph and caption. If it is so that the camera cannot lie, it must be so for the sufficient reason that the camera cannot tell the truth either: we look at a picture of a crowd, blurred whitish faces, blurred black clothing. Are they laughing? Praying? Watching a ball game? The caption tells us they are the survivors off a sunken ferry.

This relation of image and meaning is not only the plainest but also the least elegant and the least favored in modern times, yet it is the relation that obtains in a great deal of poetry, including, rather surprisingly, The Sonnets, many of which look as though Shakespeare wrote twelve lines and handed them to an apprentice — Here, boy, you've got two lines to say what this is all about. Modern readers are sometimes disappointed, not only because this relation of image and meaning is out of fashion but much more because Shakespeare's way of handling image, metaphor, and meaning in The Plays is one of the strongest reasons for the simpler relation's being out of fashion. Perhaps one way of accounting for the difference is overlooked: in The Plays the development of the plot and the behavior of the persons in relation to it steadily provide a rough approximation of meaning for the most complex figures in the verse, even in passages corrupt beyond emendation, such as Hamlet on the dram of ale and Othello on the green-eyed monster. In the context of speech and action the phrases are so clear and striking as to have become proverbs, though in strictness they have no assignable meaning. But in The Sonnets, meaning is rather baldly asserted, and the very form of the Shakespearian sonnet seems designed with this in view.

Dante, the complexity of whose poetic theory no one will dispute who had looked at the letter dedicating the *Paradiso* to Can Grande, nevertheless is quite firm on the plain separability of figure and meaning at least in the poet's mind: it would be a great shame, he says, for anyone to hide his subject under the clothing of metaphor or the colorings of rhetoric, and not be able later on to demand to strip his words of these garments in such a way as to produce a true understanding (*Vita Nuova*, XXV). Closely attended to, he seems to say that the meaning need not be supplied *in the poem,* and yet that the poem must have a plain — and separable — meaning.

It is a major tenet of modernism in literature that in one way or another — and I shall soon inspect examples of the ways — this assertive relation of image and meaning can be avoided and must at all costs be avoided. The cost is sometimes high indeed, and I find myself wondering if the progress of our explorations may not lead us round in a circle and back after all to the picture and the caption. But we shall see about that later. For the present I shall begin with the hypothesis that what modernism in writing is chiefly about is *seeing,* seeing as superior to thinking, as opposed to thinking, and something the poet must do instead of thinking if necessary. One notes already the suspicion of a difficulty, that all this affirmation of the eye at the mind's expense is an operation carried out and a decision taken by the mind, not by the eye. Nevertheless, this aspect of the Modern seems to be present about equally in the program of The Imagists, in Eliot's 'objective correlative,' in Joyce's 'epiphany' and in Hemingway's insistence on 'the way it was.' It is what Conrad believed about his art: 'It is above all in the first place to make you see.' One of the most celebrated recent definitions, or slogans, occurs in a little poem by William Carlos Williams, called 'A Sort of a Song.' I give it entire, though it is the second stanza I am chiefly concerned about.

A SORT OF A SONG

Let the snake wait under
his weed
and the writing
be of words, slow and quick, sharp
to strike, quiet to wait,
sleepless.

—through metaphor to reconcile
the people and the stones.
Compose. (No ideas
but in things) Invent!
Saxifrage is my flower that splits
the rocks.

This little piece, whose enthusiastic assertiveness contrasts so oddly with the diffidence of its title, looks to be a very fair sample of a modernist poem, of the claims of modernist poetry in general, and of some of the difficulties the program imposes on the poems. I shall try to tell you some of the ways in which I think it is characteristic of a large and definite part of the mixed bag that gets labeled Modern Poetry.

First I observe that there is no point in saying it is written in free verse, for someone of the opposed persuasion would point out that it comes in two six-line stanzas; and if I objected that the stanzas didn't really match and indeed weren't really stanzas, he might bring in Dr. Williams's notion of the 'variable foot,' which is allowed to vary from one to ten syllables, leaving me speechless. The only thing the idea of free verse does for us here is to tell us that we have become free with respect to definitions and minimal with respect to forms.

The poem is about poetry, and this too is very modern, this reflexiveness. It has always been a possibility for poetry, but never so exploited as in the present century. There has even been collected a fine anthology of poems on poetry, and the flap copy gives me the information I should otherwise have had to spend an hour counting up for myself: of nearly 250 poems by 121 poets chosen from all periods and going as far back as the fourteenth century, half are by twentieth-century poets. One of the things this preoccupation of poetry with itself has seemed to me to mean is the end of poetry; but of that in another place.

The poem is about poetry, and wants to say what poetry ought to be, how poetry ought to go, and must be meant for an example of what it asserts on the subject. The first stanza says that writing, good writing presumably, should resemble a snake in being both slow and quick, sharp and quiet, sleepless. The second stanza offers more abstractly a program for poetry which involves imagism (no ideas but in things) but goes beyond imagism in having for its object

through metaphor to reconcile
the people and the stones.

The climactic image, though less reconciling about stones — of people nothing is said — is a happy one, and yet so narrowly or marginally so as to look a bit like special pleading. For a man to say in one breath 'no ideas but in things' and in the next to give saxifrage as his example is to triumph, but at some cost. Saxifrage is a good example for the excellent reason that its idea does happen to be in its name, which is Latin for *rock-breaker.*

And here is the main difficulty that imagism and its derivatives and variations run into every time. Most ideas are not contained in the mere names of things, nor even in the description of things, and have to be supplied from elsewhere. If you are and say you are in principle against any ideas save such as come packaged in things and the names of things, you will have to bootleg your ideas in somehow-anyhow and spatchcock them onto your poem somehow-anyhow, while continuing to proclaim you are doing no such thing. And that is what happens here.

Moreover, even in the fortunate choice of saxifrage — asphodel would not have done nearly so well in this poem, though it served the poet splendidly in a much better one — Dr. Williams is not at all content to let the idea arise from the thing; instead, he explains that saxifrage is a flower that splits the rocks. To be consistent with theory and program he should have ended the poem simply with the flower's name; and to be consistent with other of his views on an indigenous American poetry he should have said plainly: Sassafras.

Dr. Williams was on occasion a marvelous poet, and I shall come back to a few of his works to exemplify not only the difficulties of imagism but also, in one instance at least, the triumphant resolution of these. As to the present example, however, I will add that one can love a poet without being either cajoled or bulldozed into believing his theories. In fact, one of the hardest things about studying Modern Poetry is that you can write a far more coherent and plausible account from what the poets said they were doing than from their poems. This difficulty is compounded when the poems keep talking about themselves and their intentions for poetry as a whole.

The trouble with 'no ideas but in things' is much the same as the trouble with an earlier attempt of a similar sort, Archibald MacLeish's celebrated 'Ars Poetica,' with its slogan 'a poem should not mean but be.' As one of his exempla the poet gives us this image:

An empty doorway and a maple leaf,

which we might either be puzzled by or so bemused by that we spend a long time listening to its reverberations in memory — except that he has prefaced the image by telling us it stands 'for all the history of grief.' The picture and the caption again, even if the caption has come first. Eliot assigned explicit meaning a low enough value for poetry when he compared it to a piece of meat that a burglar carries to quiet the watchdog; he did not suggest that burglars were likely to succeed better without such a sop. Yet something very like that, doing without meaning altogether, is what pure imagist theory demands, so that one consequence of pure imagist theory is that there could not be a pure imagist poem because it could not be as long as a line, else you would find you were talking about the object instead of presenting its image. Pound saw this when he defined an Image as 'that which presents an intellectual and emotional complex *in an instant of time.*' (My italics.) And he faced its extremest consequences: 'It is better to present one Image in a lifetime than to produce voluminous works.' After which he sat down to write the *Cantos*. Before doing so, however, he produced the example most often cited as the triumph of imagism, 'In a Station of the Metro.'

> *The apparition of these faces in the crowd;*
> *Petals on a wet, black bough.*

But in fact this is not an imagist poem at all, it is the statement of a relation, or what is traditionally called a metaphor, and as such suggests that the way out of the impasse offered by imagist programs is really the way back, modified by a few precepts such as Pound's insistence on "Direct treatment of the 'thing' whether subjective or objective," his "the natural object is always the *adequate* symbol," and so on, some of them excellent instructions to keep tacked on the workshop wall but in no way remarkable for theory.

One striking thing about modernism in literature is its recurring or even nagging worry about diction, or what Henry James called 'rendering.' How to perceive, how to represent perception in language, how one's representations may rise into meaning and through meaning, one hopes, into revelation, all this is critical for the modern poet and suggests one affinity at least with the Romantics. Eliot shows it particularly by devoting one section of each Quartet to the struggle with language; Pound returns to it over and over; Wallace Stevens, one might say without greatly exaggerating, made it his subject matter. It is an aspect of that reflexiveness of poetry in this age that I spoke of before. But instead of appealing to poems that discuss themselves explicitly, I shall try to illustrate the problem of representation and meaning by three poems of William Carlos Williams that go about resolving that problem in three distinct ways.

YOUNG SYCAMORE

I must tell you
this young tree
whose round and firm trunk
between the wet

pavement and the gutter
(where water
is trickling) rises
bodily

into the air with
one undulant
thrust half its height —
and then

dividing and waning
sending out
young branches on
all sides —

hung with cocoons
it thins
till nothing is left of it
but two

eccentric knotted
twigs
bending forward
hornlike at the top

Williams wrote a good many poems of this somewhat non-commital sort, poems that say in effect scarcely more than Look! you must look, or, in this instance 'I must tell you.' They appear to me as expressing, on the negative side, a fear that not only the secondary imagination, the one that writes poems, but the primary one, which gives us the world instead of a congeries of electro-chemical and sense-specific stimuli, is in serious likelihood of being lost — perhaps by being geometrized and climate-controlled out of existence as the world tends to become ever more like a city or an airport. I chose this example out of many, however, because a spirited and in many ways illuminating defense of it has been written by J. Hillis Miller in the Introduction to a volume of essays on Williams which he edited (*William Carlos Williams* [New York: Prentice Hall, 1966]).

I do not have space to do justice to the force of Professor Miller's argument, which you should read entire if the question continues to interest you. And though I shy away from the general conclusions as to poetic purpose to which it seems to lead, I am unable to refute it on its own grounds; I shall have to resort to a craven retreat upon differences of temperament and taste, maintaining sadly that 'Young Sycamore' continues to seem unremarkable to me even after Professor Miller's justifications. What these are I must now indicate as briefly and as clearly as I can.

We fail to respond to this poem, he says, because we come at it with traditional presuppositions related to Romanticism in the first place, and to the Christian and Platonic traditions to which Romanticism appeals for justification. In these traditions, 'things of this world in one way or another stand for things of the other world.' But 'in Williams's poetry this kind of depth has disappeared and with it the symbolism appropriate to it.'

> There can also be for Williams little figurative language, little of that creation of a 'pattern of imagery' which often unifies poems written in older traditions. Metaphors compare one thing to another and so blur the individuality of those things. For Williams the uniqueness of each thing is more important than any horizontal resonances it may have with other things.

Again,

> Romantic and symbolist poetry is usually an art of willed transformation. In this it is, like science or technology, an example of that changing of things into artifacts which assimilates them into the human world. Williams's poetry, on the other hand, is content to let things be. A good poet, he says, 'doesn't *select* his material. What is there to select? It *is*.'

Such a poem, says Miller, 'seems recalcitrant to analysis. The sycamore is not a symbol.' And he recurs to this thought, expressing it a bit more fully as well as, one thinks, with a touch of quiet desperation, a couple of pages later:

No symbolism, no depth, no reference to a world beyond the world, no pattern of imagery, no dialectical structure, no interaction of subject and object — just description. How can the critic 'analyze' such a poem? What does it mean? Of what use is it?

One realizes, seeing that the critic has six or seven pages still to go, that this is part of the drama. Moreover, he has already said that what Williams is up to in this as in each of his poems 'can only be discovered by that immersion in his writing which must precede interpretation of any part of it.' This is a sound maxim for the scholar, though a person accustomed to now and then reading a poem and maybe liking it may feel a touch put off by its austerity.

For Miller, the representative anecdote of Williams's poetics is an early poem, 'The Wanderer,' which 'ends with the protagonist's plunge into "the filthy Passaic." He is swallowed up by "the utter depth of its rottenness" until his separate existence is lost, and he can say, "I knew it all — it became me." ' And he quotes from a letter the poet wrote to Marianne Moore about ' "A sort of nameless religious experience," "a despair which made everything a unit and at the same time a part of myself." ' That fall into the river, that resignation to being one with the river and its filth as a means to knowledge, Miller suggests, is at the basis of Williams's mature poetry, in which 'there is no description of private inner experience' and 'no description of objects which are external to the poet's mind. Nothing is external to his mind.'

There is a good deal more, but I had better limit myself to quoting the most concentrated passage of particular interpretation I can find:

A grammatical peculiarity of the poem may be noted here as a stroke of genius which makes the poem a perfect imitation of the activity of nature. When the undulant thrust from trunk to twigs has been followed to its end the sycamore seems to stand fixed, its energy exhausted, the vitality which urged it into the air now too far from its source in the dark earth. But this is not really true. The inexhaustible force of the temporal thrust of the tree is expressed not only in the cocoons which promise a renewal of the cycle of growth, but also in the fact that there is no main verb in the second clause of the long sentence which makes up the poem. The poem contains so much verbal action that this may not be noticed, but all these verbs are part of a subordinate clause following 'whose.' Their subject is 'trunk' not 'tree,' and 'trunk' is also the apparent referent of 'it' in line eighteen. All the movement in the poem takes place within the confines of the subordinate clause. The second line, 'this young tree,' still hovers incomplete at the end of the poem, reaching out toward the verb which will complement its substantiality with an appropriate action. If the subordinate clause is omitted the poem says: 'I must tell you this young tree' — and then stops. This is undoubtedly the way the poet wanted it. It makes the poem hold permanently open that beauty which is revealed in the tree . . . .

And one more passage in summation:

Here is a concept of poetry which differs both from the classical theory of art as a mirror held up to nature and from the romantic theory of art as a lamp radiating unifying light. The word is given reality by the fact it names, but the independence of the fact from the word frees the word to be a fact in its own right and at the same time 'dynamizes' it with meaning. The word can then carry the facts named in a new form into the realm of imagination. In this sense poetry rescues and completes. It lifts things up . . . as the words are liberated, so are the facts they name . . . .

O dear, it feels very strange to be quoting all this at you when I don't seem to understand it at all well myself . . . especially that last passage, which seems to me written in the lofty language of Art Criticism. But I suppose that if you care for the poem the interpreter's dry enthusiasm over missing verbs and the like will perhaps be your enthusiasm also.

Nevertheless it seems right to have given Hillis Miller's argument for the poem and its principles a fairly full account, for it is an argument much heard of these days. A near equivalent for fiction is Alain Robbe-Grillet's essay 'Toward a New Fiction,' though there, oddly enough, the rejection of metaphor — and on the basis of such examples as 'the village *crouching* at the mountain's foot,' yet — is said to lead, not to oneness with things, but precisely to separation and distance from things. It's a hard game, the art game, where they change the rules before you half get started. Some bright fellow once said this in a somewhat more sparkling

manner: the artist, he said, is like the crooked gambler who turns
up with his marked cards and loaded dice only to find he is
entered in the six-day bike race; he will be breathless before he can
rest on the seventh day.

But onward.

My second example is of a kind quite rare in Williams's work,
for it represents him as trying to come to terms with traditional
values of verse and construction that for the most part he rejected,
often violently; yet it seems to me a beautiful poem.

THE YACHTS

contend in a sea which the land partly encloses
shielding them from the too-heavy blows
of an ungoverned ocean which when it chooses

tortures the biggest hulls, the best man knows
to pit against its beatings, and sinks them pitilessly.
Mothlike in mists, scintillant in the minute

brilliance of cloudless days, with broad bellying sails
they glide to the wind tossing green water
from their sharp prows while over them the crew crawls

ant-like, solicitously grooming them, releasing,
making fast as they turn, lean far over and having
caught the wind again, side by side, head for the mark.

In a well guarded arena of open water surrounded by
lesser and greater craft which, sycophant, lumbering
and flittering follow them, they appear youthful, rare

as the light of a happy eye, live with the grace
of all that in the mind is feckless, free and
naturally to be desired. Now the sea which holds them

is moody, lapping their glossy sides, as if feeling
for some slightest flaw but fails completely.
Today no race. Then the wind comes again. The yachts

move jockeying for a start, the signal is set and they
are off. Now the waves strike at them but they are too
well made, they slip through, though they take in canvas.

Arms with hands grasping seek to clutch at the prows.

> *Bodies thrown recklessly in the way are cut aside.*
> *It is a sea of faces about them in agony, in despair*
>
> *until the horror of the race dawns staggering the mind,*
> *the whole sea become an entanglement of watery bodies*
> *lost to the world bearing what they cannot hold. Broken,*
>
> *beaten, desolate, reaching from the dead to be taken up*
> *they cry out, failing, failing! their cries rising*
> *in waves still as the skillful yachts pass over.*

The verse hovers irregularly around a pentameter norm, but is not iambic; more likely its principle is alliterative, again irregularly so. You can see from the beginning that the poet may even have meant to cast the whole into *terza rima*, but by line five he is seen to abandon that idea, perhaps because the alliterative enters so powerfully with the punning resonance of 'pit . . . . pitilessly." And in the next line he even becomes rhapsodic and as it were abandoned to lyricism to a degree unusual indeed in this poet of so resolute a plainness:

> *Mothlike in mists, scintillant in the minute*
> *brilliance of cloudless days . . . .*

Later on you have the rhapsodic and climaxing release of energy in the series of comparisons in which the yachts

> *appear youthful, rare*
>
> *as the light of a happy eye, live with the grace*
> *of all that in the mind is feckless, free and*
> *naturally to be desired.*

Now the poem appears at a first reading to divide rather simply into description, in the first eight tercets, and meaning, or moral, in the last three. The picture and the caption again, although we may be surprised and even a little chagrined at seeing so grim a caption under so pretty a picture. If that is the best Williams can do with tradition, we may think, he was quite right to abandon tradition and do something else. Or if that is indeed what the tradition looks like, we had better agree to abandon it ourselves.

But if now, knowing what the poet will assert at the end, we go back and inspect his poem more attentively than at first we shall see, I think, that the picture and caption idea will not cover his procedures. For what the concluding passages of explicit prophetic fury and denunciation say so plainly has been developing from the beginning, making it clear that the poem is metaphysical and emblematic, working on the principle of metaphor that says: What men do is the visible sign of what they are.

It is not so much that yachts and yacht-racing form an allegory of the workings of society, in this instance a society based upon free enterprise capitalism, but that these institutions and their associated imagery are in themselves the making visible of the beauty and the horror of a competition claimed to be held under the laws of nature but where the laws of nature are rigged in favor of great wealth.

Consider if that not the meaning of the first thing we are told, that the yacht race is not held out in the open water where the yachts would be exposed to the force of 'an ungoverned ocean' too great for them. The same idea returns, with a more overt sarcasm, in 'a well guarded arena of open water,' which invites us to read an equivocation in the 'lesser and greater craft' of the following line. It is not necessary to make explicit the equation: yachts are, say, business enterprises, family fortunes. They are yachts, and what is said of them applies to yachts and yacht-racing; nevertheless what is said of them makes them stand forth as symbolic of certain characteristics of the marketplace from which they come.

And then with superb outrage the poet throws aside the veil of the visible as he sees it will no longer satisfy the demands of his figure. The figure, rather, works for the undeniable beauty of the scene, which is a part of the paradox that makes the poem tragic. But the boats with their sharp prows cutting the waters have by now developed by the poet's perception of them into a further metaphor representing the pitiless and unequal warfare carried on by the rich against the poor. To be 'live with the grace of all that in the mind is feckless, free and naturally to be desired' requires, alas, this cruel corollary, that it can be done only by those who inflict massive sufferings on others and who remain massively indifferent to these sufferings.

It is not, I should say, the moral of the poem that makes it a success, but rather the process whereby first the poet and now his readers come to perceive a developing relation. The perception is at first implicit in natural things, by the language employed to tell of them, which cannot rid itself of an insistent undertone of symbolism that finally breaks openly into revelation.

In my view, 'The Yachts' is a superior poem to 'Young Sycamore.' But I feel uncomfortably as if Hillis Miller may be right about the premises upon which I base my preference; tersely, that I can 'do more' with the one poem than with the other, and that this about doing more with a poem reflects the fact that I am a teacher, defined by Ezra Pound as a man who must talk for an hour. In a social situation where the appropriate response to poetry was to keep quiet in its presence my liking might go the other way, and I might prefer the poem that has, so to say, nothing behind it, nothing underlying, no 'depth,' but simply is. People who do not much care for 'The Yachts,' or for the sort of traditional enterprise I find it to represent, might easily enough condescend to it by calling it a rationally appreciable schoolroom good poem, a description which they would easily enough condense to calling it worthless. Indeed, I myself do not think 'The Yachts' either representative of Williams's work in poetry or an instance of Williams at his best; I chose it because it is uncharacteristic and therefore, I hope, illuminating about our general question of the relation of image and meaning.

So to finish up with, here is a poem by Williams that for me is a masterpiece, and about as far superior to 'The Yachts' as I believe that poem is to 'Young Sycamore.'

THE SEMBLABLES

The red brick monastery in
the suburbs over against the dust-
hung acreage of the unfinished
and all but subterranean

munitions plant: those high
brick walls behind which at Easter
the little orphans and bastards
in white gowns sing their Latin

responses to the hoary ritual
while frankincense and myrrh
round out the dark chapel making
an enclosed sphere of it

of which they are the worm:
that cell outside the city beside
the polluted stream and dump
heap, uncomplaining, and the field

of upended stones with a photo

under glass fastened here and there
to one of them near the deeply
carved name to distinguish it:

that trinity of slate gables
the unembellished windows piling
up, the chapel with its round
window between the dormitories

peaked by the bronze belfry
peaked in turn by the cross,
verdegris — faces all silent
that miracle that has burst sexless

from between the carrot rows.
Leafless white birches, their
empty tendrils swaying in
the all but no breeze guard

behind the spiked monastery fence
the sacred statuary. But ranks
of brilliant car-tops row on row
give back in all his glory the

late November sun and hushed
attend, before that tumbled
ground, those sightless walls
and shovelled entrances where no

one but a lonesome cop swinging
his club gives sign, that agony
within where the wrapt machines
are praying . . . .

Now this is in no way the rationally appreciable schoolroom good; it is, to me at least, beautiful with that mysterious beauty that only high art can make arise from sorrow, pity, horror, ugliness itself. For the most part as casual, low-keyed, and 'objective' as 'Young Sycamore,' it seems to represent only such architecture as one might naturally encounter while walking around just at the edge of town. The notation is spare and not insistent, unemotional except for one sardonic comment near the beginning and the breaking forth of the hitherto suppressed feeling in 'that agony' at the end. Yet it is all metaphor, all relation, and working throughout on that principle of **metaphor I mentioned earlier,** that what men do — the buildings they build, for instance — is the making visible of what they are. The poem says almost nothing aloud, limiting itself to rather bare description, yet idea is everywhere radiantly present. The buildings are put together — *composed* — in the poem, one feels, because that is the way they are put together in the world. The relations among them — munitions plant, orphanage, monastery, cemetery — silently *are* the relations that compose this hopeless, hideous world; and yet, in that strange and decisive image of the brilliant car-tops seen as worshippers of some sacred and doubtless horrifying principle enshrined in the munitions plant, everything — without in the least denying the horror and the hideousness — becomes beautiful.

Something like that, I think, is what imagism must always have meant but almost never done. It is, in the hands of a master of our time, a property of poetry that was scarcely available to earlier poetry with its more explicit — and perhaps less adventurous — attachment to meaning. For in 'The Semblables,' meaning — in the form at first only of relation — appears to arise from the collocation of things all by itself. The poem shows what can be done by a humble and accurate attention to the things of the world in their places in the world; it is the product of what I shall call, paradoxically, a disinterested passion, a love that is able to let go, maybe even a love of letting go. Its program is eloquently set forth by another master of the present time, Pablo Neruda:

> It is well, at certain hours of the day and night, to look closely at the world of objects at rest. Wheels that have crossed long, dusty distances with their mineral and vegetable burdens, sacks from the coalbins, barrels and baskets, handles and hafts for the carpenter's tool chest. From them flow the contacts of man with the earth, like a text for all harassed lyricists. The used surfaces of things, the wear that the hands give to things, the air, tragic at times, pathetic at others, of such things — all lend a curious attractiveness to the reality of the world that should not be underprized.

In Dr. Williams's homelier diction, it is indeed

through metaphor to reconcile
the people and the stones.

Robert Hass

Listening and Making

I told a friend I was going to try to write something about prosody and he said, "Oh great." The two-beat phrase is a very American form of terminal irony. A guy in a bar in Charlottesville turned to me once and said, loudly but confidentially, "Ahmo find me a woman and fuck her twenty ways till Sunday." That's also a characteristic rhythm: ahmo FIND ME a WOman/and FUCK her TWENty WAYS till SUNday. Three beats and then a more emphatic four. A woman down the bar doubled the two-beat put-down. She said, "Good luck, asshole." Rhythms and rhythmic play make texture in our lives but they are hard to talk about and besides,people don't like them to be talked about. Another friend wrote to me about an essay of mine in which I commented at some point on a "metrical inversion" in a line from a poem by Robert Lowell. He said he liked the piece well enough, but that one phrase—that finical tic of the educated mind—had filled him with rage. I think I understand why.

For a long time anthropological theory treated shamanism and spirit possession as separate phenomena. Shamanism was seen as a priestly tradition, a repertoire of techniques for acquiring vision. Spirit possession was a peripheral phenomenon, occurring mostly among women on some borderline between hysteria and Pentecostal religion. Or so it seemed until an English anthropologist, Ian Lewis, began to study the continuities between them. At which point it became clear that shamanism was usually a fully developed, male-dominated, politically central evolution of spirit possession; and that, in the harshly repressed lives of women in most primitive societies, new songs, chants, visions and psychic experiences keep welling up into cults which have their force because they are outside the entrenched means to vision. Because rhythm has direct access to the unconscious, because it can hypnotize us, enter our bodies and make us move, it is a power. And power is political.

That is why rhythm is always revolutionary ground. It is always the place where the organic rises to abolish the mechanical and where energy announces the abolition of tradition. New rhythms are new perceptions. In the nineteenth century, blank verse, the ode and ballad forms overthrew the heroic couplet. In the twentieth, vers libre overthrew the metrical dexterities of the Victorians. The latest of these revolutions occurred in the 1950s. It is variously dated from Charles Olson's essay *"Projective Verse,"* from Allen Ginsberg's *Howl* and Jack Kerouac's *Spontaneous Poetics* or from Robert Lowell's conversion to William Carlos Williams in *Life Studies.* In the second generation of poets since 1950, the same slogans have been advanced and there is, in the magazines, an orthodoxy of relaxed free verse. Statements about rhythm emphasize its natural character. The rhythm of poetry is sometimes said to be based on the rhythm of work, but no one wonders then why we work rhythmically. The heartbeat—pa-thunk, pa-thunk, pa-thunk—is pointed to as a basis for rhythm, but if you think about it for a minute, it seems obvious that it is a little monotonous to account for much. Prosody is not much taught or talked about, since it was a form of institutional terrorism in the previous, metrical orthodoxy. And during this time, I think, there has been an observable falling off in the inventive force of poetry. A likely outcome would be an equally mindless metrical revival. And I think that would be too bad. The range of possibilities for the poem—from chant to prose—have been extended enormously in English in the past seventy years. Very few living poets—Robert Duncan comes to mind—work with that full range. What I want to try to do in this essay is talk about the part rhythm plays in the work of the imagination and suggest a way of thinking about the prosody of free verse. It is listening that I am interested in—in writers and readers—and the kind of making that can come from live, attentive listening.

Here is a poem by Gary Snyder, "August on Sourdough, A Visit from Dick Brewer":

> You hitched a thousand miles
> north from San Francisco
> Hiked up the mountainside   a mile in the air

The little cabin—one room—
                    walled in glass
Meadows and snowfields,   hundreds of peaks.
We lay in our sleeping bags
                    talking half the night;
Wind in the guy-cables   summer mountain rain.
Next morning I went with you
                    as far as the cliffs,
Loaned you my poncho—   the rain across the shale—
You down the snowfield
                    flapping in the wind
Waving a last goodbye   half-hidden in the clouds
To go on hitching
                    clear to New York;
Me back to my mountain   and far, far, west.

This poem is beautifully made, casual, tender, alive with space. It is worth remembering, since I want to argue that rhythm is at least partly a **psychological** matter, that twenty-five years ago the editors of most American literary magazines would have found it thin, eccentric, formless.

It belongs to a tradition of poems of leave-taking in China and Japan. Buson provides an instance:

              You go,
          I stay;
              two autumns

And Basho another:

              Seeing people off,
          Being seen off,—
              autumn in Kisco

Goodbyes are powerful, and Americans, who say them all the time, don't seem to write about them very much. In *A Zen Wave*, Robert Aitken's book about Basho, he observes that the Japanese, customarily, wave until a departing guest has disappeared from sight. We are more likely to turn away before that happens, not so much erasing the other person as turning inward, toward our own separateness, and getting on with it. Buson doesn't do that; he lets the moment define itself, lets the distance speak. And, in imagining his own separateness, he imagines his friend's. That last image—two autumns—speaks absolutely of the way in which each of us is alone, but it also tends to multiply, expand: two autumns, dozens of autumns, a million autumns, worlds and worlds, and whether that fact is happy or unhappy, he doesn't say; he says it is. Basho makes something different but similar of the fact that parting is like the process of individuation. The second line of his poem in Japanese reads *okuritsu hate wa,* literally *okuri* (seeing off) *tsu* (now) *hate* (goal, outcome, upshot) *wa* (particle indicating the subject). In the version I quote, R. H. Blythe has, nicely, rendered *hate wa* as a dash; comings and goings resolve into a time and a place, the ongoing world without subject or object. Basho's insight moves us a step further than Buson's. Many worlds, many subjectivities become one world which includes, among other things, all the individual worlds. How sharply you feel that world emerging, how sharply the self dissolving into it, he leaves up to you.

Robert Aitken has written a fine, brief commentary on this poem:

> Now being seen off; now seeing off—what is the upshot? **Autumn in Kiseo, rain** in Manoa Valley, a gecko at the Maui zendo—*chi chi chichichi.*
>
> Paul Gauguin asked: "Where do we come from? What are we? Where are we going?" You will find these words inscribed in French in the corner of one of his greatest paintings, a wide prospect of Tahiti, children, young adults, old people, birds, animals, trees, and a strange idol. What is the upshot after all? Paul Gauguin painted it very beautifully.

Snyder's "August on Sourdough" seems to say something like what Buson says: you go, I go. And in its evocation of space and movement, something of what Basho says; it creates a wide, windy world whose center is no particular person. One understanding of it might come from looking at the personal pronouns, at the way American speech distinguishes the self as subject from the self as object. But another way that Snyder tries to discover what he means is rhythmically. *Chi chi chichichi.* One two onetwothree. What does the sound have to say about wholeness or endings or movement or separation? What rhythm heals? To ask these questions, we have to ask what rhythm is and how it engages us.

2

Some ideas first. I want to suggest that our experience of rhythm has three distinct phases. Clear enough that it implies the apprehension of a pattern. We hear

one two

and we are hearing a sound. When we hear

one two
one two

we are beginning to hear a rhythm. If we listen to something like this,

one two
one
one two
one two three
one two
one two three
one two
one
one two

we attend to and can pick out three patterns of repetition:

one	one two	one two three
one	one two	one two three
one	one two	one two three
one	one two	one two three

Part of the explanation for this is that we are pattern-discerning animals, for whatever reason in our evolutionary history. We attend to a rhythm almost instinctively, listen to it for a while, and, if we decide it has no special significance for us, we can let it go; or put it away, not hearing it again unless it alters, signaling to us—as it would to a hunting or a grazing animal—that something in the environment is changed. This process is going on in us all the time, one way or another. It is the first stage, wakeful, animal, alert, of the experience of rhythm. And it is the place to which we are called by the first words of any poem or story. *Once upon a time; how many dawns chill from his rippling rest; it is a law universally acknowledged . . .; fishbones walked the waves off Hatteras:* it calls us to an intense, attentive consciousness. Probably that is what attracts some people to poetry, to writing generally, and it is probably what repels them, since the last thing many people want is to be conscious.

This threshold alertness is only the first phase of the experience of rhythm. The second includes the whole range of our experience of recurrent and varying sound. We enter, are made attentive, then something else begins to happen:

one two
one
one two three
one two
one two three

or this, from a musician-poet:

> Whenas in silks
> Whenas in silks
> My Julia goes
> My Julia goes
>
> Then, then methinks (methinks)
> How sweetly flows
> Sweetly flows
> The liquefaction (faction) (faction)
> Of her clothes
>   her clothes her clothes

We move from attention to pleasure, from necessity to a field of play. The principle is recurrence and variation. The effect is hard to describe. Interplay, weaving, dialogue, dance: every phrase that comes to mind is a metaphor. This need to speak metaphorically suggests that rhythm is an idiom of the unconscious, which is why it seems an echo of many other human activities.

When we listen to a rhythm, especially an insistent rhythm, there is often a moment or more of compelled attention in which the play and repetition of the sounds seem—I am pulled toward metaphor again—to draw us in or overwhelm us. That kind of listening can lead to something like trance. It is the feeling out of which comes another set of metaphors—magic, incantation—and practices. We know that rhythm has always been a mnemonic device, that metrical compositions are usually easier to remember than non-metrical ones, that in ancient times all laws were expressed in incantatory rhythms, that the oldest Greek and Latin words for poetry were also the oldest words for law. This is part of the basis for the connection between memory and inspiration: *O musa, memora mihi,* the Aeneid begins. Far back rhythm, memory, trance are connected to authority and magical power.

An instance from the Plains Sioux, in Frances Densmore's translation:

> The whole world is coming
> A nation is coming
> A nation is coming

This song was made after the buffalo had been massacred by hide hunters. It is chant, magical invocation, designed to bring the herds down from Canada in the spring as they had always come.

> Eagle has brought the message to the tribe

> The father says so
> The father says so

It is rhythmic repetition moving toward magic. *Enchantment,* we say, *incantation,* singing the song inward. Often it is accompanied by a slight rocking of the body.

> From the north they are coming
> The buffalo are coming
> The buffalo are coming

At some point chant becomes hypnotic; it begins to induce the trance state, identified with possession.

> Crow has brought the message to the tribe
> The father says so
> The father says so

Its effect can begin to be a feeling of terror and confinement. In medieval Europe you could ward off the devil by repeating a small prayer three hundred or five hundred times. The medical histories of hysteria describe instances when the chanter, once begun, was unable to stop.

> The buffalo are coming
> The buffalo are coming
> The father says so
> The father says so

Repetition makes us feel secure and variation makes us feel free. What these experiences must touch in us is the rhythm of our own individuation. It's easy enough to observe in small children the force of these pulls between the security of infancy and the freedom of their own separateness. When my oldest child was two or so, we used to take walks. He had a zen carpenter's feeling for distance, running ahead of me in an abandoned waddle, coming to an abrupt stop when he felt he had come to the very edge of some magical zone of protection which my presence generated, and then gazing back at me over his shoulder with a look of droll glee. He knew he was right out there on the edge—the distance seemed to be about eleven or twelve squares of sidewalk. Sometimes he would take one more step, then another, looking back each time, and if I uttered a warning sound he would collapse in hilarity which seemed to be a celebration of his own daring. I was listening at the same time to Miles Davis, to how far he was willing to move away from the melody, to the way the feeling intensified the further away from it he got, as if he were trying to describe what it is like to get out there so far into the wandering hunger for the next note that it seemed at the same time exultant and explosively lonely and probably impossible to come back ever. I was also reading Theodore Roethke, the long poems with their manic inward-driven nursery-rhyme rhythms:

> The shape of a rat?
> It's bigger than that.
> It's sleek as an otter
> With wide webby toes.
> Just under the water
> It usually goes.

And it made me feel that there was not, in this, much difference between child and grown-up, between my son's impulses and the tidal pulls of adult life, the desire for merger, union, loss of self and the desire for freedom, surprise, singularity. I think it is probaby the coming together of our pattern-discerning alertness with this pull between polarities in our psychic life that determines our feelings about rhythm.

It is important that we both want a rapt symbiotic state and don't want it; that we want solitariness and self-sufficiency and don't want it. Rhythmic repetition initiates a sense of order. The feeling of magic comes from the way it puts us in touch with the promise of a deep sympathetic power in things: heartbeat, sunrise, summer solstice. This can be hypnotically peaceful; it can also be terrifying, to come so near self-abandonment and loss of autonomy, to whatever in ourselves wants to stay there in that sound, rocking and weeping, comforted. In the same way, freedom from pattern offers us at first an openness, a field of identity, room to move; and it contains the threat of chaos, rudderlessness, vacuity. Safety and magic on one side, freedom and movement on the other; their reverse faces are claustrophobia and obsession or agoraphobia and vertigo. They are the powers we move among, listening to a rhythm, as the soul in the bard state moves among the heavens and the hells, and they are what make the relation between repetition and variation in art dialectical and generative.

An example, from a metrical poem:

> A slumber did my spirit seal,
> I had no human fears;
> She seemed a thing who could not feel
> The touch of earthly years.
>
> No motion has she now, no force.
> She neither hears nor sees,

Rolled round in earth's diurnal course
With rocks and stones and trees.

In this poem of grief at the death of a young girl, Wordsworth brings us in the last lines to a small, majestic, orderly music in which we feel reconciled to the way the child has entered the natural universe. Like a cradle rocking, bringing us to rest. At least that is how I read the poem for a long time, until someone pointed out to me the randomness of the last sequence: rocks, stones, trees. What is the difference between a rock and a stone? Who knows? What difference could it make? Rocks and stones. She has passed into brute matter, into the huge, mute spaces that terrified Pascal. For a while, with all the bad habits of education, I wondered which was the correct interpretation. I've come to see that the poem is so memorable and haunting because the two readings and feelings are equally present, married there, and it is the expressive power of rhythm that makes this possible.

First we hear: an order is insisted upon by the meter; then we listen, for that order is questioned immediately by the arrangement of the stanzas. Four beats in the first lines, an insistent order; three beats in the second line, the same order but lighter, easier to live with. Four beats in the third line: the heavier order enters again, intensified slightly by the almost audible extra stress of "not feel." Three beats again in the fourth line, a lightening. The fifth line is interesting because the pause seems to promise an alteration in the pattern, to give us three beats, the lighter order, but no, after the pause we get two heavy stresses, "no force"; it almost says: were you wondering if "not feel" was two stresses? "Not feel" is two stresses. It is like a musical theme; we have begun to hear not just a play between three- and four-stress phrases, but a secondary drama of the four stresses tending toward a heavier and menacing five. In the sixth line we return to the three-stress pattern. In the seventh line the five stresses appear in full force, made large and dizzy by the long vowel sounds. They say, in effect, that from a human point of view an insistent order is equivalent to a chaos, and they are at the same time wondering, wonderful. In the last line we return to three stresses, the bearable rhythm, but we have already been made to hear the menace in the idea of order, so that last phrase, deliberate and random at once, leaves us with a deep and lingering uneasiness.

To speak of a sense of closure brings us to the third phase of rhythmic experience. Many things in the world have rhythms and many kinds of creatures seem to be moved by them, but only human beings complete them. This last phase, the bringing of rhythmic interplay to a resolution, is the particular provenance of man as a maker. A rhythm is not a rhythmic form; in theory, at least, a rhythmic sequence, like some poetry readings, can go on forever, the only limits being the attention of the auditor and the endurance of the performer. Meter is that kind of sequence. The flow of blank verse suggests no natural stopping place of itself and most of the other metrical shapes, sonnets and the various stanzaic forms, are defined by their rhyme schemes. Daydream and hypnotic rhythm have it in common that their natural form is exhaustion. The resolution of rhythmic play, not just the coming down on one side or the other but the articulation of what ending feels like, is active making.

Think of the words you might want to use. *End:* to die. *Finish:* to be done with. *Conclude:* obligation over. *Complete:* to fulfill. *Consummate: really* to fulfill. *Close, terminate, arrive, leave off, release.* There are many senses of ending and they are drawn from our different experiences of it. There are rhythmic forms in nature —the day, a season, the life of a blossom. In human life, orgasm, the sentences in which we speak, falling asleep, the completion of tasks, the deaths we all see and the one death each of us must imagine. Many of our senses of ending are conventional—imagine the sound of a door opening: anticipation; of a door closing: finality. There are many possibilities of ending. In that way, each work of art is a three-line haiku. You go, I go—and the artist must provide the third line.

What hovers behind all this, I would guess, is a wish. Formally, the completion of a pattern imitates the satisfaction of a desire, a consummation, which is why orgasm is a preferred metaphor of conclusion. And because the material of poetry is language, it seems inevitable that an ending would also imitate the experience of insight. And because it is an ending, it will be death-obsessed. Sexual pleasure is a merging, a voluntary abandonment of the self; insight is a freeing, the central experience of our own originality. We don't know what death is. The wish behind the human play of artistic form is to know how these three are related: probably it is the hope that they are, or can be, the same thing. And there is another element to be added here, which belongs to the riddles of completion. When poet or reader listens through to the moment of resolution, it is over. The poet has not created until the thing is gone from his hands.

It's possible that what humans want from works of art are shapes of time in which the sense of coming to an end is also, as it very seldom is in the rest of life, a resolution. Hence the art formula common to television comedy and Wagner and the Shakespearean sonnet: tension, release; tension, release; tension, more tension, release. There is a large and familiar repertoire of formal techniques which produce this effect. It is probably a definition of a rigidifying art-practice that it has more answers than it has questions. In the early twentieth century, painting got rid of perspective, music of tonality, poetry of meter and rhyme so that they could tell what ending felt like again, and give it again the feel of making. It is this feeling of the made thing, of craft and of an event in time, that gives the poem—and the world—the feeling of historicity, of having been made by men, and therefore in movement, alive to our touch and to the possibility of change which the familiarity of convention is always deadening. The task is to listen to ourselves and make endings true enough to experience that they eliminate the ground for the old senses of completion or renew them.

So, there are three phases of the experience of rhythm: hearing it, developing it, bringing it to form. And real listening, like deep play, engages us in the issues of our lives. I want to look now at prosody, at ways of talking about how a rhythm is developed and brought to closure.

3

Some definitions. Metrical verse is a fixed pattern of stressed and unstressed syllables. In accentual verse, the number of strong stresses in a line is fixed, but the position of the stressed syllables is not and neither is the number or position of unstressed syllables. In free verse, neither the number nor the position of stressed and unstressed syllables is fixed. I have already remarked that meter is not the basis of rhythmic form. It is a way to determine the length of the line, but it is not, by itself, a way to shape a poem. For example, these lines by Yeats:

> When you are old and grey and full of sleep
> And nodding by the fire, take down this book,
> And slowly read, and dream of the soft look
> Your eyes had once, and of their shadows deep.

That is the metrical pattern. But what gives the passage the articulation of form is the pattern of pauses and stresses. It looks very different if we just indicate those:

> When you are OLD and GREY/and FULL of SLEEP
> And NODding by the FIRE,/TAKE DOWN this BOOK
> And SLOWly READ,/and DREAM of the SOFT LOOK
> Your EYES HAD ONCE,/and of their SHAdows DEEP.

It seems clear that the main function of the meter is to secure the

168

lulling sound of the first line and a half. The sense of pattern is created by two- and three-stress phrases which tend to have thematic associations. The three-stress phrases, "take down this book," "dream of the soft look," "your eyes had once," carry the energy and urgency: the two-stress groups convey balance or resignation or fatality, "old and grey," "shadows deep." The three-stress phrase appears when it disrupts the balance of the first line and a half. The pattern looks like this:

2/2
2/3
2/3
3/2

The third line replays the theme; in the last line the pattern is reversed. Life and death, odd and even are the terms of play. Even, says the first line. Odd, say the second and third lines. Even, says the fourth line, rhyming with the idea that the shadows of desire in young eyes are the shadows of mortality.

In many modernist poems, technically metrical, the use of the effects of metrical rhythm is extraordinarily powerful—they feel hacked out, freshly made—but the metrical pattern as a whole counts for very little: the rhythmic articulation exists almost entirely in the pattern of stresses and pauses:

Turning and turning in the widening gyre
The falcon cannot hear the falconer;
Things fall apart; the centre cannot hold;
Mere anarchy is loosed upon the world,
The blood-dimmed tide is loosed, and everywhere
The ceremony of innocence is drowned;
The best lack all conviction, while the worst
Are full of passionate intensity.

It doesn't take a very refined analysis to see that this varies three- and four-stress phrases. If Yeats had written:

The blood-dimmed tide is loosed;
And everywhere the ceremony of innocence is drowned;
The best lack all conviction,
While the worst are full of passionate intensity

the passage would not be less regular, but the sound has gone dead. The extra unstressed syllables in the second and fourth lines make them seem to sprawl out and the pattern of stresses feels leaden, fatal: 4, 4, 4, 4. As it is, Yeats gets the fatality but also a sense of something broken, unbalanced: 4/1, 3; 4/1, 3. The inference to be drawn from this pattern is that at the level of form the difference between the strategies of free and metrical verse is not very great.

The difference lies, rather, in the stages of announcing and developing a rhythm. Every metrical poem announces a relationship to the idea of order at the outset, though the range of relationships to that idea it can suggest is immense. Free-verse poems do not commit themselves so soon to a particular order, but they are poems so they commit themselves to the idea of its possibility, and, as soon as recurrences begin to develop, an order begins to emerge. The difference is, in some ways, huge; the metrical poem begins with an assumption of human life which takes place in a pattern of orderly recurrence with which the poet must come to terms, the free-verse poem with an assumption of openness or chaos in which an order must be discovered. Another way to say this is to observe that most metrical poems, by establishing an order so quickly, move almost immediately from the stage of listening for an order to the stage of hearing it in dialogue with itself. They suppress animal attention in the rush to psychic magic and they do so by laying claim to art and the traditions of art at the beginning. The free-verse poem insists on the first stage of sensual attention, of possibility and emergence—which is one of the reasons why it has seemed fresher and more individual to the twentieth century. The prophetic poems of Yeats and the loose blank verse of the younger Eliot, by staying near to traditional prosodies, say in effect that there has been this order and it's falling apart, while Williams and the Pound of the *Cantos* say—to paraphrase Robert Pinget—listen, there is no lost feast at the bottom of memory, invent.

The free-verse poem, by stripping away familiar patterns of recurrence and keeping options open, is able to address the forms of closure with the sense that there are multiple possibilities and that the poem has to find its way to the right one. Here is a simple example of how this might work. We can begin with a small poem of Whitman, "Farm Picture":

> Through the ample open door of the peaceful country barn,
> A sunlit pasture field with cattle and horses feeding.
> And haze and vista, and the far horizon fading away.

As I hear it, there are six stresses in the first line, and a brief pause after "door", in the second, six with a pause after "field"; in the third, six again with a pause marked by the comma. You could call this accentual verse. You could even argue that it's metrical, a relaxed mix of iambs and anapests. But that won't tell us why it

170

feels complete. Notice the pattern:

3/3
3/3
2/4

The principle is that for a thing to be complete, it has to change. And the kind of change indicates how you feel about that fact. Suppose the poem ended "and haze and vista." It would be an ending and it would radically change the meaning of the poem. That is the possibility open to the poet who has not decided how many stresses each line should have. Let's look at the possible endings. They make four or five different poems:

Through the ample open door of the peaceful country barn,
A sunlit pasture field with cattle and horses feeding.
And haze, and vista.

*

Through the ample open door of the peaceful country barn,
A sunlit pasture field with cattle and horses feeding.
And haze and vista, and the far horizon.

*

Through the ample open door of the peaceful country barn.
A sunlit pasture field with cattle and horses feeding.
And haze and vista, and the far horizon fading.

*

Through the ample open door of the peaceful country barn,
A sunlit pasture field with cattle and horses feeding.
And haze and vista, and the far horizon fading away.

All of these poems seem to me plausible. Three of them, at least, are interesting. The first poem is balanced: 3/3, 3/3, 1/1. To my ear, the last line is not excessively abrupt, but it throws a terrific weight of disappointment or longing onto what is not present, so that the balance of the last line, thunk/thunk, seems an ironic echo of the amplitude of the first two lines. (Though this hovers at the edge of something else because of that dialectical play in rhythm. A little punctuation could make the poem feel like a gasp of surprise such as Dr. Williams might feel:

Through the ample open door of the peaceful country barn,
A sunlit pasture field with cattle and horses feeding.
And haze, and vista!)

171

The second poem is also balanced: 3/3, 3/3, 2/2. It feels to me too much so. If there is such a thing as sentimental form, this is sentimental form. It invokes the idea of horizon, but prettily, so that there is no tension between the solidity of the barnyard and the hazy vista. It is like bad genre painting, nothing is problematic; distance is pretty, closeness is pretty. The third poem is unbalanced: 3/3, 3/3, 2/3. The extra stress seems to evoke the asymmetry of what fades away and is lost. Three-stress phrases usually feel more open than two-stress phrases. (I think of Leonard Bernstein's remark: two is the rhythm of the body, three is the rhythm of the mind.) The first lines, two sets of three, reconcile those two rhythms, openness and the earth. The third line says unh-uh. We have to let go of the horizon in return for the presence and solidity of the earth. It is a melancholy poem. Whitman's poem is also balanced, but it contains the asymmetrical 2/4 line. Its feeling is most inclusive. The odd rhyme of "feeding" and "fading," which is an aspect of the theme of presence and absence, is muted and, though we take note of what is lost on the horizon, the rhythm is willing to include that loss in the solidity and presence of the scene.

The point of this should be obvious. All four, or five, poems say different things. A poet in a poem is searching for the one thing to be said, or the many things to be said one way. As soon as we start talking about alternative possibilities of form, we find ourselves talking about alternative contents. It is exactly here that the truism about the indissolubility of content and form acquires its meaning. The search for meaning in the content and shape in the rhythm are simultaneous, equivalent. That's why it doesn't matter too much which a writer attends to in composition, because the process attends to both. It is possible—the testimony on this seems pretty general—to pay attention consciously to one or the other exclusively; more often, writers experience a continual shifting back and forth between formal problems and problems of content, carrying the work forward at whichever level it wants to move. In the long run, though, no work can be alive, intelligent, imaginatively open, intense, at one level and not the other.

It should be clear by now that free-verse rhythm is not a movement between pattern and absence of pattern, but between phrases based on odd and even numbers of stresses:

I loaf and invite my soul,
I lean and loaf at my ease, observing a spear of summer grass.

Three stresses in the first line, seven in the second with a strong pause after *ease*. The pattern is 3, 3/4. The first two clauses are almost equivalent. *I loaf and invite my soul.* Then, *I lean and loaf at my ease.* Had he written *observing a spear of grass,* all three phrases would be nearly equivalent and they would begin to build tension; instead he adds *summer,* the leaning and loafing season, and announces both at the level of sound and of content that this poem is going to be free and easy.

The line comes into this and so does the stanza. It is with them that we approach Pound's definition of rhythm, a form carved in time, and Williams' notion of the variable foot. Talking about the line as a "beat," as everyone who has struggled with the idea has been compelled to admit, doesn't make much sense if you are thinking of stress. But looked at from the point of view of rhythm as I've tried to describe it, I think it does. The metrical line proposes a relationship to order. So does a three- or four-line stanza. Imagine, it says, a movement through pattern. The stanza is a formal proposal, Apollonian and clear. In this, it says, I want to catch light or court a shaping spirit. Look at these lines from Louis Zukofsky's "4 Other Countries":

La Gloire in the black	2
flags of the valley	2
of the	-
Loire	1
A lavender plough	2
in Windermere	1
The French blue	2
door	1
Of a gray	1
stone	1
house in	1
Angers	1
Walled farms,	2
little lanes	2
of entry, orange-	2
red roofs	2

The rhythm of this passage is based on the strong three-beat phrase:
stone house, little lanes of entry, orange-red roofs; it doesn't appear in the notation of the rhythm because Zukofsky has broken it across the line, everywhere, into units of one or two stresses and passed the whole through the balanced proposal of the four-line stanza. Three here is the beat of the bodily world and it is resisted and shaped otherwise by the rhythm the poet cuts in

time, in imitation, I think, of the perceptions of travel. At the level of content it is straightforward description but it is given the quality of insight because the aural and visual imaginations are so freshly and attentively at work. The line, when a poem is alive in its sound, measures: it is a proposal about listening.

4

It should be fairly easy to turn now to a poem like Gary Snyder's "August on Sourdough" and listen to what's going on. The first thing to notice about it is that it is made from paired lines or half-lines which imitate and underscore its theme. *You hitched a thousand miles,* then *north from San Francisco; hiked up the mountainside,* then *a mile in the air.* Sets of two. The one break in this pattern comes in the next pair of lines: *the little cabin—one room —walled in glass.* A set of three with the poem's place of communion at its center. Two and three. You go, I go, what is the upshot? It is, when we look at the pattern of stresses, a transformation of the two stress rhythms into three stress rhythms:

YOU HITCHED a THOUsand MILES
                              NORTH from SAN FranCISco
HIKED up the MOUNtainside   a MILE in the AIR
The LITtle CABin—ONE ROOM—
                     WALLED in GLASS
MEAdows and SNOWfields   HUNdreds of PEAKS.

Stress is relative and I have marked what I hear as the main stresses. The pattern looks like this:

4

3

2/2

2/2

2

2/2

The base rhythm is the paired two-stress phrases. The variation comes in the one three-stress phrase and in the set of three two-stress phrases. The paired phrases with a pause in between insist on twoness, on the separateness of the two friends. There is just enough variety to convey a sense of movement, and the overall effect is balanced, relaxed. It is very deft work.

We LAY in our SLEEPing BAGS
                         TALKing HALF the NIGHT;
WIND in the GUY CABLES   SUMmer MOUNtain RAIN.

This is the interlude in which the images and rhythm speak of the communion of friends. It is a quiet expansion from two- to three-stress phrases, and a different balance:

<pre>
            3
            3
           3/3
</pre>

And then the parting:

<pre>
NEXT MORNing I WENT WITH you
                 as FAR as the CLIFFS
LOANED you my PONCHo   the RAIN aCROSS the
   SHALE
YOU DOWN the SNOWfield
                 FLAPping in the WIND
WAVing a LAST GoodBYE   HALF-HIDden in the
   CLOUDS
To GO ON HITCHing   CLEAR to NEW YORK;
ME BACK to my MOUNtain   and FAR, FAR, WEST.
</pre>

This is a more intricate restatement of the play between two and three stresses, but it ends emphatically with a rhythm based on threes. Two is an exchange, three is a circle of energy, Lewis Hyde has said, talking about economics. I would mark the primary pattern like this:

<pre>
           4
           2
          2/3
          3/2
          3/3
          3/3
          3/3
</pre>

and that last phrase is carefully punctuated to sing it out: 1/1/1. It insists, finally, on a rhythmic pairing of open three-stress elements. This is, formally, the solution it offers to the problem of identity and separation in partings and—as we've seen—in ending poems.

The articulation of rhythmic form, though, doesn't indicate what are for me the small miracles of feeling in the rhythm throughout. There are at least three musical phrases in the poem that are announced and then transmuted. One of them is *a mile in the air* which is echoed in *hundreds of peaks* and again in *as far as the cliffs,* and then changed to a three-stress cadence in *clear to New York.* (NEW YORK is a West Coast pronunciation of N'York —the emphatic *new* is a celebration of movement.) In the same

way, *meadows and snowfields,* a playful pair of falling rhythms—
MEAdows, SNOWfields—like the falling rhythms of nursery
rhymes, Bobbie Shaftoe, Humpty Dumpty, is repeated in *loaned
you my poncho* so that it has become a memory of playful reci-
procity, and then it is transformed by the urgency of movement
into *you down the snowfield.* Most brilliant and moving to me is
the sudden iambic phrase, *the rain across the shale.* It is suggested
in the first line, *you hitched a thousand miles,* echoed in *talking
half the night* and *summer mountain rain.* And then, clearly, the
old orderliness of iambic meter rises up to make us feel an order
of nature older than us and steadier in which our comings and
goings mean very little. "Hailstorm on the rocks at Stony Pass,"
Basho said. "The rain it raineth every day," Shakespeare said.
"Rocks and stones and trees," said Wordsworth. The juxtaposition
of rhythms and orders, *loaned you my poncho, the rain across the
shale,* before the poem's open windy farewell is a lyrical hesitation, a moment of hearing really astonishing, I think, in its
warmth, sharp pathos, and clear intelligence:

> Loaned you my poncho   the rain across the shale
> You down the snowfield . . .

It recapitulates the two worlds the poem speaks of, the little one,
one room, walled in glass, and the big one, half-hidden in the
clouds.

The freshness and life of this poem is not uncommon in the
work of the 1950's when the younger poets were writing in the
teeth of an institutionalized and deadening metrical facility. It was
in those years, somewhere, that William Carlos Williams delivered
a lecture to Theodore Roethke's students at the University of
Washington, "The Poem as a Field of Action." "Imagism," he told
them, "was not structural: that was the reason for its disappearance . . . . You can put it down as a general rule that when a poet,
in the broadest sense, begins to devote himself to the *subject
matter* of his poems, *genre,* he has come to the end of his poetic
means." There is a wonderful sense of momentum in his talk and
it is hard not to feel, though almost everyone writing now would
claim him as a master, that that momentum has been lost. I think
he identifies the symptom. Almost all the talk about poetry in the
past few years has focused on issues of image and diction. There
was a liveliness in the idea of hauling deep and surreal imagery into
American poetry, but the deep image is no more structural than
imagism: there was hardly any sense of what the rhythmic ground
might be. Hence, stuff like this:

176

He played banana drums and dreamed of felt.
He discerned a tin angel in a caulking gun.
His bounced checks and their imaginative *noms de plume*
Glittered in the cash registers of abandoned motels.

etc. Five beats to the line. The imagery is unusual enough; the rhythm is absolutely conventional. The counterattack on this kind of writing has been that it should have a different content. So we have gotten an aggressive return to the conscious mind:

Pets are a creation of the industrial revolution.
And so is 'projective identification.'
You feed the useless animal to remind you of animals
While the terminology of relationship is elaborated.

One of these is writhing rebelliousness in the face of terminal ennui, the other is ironic intelligence in the face of same. The ennui is expressed by the simple, orderly, conformist, free-verse rhythms; that is the main message, and it can't be talked about if poetry is a matter of kinds of imagery and kinds of diction. Way below the content of a particular poem, the idea that rhythm is natural, bodily, spontaneous, has been transformed into the idea that it is simply a given, invisible or inevitable. What this expresses is a kind of spiritual death that follows from living in a world we feel we have no hope of changing.

I have it in mind that, during the Vietnam War, one of the inventions of American technology was a small antipersonnel bomb that contained sharp fragments of plastic which, having torn through the flesh and lodged in the body, could not be found by an X-ray. Often I just think about the fact that the bomb works on people just the way the rhythms of poetry do. And it seems to me then that there really are technes on the side of life and technes on the side of death. Durable and life-giving human inventions—tragedy, restaurants that stay open late at night, holding hands, the edible artichoke—were probably half discovered and half invented from the materials the world makes available, but I think that they were also the result of an active and attentive capacity for creation that humans have, and that a poetry that makes fresh and resilient forms extends the possibilities of being alive.

Stanley Plumly

Dirty Silences

Tell X that speech is not dirty silence
Clarified. It is silence made still dirtier.
It is more than an imitation for the ear.

—Wallace Stevens, "The Creations of Sound"

Stevens never quite tells us what his silence made still dirtier is, but he does suggest later in the poem that it is the visible made a little hard to see and the audible a little hard to hear. The actual lines are addressed to a poet X, who is the villain of the piece, a man too exactly himself, a man too much in the way of the poem, and they go something like this:

> His poems do not make the visible a little hard
> To see nor, reverberating, eke out the mind
> On peculiar horns, themselves eked out
> By the spontaneous particulars of sound.

I would like to be able to say to you this morning that *dirty silence* is an accurate gloss of free verse and that blurred vision, accompanied by the spontaneous particulars of sound, played on peculiar horns, is, collectively speaking, the very language of free speech. That, of course, would not be true. Stevens' answer to the issue of "naked poetry" is his blank-verse answer to the issue of dirty silence clarified. . . . "We do not say ourselves like that in poems." Dirty silence may not be a pure oxymoron; nevertheless, it is a metaphor describing a certain kind of tension necessary to the "music of a poem" — to use another Stevens phrase — if by music we mean a poem's total vocal and visual rhythm.

We have been hooked for so long on the two-party system in poetry, on the argument between so-called formalism and so-called free verse, between reactionary and radical, conservative and visionary, that we have tended to look at the American version of the art as political — the Dickinsons and Frosts and Stevenses and Wilburs on one side of the aisle, the Whitmans and Pounds and Williamses and Lowells on the other. And every so many years, sometimes in as little time as four, each side has nominated and tried to elect a president of poetry. Indeed, the debate has gone on so much from the start of our entry into the "modern world" — in the period right after the Civil War — that our national poetry often appears to exist less as a historical experience and more as a continuing contemporary condition, less as a linear development of action and reaction (as in the linkage of a Spenser-Milton-Dryden-Pope-Wordsworth, et al.) and more as a series of concentric circles, within a single cylinder of time, with various figures placed at pole and antipode.

Critics fond of the overview have tended to see this debate as a dialectic rather than as a strict dichotomy — especially in terms of proper English as our ghost language. If my configuration of circles is correct, such critics have more often than not placed egalitarian Emerson at the center of gravity. Because if as a Transcendental theologian, Emerson appeals to our vanities about our vital relations with nature, it is as an astute and pragmatic reader of poetry that he appeals to our vanities about verse. You will remember his famous complaint against "a recent writer of lyrics" (Emerson's own poet X) for whom "the argument is secondary, the finish of the verses primary" — Emerson declares that "it is not metres, but a metre-making argument that makes a poem, — a thought so passionate and alive that like the spirit of a plant or animal it has an architecture of its own, and adorns nature with a new thing." He continues that "the thought and form are equal in the order of time, but in the order of genesis, the thought is prior to the form." Even as a poet Emerson cannot avoid essaying. There is that high moment in "Merlin" in which he states that

> The trivial harp will never please
> Or fill my craving ear;
> Its chords should ring as blows the breeze,
> Free, peremptory, clear.

An architecture of its own, free, peremptory, clear. Lest it sound as if I am putting words in Emerson's mouth: it should be obvious that he is not, no more than was Stevens, promoting a free verse over a formal one. He is, however, drawing — in theory at least — a line between mere verse or "lyricism," as he calls it, and real poetry, poetry tied inevitably and effectively to its intellectual and emotional sources.

If Emerson and Stevens seem to be talking out of both sides of their mouths at once, they are. To make the full generalization: they would seem to want us to write formal verse as if it were free and so-called free verse as if it were formal. A familiar, if not always possible, aesthetic assignment. Yet as references in the history of our critical thought concerning rhythm in poetry, I would choose these two fundamentalists over a Pound or a Williams just because they absorb rather than disavow our national debt to an inherited language and a distinctly inherited rhythm. I would choose them, as I would choose the reader in Eliot or in Roethke, because they are far less interested in the political debates between poets than in the formal dialectics within poems.

What Emerson's meter-making argument offers us is a coherent basis for reading both, say, a Whitman and a Dickinson; and what Stevens' dirty silence offers us is a coherent metaphor for reading the conflicting evidence of our contemporaries.

The poems of Whitman's, for example, that many of us feel most satisfied with are those that *inhere* to a stable rather than a shifting center — poems that hold the line, in Poe's phrase, toward a single, illuminating effect — that supply the reader with the connecting rhythm and closure of a presiding metaphor. As wonderful as "Song of Myself" is, for me it remains an anthology, a manifesto, a great rangy text, compared to the greater gifts of "Crossing Brooklyn Ferry" or "This Compost" — two poems that develop themes of disintegration and regeneration through the terms of their inherent and limited raw materials; two poems that confront us indirectly rather than resort to the poetry of bravado; two poems that allow the accent to rise as well as fall. Organic or invented, Whitman, at his most interesting, works hard toward singular unity, wholeness; he does not attack the architecture for the sake of being free, peremptory, and clear.

Dickinson too has suffered from stereotype. If too many of her poems scan to the tune of "The Battle Hymn of the Republic" or "The Yellow Rose of Texas," the fault may lie with our hearing of the essential 4/3 hymnal line. The fact is that in her finest work Dickinson struggles against her apparent need for metrical closure and metaphysical purity by opening and shutting the line unexpectedly and by mixing up her metaphor as if she were taking psychological shorthand. Number 640, for instance, is a direct address to the Reverend Charles Wadsworth — a painful, beautiful love poem, and, at fifty lines, one of her longest. It is the poem that begins

> I cannot live with you—
> It would be Life—
> And Life is over there—
> Behind the Shelf
>
> The Sexton keeps the key to—

and concludes by breaking the poet's hymnbook quatrain pattern with a six-line emphatic stanza, four rhyming lines of which drive the same nail in.

> So we must keep apart—
> You there—I here
> With just the Door ajar
> That oceans are—and Prayer—
> And that pale Sustenance—
> Despair.

In one of her last poems, number 1670, Dickinson pursues the key sexual rhyme of Room/worm/warm/home/Form/swim/him/dream through four uneven stanzas in such a way as to let the dream, the pursuit, the transformation of a worm into a snake in her chamber, take over. By insisting on her repetitions and clipped lines, her quick surprises, Dickinson frees the form, freeing it to become her real antagonist.

I am not, by the way, sponsoring a simpleminded law of contraries, in which form is supposed to act as an anchor to content, content the current trying to carry the boat out to sea. I am talking about the dialectic of form itself, an argument of the energies within a poem. It may be true that Whitman needed a father figure — literally, as in his love of Lincoln, or figuratively, as in his use of a presiding metaphor and meter. It may be true that Dickinson needed a demon lover and that the underlying energy of her poems is suspended sex. But these are issues for the biography of content. They do not address directly enough the poetry of the poem. And neither am I attempting to describe a Chinese jar moving perpetually in its stillness, though it is true that I believe words move only in time, and that, after speech, they reach into the silence, make it still dirtier.

I am trying to pay attention to a phenomenon that has pre-occupied our poetry from the beginning. The first phrase of Eliot's landmark essay, "Tradition and the Individual Talent," reads "In English writing. . . ." He does not say, "In writing in English. . . ." I know I am waxing the point a bit. Nevertheless, expatriate Eliot does go on to define poetic relationships, whatever the relative tensions, that exist *within* the tradition rather than relationships that exist outside and against the tradition. Our American meter-making arguments with our English antecedents are too well documented for me to bother with here; but I do want to stress that our witness of what our language is and what a line of poetry means comes from a culture, king, and country that we rejected. Yet as we could not invent an absolute alternative we did adjust one. We discovered a whole new landscape, new skies, a different sense of time and space, extreme weather, Indians, and eventually Europeans. When Williams was asked by an Englishman, "But this language of yours, where does it come from?" Williams replied, "From the mouths of Polish mothers." Whatever the anxiety of influence within the Romantic tradition, there is in our poetry a present tense conditional with the past, a past that, like it or not, provides us with a ghost language, a ghost form, be it sonnet, elegy, or ode, be it epic or pentameter rising; a past that has left us with a shadow line and line of thought. From Whitman to Williams, the argument has really been a matter of a difference of diction and syntax, a language of our experience, a language within a larger, mother tongue. In lieu of an original language for poetry, we have been perennially forced, with Emerson, to realize a new dialectic of rhythm — Anglo and American, monarchical and democratic — if by rhythm we mean movement, or by movement we mean form.

Yet, as my own comments suggest, we have tended, historically, to talk about form in the limited terms of the movement of a line, and from that assumption we have tended to speak of lines adding up to something: the bottom line. Whether it is Emerson looking for its counterpart in nature or Pound telling us to compose in the sequence of the musical phrase and not in the sequence of the metronome or Williams asking us to believe in a variable foot as well as a triadic "stanza" or Olson claiming all the white space of the page; whether we are discussing biorhythms or breath pauses, caesuras or enjambments, accents or syllabics — we have focused on the science of the line. We have tended to speak of form in poetry in terms of the way we write or type it, across the page, and according to the determinations of line break. We have, in fact, and more often as critics and theoreticians than as poets, tried to beat the Tradition at its own game. We have tried more than once to make an American line. Of course, considering the achievement of our ancestry, we have had little choice but to deal with what is primary. . . . Poetry, as form, is a problem of movement across a measured space. But as form, that is not all it is.

Still, I am reminded of a little panegyric of Pound's celebrating the American virtues of Whistler, who like Pound was a sometime Londoner. The third stanza goes:

> You had your searches, your uncertainties,
> And this is good to know—for us, I mean,
> Who bear the brunt of our America
> And try to wrench her impulse into art.

I hope you could hear the measure of this quatrain — four lines of ghost pentameter, half of which is sure iambic. There is even a little assonant rhyme going on, in couplets. And the poet even manages to interrupt himself ("for us, I mean") without interrupting the "music" of the line. Indeed, it is a technique, this talking back against the metrical potential of the line, that Pound was to later perfect in that matrix of meters, *The Cantos.* It is a technique that feels particularly American: speech barking back at song.

The trouble with concentrating the discussion of rhythm in American poetry on the line is that it continually shifts the balance toward the weights and measures of the form we have inherited and away from the idiom in which we live and move and have our being. Even a poet as fed up as Williams, in a poem as gorgeous as "Asphodel, That Greeny Flower," ends up substituting the artiface of his triadic formula for that of another. His formations impose upon rather than reveal variations in rhythm. "Of love, abiding love it will be telling though too weak a wash of crimson colors it. . . ." is one kind of clear music, whereas the lines that immediately follow support a different music — "There is something urgent I have to say to you. . . ." Free verse ought to be flexible enough to handle such juxtapositions *in kind,* without the form aggrandizing. "Asphodel" reads better than it is written, better than it is affixed to the page. Ironically, the harder Williams works against the regularity of the stress, the more he emphasizes its place in his poem.

If 1855 and 1912 are the important dates in the history of our struggle with the conception of the line — from Whitman's long yawp to Pound's announcement of an "absolute rhythm" — then sometime in the middle 1950s through about the term of John Kennedy, we began to extend our aesthetic to include the whole length of the sentence. Whether we are talking about Projective verse or Beat or Confessional or Deep Image, and whether the phenomenon has received much critical attention, the fact is that along about then we began to divide up into category and constituency, armed against the academics, and ready to try to deal with the poem as a whole — a discontinuous rhythm, often with the verbal surface at odds with the content — whether it was composition by field, poetry by protest and confession, or poetry as the interpretation of dreams. We began to look beyond the inherent demands of the line toward the total spatial and temporal needs of the poem. We began to read past the rhythms moving across the page to those moving down as well. Olson's "The Kingfishers," for instance, wants to find a way of including the poet's whole big body, a way of responding to the full, the literal moment — mind, heart, hair, and all. Lowell once spoke of how he arrived at the "form" for the family poems of *Life Studies:* they were written, he said, with as much formal containment and packed verbal surface as any of his earlier lines; he simply chopped them up. He did not have to tell us about the difference the chopping makes, nor the difference the content of crisis forces. And "Howl" is one long sentence long, a litany of loss in a list of losses, held together by a left-hand, anaphoric rhyme of *who's* and a right-hand answer of commas, all built on the single, wonderful statement that "Carl, while you are not safe I am not safe." As for those poets rediscovering the image — a poet like Bly seems to want to be able to operate outside the rhythm of terrestrial time altogether in favor of the poetics of an outer space, so as to create a kind of light filling the page.

There is no such thing as an American line because there can never be any fixed way of writing the free-verse line. Our argument with our forebears is really an argument against certain closure. As the examples of Whitman or Williams or Lowell or even Dickinson might show, it is not so much that our poetry has rejected the ghost forms we inherited but that the needs of our experience make demands, in every generation, that we transcend those forms. But of course we can never exactly "transcend" them, not as long as we live within the same language, the same accents and patterns; we can, however, move through them, past them, distending or extending them. (That is what idiom is all about, the language of an identity, language as "the music latent in the common speech of its time.") Free verse has about the same meaning for us as free speech: though we would never shout fire in a crowded theater, free speech is our birthright and responsibility.

And that is why the silence is getting dirtier and dirtier. As the line turns toward the completed sentence, the sentence turns toward the total structure and texture of the poem, its total rhythm, toward spontaneous particulars and particulars of sound. If the phrase "free verse" has any useful meaning, it lies in its emphatic sense of the poem as an open entity, moving by assonance and consonance, moving by rising as well as falling rhythm, moving by image and rhetoric, and moving by, most of all, surprise. The dialectic between the unit of the measured line and the unit of the full sentence might read more relaxed, yet it would still be necessary as a stay against just "one person talking to another," to quote Eliot again. From John Ashbery to James Wright, a generation of poets decided that apprenticeship is one thing but forms of closure could lead to solitary confinement. Ashbery and Wright, in fact, force us to read them whole poem by whole, for their "single effects," or not read them at all. Their ears are tuned to the sentence — certainly to the completion of image and thought, but clearly also to the richer, intimate disclosure of the emotion.

The chief distinction between the verse line and the free-verse sentence is the distinction between a poetry that continually returns and one that continues, that turns, that goes on. Whatever adjudications have to be made between persona and person in a poem, as between relative relationships the speaker has to his or her raw material, in American free verse since the 1960s we are asked to move from line to storyline in such a way that the interchange be imperceptible. Line break becomes line turn, line continuum, a sentence. As the vocalization of the line occurs *within* it, the endings of the lines begin to add up to something visual, yet something we see through. This kind of voicing over the integrity of the line into the sentence, toward the totality of the poem, is often hard to hear, not because the verse is really prose but because the verse is accumulative, acquisitional, special, and, if it is of the quality of a John Ashbery or a James Wright, understated — leaning toward or away from the predictable, the regular, never quite on the mark.

Our free verse, then, is fictive music, developed through the art of the individual idiom.

But all of this at best addresses the energy and the rhythms withheld or released in the poetry of the sentence. The sentence itself goes on. In depending on the sequence of subject-verb-complement, free verse depends on cause-and-effect connections, and therefore emphasizes, sentence to sentence, plot over pattern. If pattern is what we hear in verse, plot is what we are asked to listen for when the verse is "freed."

On Wednesday the queen died and on Friday the king died,

says E. M. Forster, and that is straight narrative; but on Wednesday the queen died and on Friday the king died of grief, that is plot. Pattern is how we move from here to there; plot is why. In emphasizing why over how, free verse further depends on its ability to dramatize, to bark back continually at the song, as when Ashbery, in "Wet Casements," tells us that he "can't have it, and this makes me angry" or when Wright tells us, in poem after poem, "Don't blame me, I didn't start this mess."

That remarkable tension between how and why, the lyric and the dramatic, between lingering and needing to go on, between the horizontal rhythm of the line and the vertical rhythm of the story, with the balance always favoring the movement down, is what gives free verse its authority. The verse itself, the lyricism, lives in the phrase, the clause, while the freedom lives in that language that completes the sentence, that extends and connects it to the next. (W. S. Merwin, for example, a poet who has played with the abridgment of the line and the syntax of the sentence better than any of his contemporaries, writes of "St. Vincent's" that "its bricks by day a French red under / cross facing south / blown-up neoclassic facades the tall / dark openings between columns at / the dawn of history / exploded into many windows / in a mortised face." The line breaks are intended to excite as much as complicate the differences between ending, enjambing, and continuing — to make us move swiftly through the emphasis of phrase to the total structure of the stanza. The tension between breaking and entering the new line is supported by the need to go on, to complete, to make whole: a whole thought, a whole perception.) In that growth lies the dramatic voice, the voice unwilling to simply sing, but nevertheless demanding to be well heard. Yet a voice not simply speech. In the achieved free-verse poem we hear the formalization of a process, as well as a progress: we hear form itself being achieved. And the form speaks, as in a dialectic of poetry against itself.

Perhaps, though, we should look at the bright side, think of our formal problems less in terms of a dialectic and more in terms of a happy correspondence. Last year the young American poet Robert Hass — a figure somewhere in the aesthetic middle ground between a contemporary poetry committed to the tight line of the image and one reinventing the longer, more flexible line of narrative — last year he published a book entitled *Praise*. The second poem, "Meditation at Lagunitas," goes as follows:

> All the new thinking is about loss.
> In this it resembles all the old thinking.

The idea, for example, that each particular erases
the luminous clarity of a general idea. That the clown-
faced **woodpecker** probing the dead sculpted trunk
of that black birch is, by his presence,
some tragic falling off from a first world
of undivided light. Or the other notion that,
because there is in this world no one thing
to which the bramble of *blackberry* corresponds,
a word is elegy to what it signifies.
We talked about it late last night and in the voice
of my friend, there was a thin wire of grief, a tone
almost querulous. After a while I understood that,
talking this way, everything dissolves: *justice,*
pine, hair, woman, you and *I.* There was a woman
I made love to and I remembered how, holding
her small shoulders in my hands sometimes,
I felt a violent wonder at her presence
like a thirst for salt, for my childhood river
with its island willows, silly music from the pleasure boat,
muddy places where we caught the little orange-silver fish
called *pumpkinseed.* It hardly had to do with her
longing, we say, because desire is full
of endless distances. I must have been the same to her.
But I remember so much, the way her hands dismantled
     bread,
the thing her father said that hurt her, what
she dreamed. There are moments when the body is as
     numinous
as words, days that are the good flesh continuing.
Such tenderness, those afternoons and evenings,
saying *blackberry, blackberry, blackberry.*

It is unlikely that you heard many line breaks. I hope, however, that the rhythms in and of the sentences were audible, if not
always certifiable; and I hope that the overall plot of the poem,
from exposition to complication to climax, could be followed.
Hass calls it a "Meditation," which traditionally has been that
chance to think aloud, brood, speculate, wander a bit, and possibly
arrive at a conclusion. However we are to look at it, as an action or
as an argument or both, there is something intellectually and
emotionally serious at stake here, something obviously painful,
local, real. The poem reads deductively, going from generalization
to the evidence as if we were being instructed, yet it is clear that
the experience at the center of the poem has itself brought the

speaker to this Pacific place — to ruminate, to set priorities. And the poem is framed by its "philosophy," yet it is also clear that all the new/old thinking about loss has been changed, affected, intimately transformed by the time we hear the word *blackberry* repeated in the last line. And the poem is arranged in four discrete units, paragraphlike, rather than stanzas, yet, again, it is clear that transitions are being offered and that the order, once headed, seems inevitable.

The title, "Meditation at Lagunitas," would have us believe in the fiction that the speaker is actually standing by the ocean thinking about loss, telling us he is thinking about loss; when in truth, to round out the tautology, the speaker is showing us that he is there thinking about loss — demonstrating, dramatizing the fact, speaking from the condition of loss. He even notices a clown-faced woodpecker for us — to reassure us. I worry the point because the greater fiction is always the form itself, the revealing, realized emblem. By dramatizing his sense of loss the speaker is formalizing it. But I will have more to say about that later. For right now, "All the new thinking is about loss. / In this it resembles all the old thinking." These two lines of wit and confidence, this thought-rhyme, will be the last two so juxtaposed, end-stopped lines in the poem. For the remainder of this first verse paragraph, the speaker will deliberate back and forth, sometimes ten, sometimes twelve, sometimes sixteen syllables, building by parallels of pronoun and antecedent, working down to the poem's essential perception — "a word is elegy to what it signifies" — a bottom line with the first full integrity of a regular statement. The passage goes again:

> All the new thinking is about loss.
> In this it resembles all the old thinking.
> The idea, for example, that each particular erases
> the luminous clarity of a general idea. That the clown-
> faced woodpecker probing the dead sculpted trunk
> of that black birch is, by his presence,
> some tragic falling off from a first world
> of undivided light. Or the other notion that,
> because there is in this world no one thing
> to which the bramble of *blackberry* corresponds,
> a word is elegy to what it signifies.

If you can imagine it, the right-hand margin is sharply angular, in keeping with but not overstating the anxiety of the thought that links *loss* and *erases* and *tragic falling off* and *no one thing* and *elegy*. Nearly all of the eleven lines are divided by caesura or comma, or interrupted by periods. The final, the summarizing, line of the passage turns out to be, of course, the best balanced, "elegy" positioned against "signifies." Save for the starting "couplet," the passage is a single, extended sentence, with the emphasis on the rationality of first this perception as opposed to that notion. It is hardly a syllogism; but the passage does play seriously with the logic of loss. This is the "music" of theory.

And it would seem, having stated all the issues, that the form is satisfied. A little speculation with illustration. But since the center of the poem and the reason for its having been written involves an emotional and sexual encounter that superfically bears no necessary connection to the beginning, a way must be found to get there to link up. In this case, through a third person, a friend.

> We talked about it late last night and in the voice
> of my friend, there was a thin wire of grief, a tone
> almost querulous. After a while I understood that,
> talking this way, everything dissolves: *justice,*
> *pine, hair, woman, you* and *I.*

If we listen closely we can hear plot developing, as the terms for loss begin to enlarge, magnify. In just these four and a half lines, Hass achieves the status of a protagonist, a presence no longer simply engaged in thinking but in talking out his thinking about loss. He gets in and out of the discussion so quickly we barely have time to notice how fully he extends his thesis. There are four references to the concern that there is in this world no one thing to which the bramble of *blackberry* corresponds: first the pronoun *it,* which sends us in reverse order back through the passage we have just made; then *thin wire of grief,* the tone of voice of the friend, then the speaker reminds us that we are, in fact, *talking this way;* and finally *everything dissolves* — presumably into words — *justice, pine, hair, woman, you and I.* Half the poem is over, and we have, in the meditating mind and mediating voice of the speaker, moved from thinking of loss to talking in the terms of you and I; and a woman. It has been a declension directed at the heart of things, the memory in the poem.

> There was a woman
> I made love to and I remembered how, holding
> her small shoulders in my hands sometimes,
> I felt a violent wonder at her presence
> like a thirst for salt, for my childhood river

with its island willows, silly music from the pleasure boat,
muddy places where we caught the little orange-silver fish
called *pumpkinseed.* It hardly had to do with her.
Longing, we say, because desire is full
of endless distances. I must have been the same to her.

Easily the poem's most lyrical moment, these lines move with the
grace of their attention — one long sentence of experience, three
short sentences of comment. Motion, with modification. The long
sentence, the central sentence, turns and turns and turns, with less
need of pause than continuation. The sense of the unit standard of
the lines would have them breaking something like:

There was a woman I made love to
and I remembered how,
holding her small shoulders in my hands (sometimes)
I felt a violent wonder at her presence . . .

Remarkably, Hass observes this standard fairly closely, even
though many such closely observed lines could go flat very fast.
The issue is that he works against the habit of the thought and
possible metrical unit to make the good sense more interesting
sense, to let us ease into the emotion with him. He also wants to
emphasize visually, as well as vocally, some of the other names
into which "everything dissolves": woman, holding, sometimes,
presence, river, boat, fish. Freeing and breaking his lines for their
best sentence sense, their plot-complicating sense, allows the poet
to discover his stresses within the phrase or the clause, while the
voice-over of the speaker, the actor in the poem, is free to carry us
through the line and storyline to completion. Hass' speaker brings
us out of our river dream, with its island willows and silly music
from the pleasure boat, rather abruptly. It — again the open pronoun — it hardly had to do with her, he says. The truth of this is
softened a bit by his asking us to remember that longing is full of
endless distances. Therefore it must have been the same with her.
But, the speaker adds,

I remember so much, the way her hands dismantled
bread,
the think her father said that hurt her, what
she dreamed.

Like so many in this poem, the lines here keep tucking in, with
"bread" and "what" and "dreamed." Bread and a thing said: they

may be the source of dreaming, but the consonant endings of *d* and *t,* the rhyme of *bread* and *said,* drive home the hurt for both speaker and lover. The speaker concludes, in something close to a quatrain, that the bread is the body, just as the word is inevitably, elegiacally, flesh, and flesh, word. A fair exchange.

> There are moments when the body is as numinous
> as words, days that are the good flesh continuing.
> Such tenderness, those afternoons and evenings,
> saying *blackberry, blackberry, blackberry.*

If this poem is successful it is successful because it moves convincingly from the easy wit of thinking about loss to a condition of fullness, tenderness, from the melancholy of the word to a belief in the body, from blackberry as sign to blackberry as speech. Yet vocally, and emotionally, the poem grows through the internal strength of its sentences, through a music worked out within the completed sentence structure. The line is determined more by its aural good sense than by its sense of measured sound. As the primary combining and cohering rhythm in the poem, the sentence naturally extends into the verse paragraph, the paragraph into the poem.

Nevertheless, "Meditation at Lagunitas" is one stanza in duration, a single, continuing embrace of its tensions — and not just those tensions between the line holding and the sentence going on, between the visual and vocal rhythms, and not just between the word and its corresponding flesh, and not just between the idea and the emotion. This piece seems to want to travel the distance from meditation to love poem, from one temperature to passion. It seems to want to be organized around alternating parts of its speech, a longer passage to short, longer to short; that is, eleven lines to five, thirteen lines to four. It seems to want to achieve, to complete its *blackberrying* yet to remain open-ended. The poem is plotted, certainly, from, through, and to something. And it does move within a time frame of causal relations, from thinking to talking to remembering to realization, from here to there, through a list of synonyms for loss — until loss itself is transformed.

One of the advantages of fixed or invented forms is that they secure the reader in space as well as time; line by line they reassure the reader of an order, past and passing and to come, within the void of the page. So in a sense, no matter how we vary those forms, so long as they are surefooted we are potentially aware of the whole of the poem, its plan, and its commitment to closure, from the start. We can sit back and enjoy the music that much more. We can anticipate.

Free verse is famous for reassuring no one of anything, least of all the reader. Yet when it is done well, its ambition, and its ability, I would like to think, is to find a form as secure in its space on the page as it pretends to be in the time it takes. The point is important because it permits us to see free verse less as a creative accident than as an earned achievement, less as attempt than as perfected art.

All the new thinking is about loss because of those afternoons and evenings when the body was as numinous as words, moments and whole days of the good flesh continuing, saying this is that to which the bramble of *blackberry* corresponds. That sentence is the plot in summary — in reduction, the cause-and-effect, temporal, ongoing rhythm of the whole. But it is not the poem as a whole brought to bear. It is not the form, achieved.

One of the worst poetry clichés, reintroduced as an aesthetic in the 60s, was that this dominant mode, free verse, should represent the spontaneous overflow of powerful feelings without much exercise in recollecting them in tranquility. Even Lowell, from out of the tranquilized 50s, would later describe his experiential *Notebook* sonnets as "the loose ravel of blank verse." The notion that free verse must be either naked or dressed for dinner does not deal with the dialectic of the phrase itself. It can be free of its verse only to the extent that it keep the faith, in sounds that are a little hard to hear, with sights a little hard to see. Its lyric values are amended by the voice, the voice normally in the middle of its dramatic circumstance. It is a voice at once preoccupied with expressing and advancing the story, of moving across the space, yes, of making us pay attention, but also necessarily committed to moving down the page, of keeping our attention. The interval of the phrase and clause may be the basic unit of its lyricism, but the sentence is the rhythm given meaning, the line a way of getting there. The parental, the ghost form may be more apparent in some free-verse poems than others: regardless, the nominal music will be invariably speech barking back at song. And the simple weight of the bottom of the page will favor passage over pause.

But there is a bottom line. Stevens ends his poem "The Creations of Sound" by offering that "We say ourselves in syllables that rise / From the floor, rising in speech we do not speak." I read these lines as referring to a language so intelligent with the source of the poem that the language seems a priori to the art. So that the poem would perform as provided with its speech rather than having learned it en route to its last line. The formalization of free verse consists in its ability to speak from the floor from the first line on — and to continue, line by sentence, to free the voice from the imitations for the ear.

And that is why Robert Hass' poem is a mediation of a meditation. At the point of entry of thinking about loss he has entered the form. He has set tone, he has reached into the silence. His medium, his agency, will act as his means; it will even allow him to write a sort of love sonnet within the whole story. The fiction of American free verse is not so much that the demands are any less formal but that they are finally any different.

Stephen Dobyns

Metaphor and the Authenticating Act of Memory

There is an old conundrum which asks, Is a bathtub a bathtub on Mars? Implied here is the suggestion that something is defined by its function. Consequently, if you take a bathtub and rocket it to Mars where it can't be used, it will cease to be a bathtub.

Art, too, can be defined partly by its function: that is, a work of art, such as a poem, seeks to communicate with an audience. If that communication does not take place, then the work of art has failed in its function, although that failure may be the fault of the audience and not the work of art.

This has not been a popular idea in modern poetics. The French Symbolist poets felt that a great poem was like a bright light. It wasn't required of a reader to understand or not understand. In that poetry dealt with the inexpressible, communication was hardly relevant. All that was needed was for the reader to be within the presence of the poem to feel its beneficial effects.

These ideas influence Eliot, Pound and other modernists with the result that their sense of an audience tends to be rather high-handed. If they think of the reader at all, it is only to say he is lucky to be there. They feel that the poet's responsibility is entirely to the poem and that to pause to guide the reader is to diminish the poet's first duty and cheapen the work.

Opposed to this is an idea found in Samuel Johnson, who wrote, "By the common sense of readers uncorrupted with literary prejudices, after all the refinements of subtlety and the dogmatism of learning, must be finally decided all claim to poetic honors."

For Johnson, the ideal reader is not simply a bystander but the final judge, and part of his judgement derives from how well the poem communicates. It is a modified version of this idea which influences Yeats and William Carlos Williams. Indeed, Yeats would study the poems of Mallarmé, trying to determine the exact line between communication and solipscism, thinking that to cross it, as he felt Mallarmé had done, would destroy the poem.

These two extremes become the extremes of modern **British** and American poetry. For the purpose of this paper, I would like to offer my own definition, which is an extension of that statement of Samuel Johnson's: that is, the most successful contemporary poem is an expression of formally heightened emotion which seeks to establish an intimate relationship with its audience by making the audience a participant in the creative process; and further, if the poem does not seek to establish this relationship or fails to establish it or is incapable of establishing such a relationship, then it fails and, at best, the audience becomes an interested witness.

By "formally heightened" I mean only to indicate a relationship between content and form without attempting to define it. Furthermore, this definition deals only with the poem's responsibility. The reader, too, has a responsibility, but that is a subject beyond the scope of this talk. In any case, within this definition, if the poem is incapable of establishing an intimate relationship with its audience, then it simply isn't a poem.

What I want to discuss here are ways in which this relationship with the reader may be strengthened. One way is through the use of metaphor, by which I mean to include the grammatical figures of metaphor, simile, allegory and analogy. Generally, they are forms of comparison which exist to heighten the object of the comparison. Another way is through the authenticating act of memory, which means that the reader must be able to recognize and respond to the world of the poem, which further requires a certain clarity as to the physical, emotional and intellectual contexts or situations to be found within the poem.

Gertrude Stein once **wrote** about the difficulty of writing in a period of late language, by which she meant a period in which people are so used to the language and meanings of words that they tend to take those words for granted, seeing them as no more than signs. She said that when the language was younger it was possible for a writer to make a statement like, "Oh Moon, I am lonely," and still have the language communicate intense loneliness. In a period of late language, however, the reader's linguistic sophistication blocks the emotion and he takes the word "lonely" only as a sign indicative of the speaker's emotional state and doesn't let it communicate any feeling of loneliness. Instead of creating a sense of emotion on the page, the words refer to an emotional state existing off the page. Consequently, the reader doesn't become a participant, if only because the simple expression of loneliness isn't enough to jar him into empathy.

The more sophisticated we become about language, the less we are moved by its simple expression. Because of this, poets are constantly seeking ways to make emotion appear fresh. One of the obvious functions of metaphor is to heighten emotion. In a poem that I will discuss later, W. S. Merwin replaces the statement "I am lonely" with "When you leave, the wind clicks around to the north." Another metaphor for aloneness is:

> **Unless** she is the one
> sail on to death
> like an empty ship.

That metaphor, along with others I will be using, comes from W.S. Merwin's *Asian Figures,* which are translations of folk-sayings from half a dozen Asian countries.

A metaphor can exist to heighten just a small part of the poem or it can be the entire poem. To be successful, however, the metaphor must be functional rather than decorative; by which I mean, it has to further and heighten the general intent of the poem and that it must be necessary to the reader's understanding and involvement in the poem. Any decorative use of metaphor is basically rhetorical; the author is trying to convince the reader by what amounts to technical effects, rather than by content.

A metaphor consists of the object half and the image half. The image half is most successful when it is open-ended or when the mind cannot fully encompass it: that is, when it creates the impression that it could give additional ramifications of meaning each time the reader returns to it. Compare, for example, the stale metaphor "as quiet as a mouse" with:

> Quiet
> like a house where the witch
> has just stopped dancing.

When it is open-ended, the image works like a symbol, which in its simplest form is only an image that represents more than its literal meaning. The witch's dance is not described and, while we might have some understanding of it, we cannot encompass it, nor what the house is like without it. In a similar way, the symbol of the cross can be to some degree understood but it cannot be encompassed, while the meaning of a stop sign, like the quietness of a mouse, can be encompassed.

This difference is partly the difference between sign and symbol, and it can be seen that the image of the mouse to represent quiet approaches being a sign. It would appear, therefore, that the image half of the metaphor has the greatest possibility of affecting the reader the more closely it works either like or as a symbol. This is similar to what Yeats says in his essay, "The Symbolism of Poetry:"

> . . . metaphors are not profound enough to be moving when they are not symbols, and when they are symbols they are the most perfect of all, because the most subtle . . . .

The open-ended quality of the image half of the metaphor allows it to become to some degree mysterious. The more we think about the possible frightening qualities of the witch's dance, think of what makes the house so silent when the dance is over and of the fear implied by that silence, then the more we continue to draw understanding from the entire metaphor.

In that metaphor, the object is obviously the word "quiet," but in more complicated metaphors the object can be an entire situation. This is true in the two Asian Figures:

> Talk about tomorrow
> the rats will laugh
>
> Spits straight up
> learns something

Since the object half of the metaphor attempts to provide a context for the image, the object itself should be entirely clear. When someone accuses a poem of being vague, he often means that the object or context of a metaphor is unclear or that the relationship between the object and image appears imprecise. Vagueness is caused by withholding information and usually no amount of thought will suppy what is missing or, if it does supply the information, the act of supplying it is basically irrelevant to the poem and does not heighten the metaphor, meaning that the information should have been there in the first place.

Consider the metaphor,

Full of danger
as an egg pyramid

If the word "danger" were removed and the reader were forced to guess at it, **nothing** would be gained by that guessing. The purpose of the metaphor is to heighten our sense of the object of the metaphor. If we don't know the object, then that heightening process cannot occur.

A mystery is potentially capable of being understood. What is mysterious lends itself to understanding, but what is vague leads primarily to frustration and confusion.

The problem with many weak poems is that they often substitute vagueness for mystery. They withhold necessary information as to the object or context of the metaphor and offer only image or what appears to be image, which then gives the poem an aura of mystery and meaning. But image without object is nonfunctional, since the contemplation of it won't increase our understanding. It is not the contemplation of the image which leads to understanding; rather, it is the contemplation of the relationship between the image and object. This is very important. Image without object is enticing but it's a dead end. The image has no function without the object, while the purpose of metaphor is not to draw attention to its parts but to the relationship between its parts.

Although what is being discussed is image as it functions within metaphor, I would like to expand this argument to include images as they were often used by the early Imagist poets and the poets who were influenced by them. These poets often felt that the image had a value entirely by itself. What they called image was very similar to what an earlier generation had called symbol. Both groups felt that the mere presence of the image or symbol energized the poem, but both, by putting little value on audience, were ignoring certain rules of communication. Even a symbol, in order to be effective, has to give a sense of what it symbolizes; the possibility of connection between image and object must be available. The Imagists attempted to erase the comparative role of the image, but it is that comparison which makes the images important. We partly go to art to learn about the world. In a metaphor, the world is represented by the object, while the comparison with the image gives us a new sense of that world. To remove the object, destroy the comparison and present the reader only with the image is to decrease his interest and limit communication.

This criticism of Imagism is also made by Graham Hough in his essay, "Reflections on a Literary Revolution." Hough writes of these Imagist poems:

In all of them we find a host of examples where immediate communication between poet and reader fails on two planes; both on the plane of reference, all that is ordinarily called the "sense" of the poem; and on the plane of feeling, the emotional attitude toward the situation presented. Whatever tradition Imagist poetry may have recalled to us, the most important tradition of all, that of a natural community of understanding between poet and reader, has been lost.

Examples of metaphors with clear objects and open-ended images are:

The mouth is
one gate of hell

Neglect is a dog
in a dead man's house

Tongue
pale pig in a bone fence

Scruples
lead you to hunger

Stepping on a long **thorn**
to me the sight of her hair

Every metaphor is based on buried or withheld information which the comparison implied by the metaphor attempts to discover. Implied in each metaphor is the question how the image is like the object. It is by answering this question that the reader becomes a participant in the poem by authenticating the comparison from his own memory.

Simplistically, every metaphor is a riddle, since, if the object is clear, then the reader always asks how is A like B. That kind of asking and answering is practically unconscious. It is as if the brain when presented with a potentially solvable question automatically attempts to solve it. Only when the brain consciously tells itself to stop trying does the questioning process come to a halt. When I ask myself what is the square root of eighty-five, I am aware of my brain beginning to question and then stopping itself because I'm unable to solve such a problem in my head. But that beginning to question is automatic.

The question implied by the metaphor forces the reader to clarify and define the relationship between the object and image, and this—one—forces the reader to participate actively in the poem and—two—gives him knowledge about something he did not know or only partly knew by making it analogous to something he can imagine. And this act of imagining increases his participation by forcing him to draw on memory to authenticate the metaphor.

When I give you the simile "A liar is like an egg in mid-air," I am trying to heighten and particularize your sense of a liar by saying how fragile and precarious and short-lived the lie is. When you hear the simile, your mind automatically asks the questions of how and why. In order to answer these questions, your mind draws on its knowledge of eggs and, equally important, it imagines a time-sense or temporal context. The egg in mid-air exists in one point of time. In order to understand the simile, you have to imagine a past and future.

Take another simile:

> Silent
> like the thief the dog bit

Again, the action exists in one point of time and you have to imagine a temporal context: a brief narrative with a past and future.

What I find particularly amazing is the speed at which the mind comes up with the information. If I were to write down how a liar is like an egg in mid-air, it could take pages, but I wouldn't be able to say anything that I hadn't already made clear to myself in a split second. We tend to take this process for granted, but if it weren't for our ability to compare one thing to another, then to draw seemingly spontaneous knowledge from the comparison, poetry would be impossible.

The speed of this process also gives the metaphor the additional advantage of surprise, as can be seen in the figures:

> The hissing starts
> in the free seats

> Rank and position
> gulls on water

> Close to death
> see how tender
> the grass is

Who looks at a mirror
to see a mirror

Life
candle flame
wind coming

In each of these cases, the speed of our understanding is so rapid that we seem to take ourselves by surprise, and the presence of this surprise helps convince us, sometimes falsely, of the accuracy of the metaphor. The surprise almost functions as a rhetorical device, since our sense of surprise can distract us and cause us to overlook the logic of the metaphor.

For a metaphor to be successful it must be logical; it has to conform to our knowledge of the known world. I expect we can accept this without further inquiry. But logic by itself isn't enough; the metaphor must also be specific and precise. To say "Ask the mouth, it says food" is certainly logical, but it does not have the precision of "Ask the mouth, it says cake." The former says what we already know, what we can already encompass, but the latter also says something about self-indulgence and how the body doesn't necessarily know or care about what is good for it. Now, in a sense, we already know this too, but it's as if we weren't really aware that we knew it until the memory surprised us with it.

The specific goes further to engage us because it evokes a clearer and **possibly** more sensual memory response. The word "food," which is a broad category, calls up only a vague memory response, while "cake," a narrower category, evokes a response that is more detailed.

Take another example: to say, "Talk about tomorrow people will laugh," is logical, but it doesn't have the precision of "Talk about tomorrow the rats will laugh." As with the mouth/cake metaphor, the first tells us something we don't have to reach for, that we already consciously know. The former we can encompass and authenticate simply with the conscious mind, but the greater complexity of the latter keeps us going back and forth between image and object, keeps engaging our memory until we fully accept the knowledge that no one knows more about failed plans than scavengers.

Look at another:

Where there's no tiger
the hares swagger

If you replace "swagger" with "call attention to themselves," you dilute the metaphor and what it says about power. It makes sense but it is also something we already know. What partly activates the memory are the questions of how and why, but the memory isn't going to bother engaging with something that we **already** know and if the memory doesn't engage with the metaphor, then the reader can't become a participant. The memory is also more actively engaged by verbs which specifically involve the senses. We can see "swagger," we cannot see "call attention to themselves." This act of engaging is how the memory authenticates the metaphor and it is **this** authenticating act of the memory which is the way the conscious mind is given a piece of information that already seems to exist in the unconscious.

What I call the unconscious may be no more than memory: that the best metaphors are those with enough complexity to need substantiating by dredging up information that one had **forgotten** one had had. On the other hand, I see nothing wrong with accepting Freud's definitions of the conscious and unconscious minds in order to explain this process, while accepting the possibility that Freud's definitions are themselves metaphors for something we still don't understand. Generally, I would say that the best metaphors are those which engage the unconscious mind: that is, that part of the mind which contains psychic material of which the ego is unaware.

The more the metaphor involves the entire mind, both conscious and unconscious, then the more successful it has the possibility of being. The figure, "When he draws a tiger it's a dog," surprises us with a new sense of the ineffectual. Yet to verify it there is a split second in which I ask myself how it is meant to mean. It is that act of questioning that seems to submit the conscious to the unconscious mind, expecting the unconscious immediately to authenticate and understand.

Sometimes the conscious and unconscious seem to authenticate the metaphor at exactly the same instant. At other times, it seems this authenticating response is not simultaneous, that the unconscious **understands** before the conscious and there is a moment of confusion.

Look at these figures:

Needle thief
dreams of spears

Leave a bit of tail
on account of the flies

I see the wind far away in flags
my heart is not patient
sick with waiting

Rough water drowns the gosling
money drives out manners
poverty drives out reason

Start to speak
lips feel the cold autumn wind

Sparrows a hundred years old
still dance
the sparrow dance

Here it seems that my unconscious understands sooner than my conscious mind. I have the sense that I understand it before I know why I understand it. The effect of this is to surprise me with myself. I suddenly become faced with myself and my view of the world. And that face-to-face quality occurs during the moment when part of me is struck by the precision of the metaphor and another part is still trying to understand it. I expect this happens with most good metaphors: there is a moment of combined knowing and not-knowing where we confront ourselves. Think again about the Asian Figures: "Ask the mouth it says cake" or "The hissing starts in the free seats" or "Spits straight up learns something." First there is a moment of recognition and ignorance, then a moment of recognition and ignorance, then a moment of asking how and why, then the ignorance resolves itself into knowledge. But that recognition, which is certainly also knowledge, was there from the first.

Knowledge mostly comes to us accumulatively; it arrives word by word, in the way that words accumulate in a sentence. We build verbal structures of argument and persuasion. But knowledge can also come through seemingly spontaneous non-verbal perceptions. For instance, if I ask myself what would happen if the Russians dropped an atomic bomb on Boston, I respond with an immediate non-verbal perception which seems detailed in all the nuances of nuclear holocaust, ranging from the destruction of the ozone layer to the roasting of old ladies in Minsk.

This is also how metaphor works and partly what makes it so effective. I don't know how to label this sort of perception, this way of immediately surprising oneself with a large body of information, but it can occur in all areas — when I am working out a problem in mathematics, when I am playing chess, when I am working on a poem, when I am trying to understand the world. In the first moments after this non-verbal perception, there is a period of confusion, of trying to understand, while the conscious part of my mind asks a number of questions. But nearly always the conscious mind comes away satisfied. It will begin to ask, Will the old ladies of Minsk really be roasted? And even before it can finish verbalizing the question, it will know the answer is yes.

A non-verbal perception of this nature is immensely convincing. It seems almost to come from outside of us, almost like a vision, an exterior voice telling us the truth. And this has the peculiar side effect of momentarily taking us out of our isolation and joining us in some larger idea of the world. I expect this sense of its being an exterior voice is somewhat caused by the fact that we think of the ego as verbal, that endless mumble in the brain — therefore, a huge, non-verbal perception appears to come from beyond the ego. This is certainly how it sometimes seems in the writing of poetry where in a moment of non-verbal perception I suddenly "see" how the poem is going to work itself out. It also helps to explain the theory we first find in Plato's dialogue "Ion," where Socrates argues that the poem does not originate with the poet, but rather the poet is the medium through which the poem passes from a higher sphere to the world.

This would seem to be straying from the subject, but it is the ability of metaphor to elicit large, non-verbal perceptions that is one of the great strengths of poetry and what can make a poem immediately convincing. Yeats, for instance, loved to entwine the non-verbal perception created by the metaphor with the intellectual argument of the poem. He would so carefully link argument and metaphor at the conclusion of a poem that the non-verbal perception completely overwhelms and absorbs the verbal argument. This is the strategy he uses to close "The Second Coming," "Among School Children" and "Sailing to Byzantium" where he leaves his argument and shifts to a metaphor which illustrates his conclusion. What helps convince us of these endings is not necessarily their intrinsic truth, but the manner of their presenting: that is, by forcing us to experience the non-verbal perception which confronts us with a moment of combined knowing and ignorance, and which through questioning we resolve into knowledge.

Roethke said that people often don't like poetry because it asks questions of their lives. But what it may really do is to present them with metaphors which make them ask certain questions of themselves: "If you're going to be a dog be a rich man's dog" or "Wait till he's falling then push" or "If it's dirty work borrow the tools." The questioning process by which the reader submits himself to the metaphor makes him vulnerable to its suggestion, while the extreme pragmatism of these particular metaphors can force him to examine the way he perceives the world.

I said originally that a poem seeks to establish an intimate relationship with its audience. I want to expand this to say that a poem seeks to establish this relationship in order to force the audience or reader to become aware of his relationship with himself by forcing him to become aware of how he sees the world.

Now this seems complicated and it's connected to what I said about non-verbal perception, but another aspect of this process is the ability of the metaphor to surprise us with a piece of information that it feels as if we knew but weren't really aware that we knew until the metaphor revealed it to us. Either the unconscious already had this knowledge or the unconscious answered the question posed by the metaphor faster than the conscious which makes it *seem* as if the unconscious already had this knowledge. The conscious tends to verbalize its thought and this process of verbalizing makes it move more slowly than the unconscious. Also, the immense speed of non-verbal perception can create the illusion that we already possessed the knowledge. Does the information already exist in the unconscious or does it only seem that way because the unconscious answered the question first?

Possibly it's a combination of the two, but if the information is already in the unconscious, then perhaps it is the questioning process of the metaphor coupled with the pragmatic honesty of the unconscious — "Wait till he's falling then push" — which confronts us with the barriers, inhibitions and rationalizations of the conscious mind. I expect that the ability to lie is an ability of the conscious mind and we lie just as much to protect ourselves from ourselves as to protect ourselves from other people. But the unconscious mind seems unable to lie. It simply takes in information and interprets it according to the knowledge that it has. It may misinterpret, but it doesn't intentionally deceive. In this sense at least it seems honest.

It would appear then that the successful metaphor confronts the conscious with the unconscious mind and this results in a heightening of the reader's relationship with himself. Consequently, the degree to which we call a metaphor precise is perhaps the degree to which the metaphor is authenticated in this confrontation between the conscious and unconscious minds. Further, it is the function of metaphor to create this confrontation.

I want to look now at three poems in order to see how metaphor functions more exactly. All three give examples of simple metaphor and our understanding of the poems comes from working out the almost linear accumulation of image.

The first is Tomas Tranströmer's "Face to Face:"

> In February living stood still.
> The birds flew unwillingly and the mind
> chafed against the landscape as a boat
> chafes against the bridge it lies moored to.
>
> The trees stood with their backs turned toward me.
> The deep snow was measured with dead straws.
> The footprints grew old out on the crust.
> Under a tarpaulin language pined.
>
> One day something came forward to the window.
> Dropping my work I looked up.
> The colors flared. Everything turned around.
> The earth and I sprang towards each other.

Here we have a clear example of the relationship between the object and image halves of the metaphor. The first line immediately states the object — living in February, which in this case would be in the author's homeland of Sweden — while the verb-adverb construction "stood still" is also a metaphoric usage. The object is then heightened by two examples — the birds flying unwillingly and the mind chafing against the landscape. These are basically realistic but contain some degree of metaphor. Do the birds really fly unwillingly or does it only seem that way? The second example is further heightened by the simile of the boat chafing against the bridge.

The first stanza is a fairly objective description of reality. The second stanza, however, describes a metaphoric reality. The link between the two seems to be the simile that concludes the first stanza: that the mind in winter chafes against the winter landscape as a boat chafes against the bridge to which it is tied. But looking more closely at lines two, three and four, we see that each contains a greater degree of metaphor until it is only a small step to line five which is pure metaphor. Without that gradual increase of metaphor the second stanza would seem only an exaggerated description of reality: that is, hyperbole.

In the second stanza, the four images have an accumulative strength. They are strange, cannot be entirely encompassed and each, by being another example of immobility, refers back to the "stood still" in line one. Along with this immobility, there is the sense of life withheld or denied; and by line eight, where language actually grieves, we see that what is also being talked about is the writer's relationship to his work. Additionally, the phrase "under the tarpaulin" returns us to the boat moored to the bridge and perhaps we think of a boat covered by a tarpaulin and put up for the winter.

The third stanza seems to return to an objective reality but the nature of the "something" in line nine is hidden from us. What we find in the stanza is the presence of movement and color where there was none earlier. By answering the question as to what caused this movement and color, we come up with the sense of that "something."

Our understanding of the poem comes from considering the relationship between the first and second stanzas, while in the third stanza a metaphoric and objective reality are joined together and confused. One could preface each of the lines in the second stanza with the phrase "it was as if," but that can't be easily done in the third stanza. It is by heightening objective reality to a point of transcendence that Tranströmer is able to communicate the poem's closing sense of wonder and joy.

The second poem I want to consider is W. S. Merwin's "When You Go Away," which was dedicated to his wife Dido.

> When you go away the wind clicks around to the north
> The painters work all day but at sundown the paint falls
> Showing the black walls
> The clock goes back to striking the same hour
> That has no place in the years
>
> And at night wrapped in the bed of ashes
> In one breath I wake
> It is the time when the beards of the dead get their growth
> I remember that I am falling
> That I am the reason
> And that my words are the garment of what I shall never be
> Like the tucked sleeve of a one-armed boy

This is a highly metaphoric poem but when we break it down we find a direct and uncomplicated subject: that is, when you leave it is my fault because I am fallible and because my words don't express an actual reality but an idealized and yearned for reality which I will never be able to achieve. He presents this subject with two clear statements of an objective reality — when you go away, in the first stanza, and at night I wake and remember that I am the reason, in the second — and eight images. Six of the images use the title as their object. Another — the eighth line about the beards of the dead — is, I think, the weakest and most decorative, while the last image uses "I am the reason" and "my words" as its object.

The three images of the first stanza represent loneliness, desolation and a kind of ennui or lethargy. Obviously they are more than this, but they work by taking those feelings and heightening them. The fourth and seventh images — the bed of ashes and falling — are variations on the first two, while the last image — "the tucked sleeve on a one-armed boy" — presents the conflict between the two realities: the idealized and the actual.

The subject of the poem is simple. If we don't recognize it from our experience, we can easily imagine it. But with this accumulation of rich and original image, Merwin is able to take a common feeling and make it fresh again, make us see it as if for the first time. The strategy of the poem is like the strategy of metaphor itself. We are presented with an object and a series of images that heighten that object; and we come to understand the metaphor — this poem — by thinking about the relationship between object and image.

The third poem I want to consider is "Signs" by the French poet, Jean Follain. The translation is by Merwin.

> Sometimes when a customer in a shadowy restaurant
> is shelling an almond
> a hand comes to rest on his narrow shoulder
> he hesitates to finish his glass
> the forest in the distance is resting under its snows
> the sturdy waitress has turned pale
> he will have to let the winter night fall
> has she not often seen
> on the last page
> of a book of modest learning
> the word end printed
> in ornate capitals?

We begin to understand this poem by asking the significance of the hand in the third line. The answer that allows the poem to unfold most simply is to say that the hand is the hand of death. Once we understand that, the poem seems perfectly direct. A man in a restaurant has a sense of his approaching death, and a waitress, watching him, sees him experiencing this awareness and she, or the narrator, relates this to seeing the word "end" or "fin" on the last page of a book.

What I like about this poem and what helps make it mysterious is that along with the concluding metaphor which strikes us consciously are indirect and hidden metaphors that touch our unconscious, which communicate subliminally. The best way to disclose these hidden metaphors is to question Follain's word-choices.

For instance, why make the nut an "almond" and why a "narrow" shoulder? This question leads us to realize that the shapes are similar, which leads us to see that as the man is so much greater than the almond that he is touching, so is death so much greater than the man who is being touched. Then Follain presents the reader with another image: the snow resting upon the trees. Thinking about it, we can see that many trees, like pine trees and poplars, have that same almond shape, and further, as the touch of snow is cold upon the living tree, so is the touch of death cold upon the shoulder of the living man.

Then with the phrase "he will have to let the winter night fall" we see that is how he will have to let his own life fall, which is also how he is letting the almond shells fall, while buried within that is the simile that his life is like the winter night. When we reread the poem, a word like "shadowy" in the first line takes on further meaning not only by foreshadowing the forest but also by describing a place between light and dark, life and death.

The poem is two small scenes about the apprehension of death, and they are woven together in the center by those two mysterious lines about the forest and letting night fall. Both of those lines modify the first scene, but by separating them with the waitress and her sudden understanding they also modify the second scene. This allows the metaphors to do extra work. For example, in the same way that the forest is reposing under the white snow, so is the customer under the regard of the pale faced waitress. Also, in the same way that he will put down or drop his glass, so he will have to let the winter night fall.

It is interesting to see how Follain lets these images shift in the poem. In the end, he further heightens our sense of life and death with the simile which compares them to the book of modest learning and the ornate capitals. Even the word "modest" becomes a small joke about the man, while the visual image of the black letters of the word "fin" surrounded by the white space of the page again evokes the black trees surrounded by white snow. What should be clear in this poem is that Follain would not be able to let his images do such an immense range of work if the objects of his metaphors — if the context and situation of the poem — were not immediately obvious.

But metaphors, no matter how precise, only form part of a poem. We must also understand how the metaphors relate to the poem as a whole. Ideally, a poem takes hold of the reader and forces him to respond to it with his emotions. Kafka wrote that literature should be an axe with which to shatter the frozen sea of the heart. As I've said, the actual subject of any poem is the reader. The poem should be where the reader sees himself afresh, momentarily freed from the trappings of the world. But for this to occur, the reader must be able to find his way into the poem as a participant. Metaphor, through its question-asking process, is a partial way to do this. But it is also necessary for the reader to apprehend and authenticate the event or situation of the poem with his memory. That is, he must take part in the poem by engaging in an act of recognition.

This recognition can be divided into three general types: intellectual, physical and emotional. When I say 5x5=25, you engage in an act of intellectual recognition. When I describe the smell of apples, the recognition is physical. When I talk of the difficulty of love, the recognition is emotional.

It is rarely so simple. Any recognition will often be made up of all three parts, although only one part may predominate. The degree, however, to which the reader is involved and becomes a participant in the poem is the degree to which he is involved in these three acts of recognition; further, another function of metaphor is to act as a bridge between these three types of recognition: for instance, to say that something is as huge as hatred or that grief is like the taste of ash or, as Robert Hass says in a poem, "White, as a proposition."

What we also notice about these types of recognition is that they engage three different aspects of the reader. The act of physical recognition involves the five senses. Intellectual recognition primarily involves the conscious mind, while emotional recognition involves the unconscious. And the more the entire mind and body, the entire entity of the reader, is involved in the recognition process, the more the reader will be involved in the poem.

Now, it seems to me, that for this authenticating act of recognition to take place, the intellectual, physical and emotional context or situation of the poem must be readily discoverable. Look at the poem "Consider A Move" by Michael Ryan.

> The steady time of being unknown,
> in solitude, without friends,
> is not a steadiness which sustains.
> I hear your voice waver on the phone:

Haven't talked to anyone for days.
I drive around. I sit in parking lots.
The voice zeroes through my ear, and waits.
What should I say? There are ways

to meet people you will come to love?
I know of none. You come out stronger
having gone through this? I no longer
believe that, if once I did. Consider a move,

a change, a job, a new place to live,
someplace you'd like to be. *That's not it,*
you say. Now time curves back. We almost touch.
Then what is? I ask. What is?

The first three lines give the intellectual context, the fourth gives the physical and the fifth and sixth give the emotional. But, again, this means that these types of recognition predominate in those places. We can see that line two also contains an emotional context; that in line four the verb "waver" also suggests emotion, and that in line six there are again elements of the physical.

If the intellectual, physical and/or emotional contexts were obscured in the poem, then the reader would be led to ask questions in an attempt to make them clear. For instance, without the physical grounding of the poem in line four — two people talking on a telephone — one would ask how the conversation took place. Obviously, such a question is irrelevant, but if the information about that physical context weren't available, then the question would be automatic and a distraction would occur. In writing, one must always guard against eliciting useless questions since they focus the reader's attention on inessentials.

Obscurity in a poem must be a tool. It is there to force the reader to ask questions which will direct him toward an understanding of the poem. Any question which does not directly increase our understanding of the poem detracts from it. It does nothing to be obscure about the intellectual, physical and/or emotional contexts of a poem in the same way that it does nothing to be obscure about the object of a metaphor. It is useless to make the reader ask questions about the nature of the context, because it is not through the contemplation of the context that we understand the poem; rather it is by thinking about the relationship between the three types of context and the narrative of the poem that some understanding is reached.

I use the word narrative in its broadest sense and I expect

every poem has one, even if it is only an implied narrative with an invisible speaker being someplace and thinking about something. There is always somebody saying the words. Even the simplest lyric, where the event occurs in one moment of time, asks the reader to imagine a narrative.

Look at the poem, "Western Wind."

> Western wind, when will thou blow,
> The small rain down can rain?
> Christ! if my love were in my arms,
> And I in my bed again!

Although the action of the poem exists only in one point of time, it is by imagining what led up to it and what may follow it that we understand the poem. And whenever we have more than one point of time, then we begin to have narrative. But the lyric poem, because its action often occurs in only one moment, seems to require the least information about its intellectual, emotional and physical contexts. The more narrative that a poem has, however, then the more information needs to be given about these three types of context. Even a tiny lyric poem like "Western Wind" lets us know that it is winter, that the narrator is away from home and that he is lonely, and it is by considering the relationship between this information and the narrative that the poem moves us.

In summary, then, it is by thinking about the relationship between the intellectual, physical and emotional contexts and the narrative of the poem that the meaning of the poem is approached; and that one of the roles of metaphor is to clarify and heighten one or more of those three types of context. Further, all three contexts must be clearly covered if only to avoid useless questions. The telephone is not very important to Ryan's poem, but without it the resulting irrelevant question would create a distraction.

When Yeats was young, he wrote a poem about a lonely Titan who lived on a rock in the ocean. A friend, criticizing it, wrote across the page: "How did it get there? What did it eat?"

Often, when one or more of these contexts is unclear, a poem will be criticized as too private, which usually means that the writer is withholding too much information, making the poem unnecessarily vague. The result is that the reader isn't able to examine the relationship between one or more of the three contexts and the narrative, which limits his access to the poem.

Another point is that there must be a balance between these three types of contexts, even though one may predominate. But if one is exaggerated to the detriment of the whole, then the poem breaks down. For instance, when the intellectual context is exaggerated, the poem becomes overly descriptive and decorative; and when the emotional is exaggerated, the poem becomes sentimental. The discursive, the decorative and the sentimental all attempt to function independently of the narrative and effect the argument of the poem in a way that is basically rhetorical.

I would now like to look at three more poems as examples of balance between intellectual, physical and emotional contexts, although each of these poems stresses one context over the others. The first is "My Sisters" by Stanley Kunitz.

> *Who whispered, souls have shapes?*
> *So has the wind, I say.*
> *But I don't know,*
> *I only feel things blow.*
>
> I had two sisters once
> with long black hair
> who walked apart from me
> and wrote the history of tears.
> Their story's faded with their names,
> but the candlelight they carried,
> like dancers in a dream,
> still flickers on their gowns
> as they bend over me
> to comfort my night fears.
>
> Let nothing grieve you,
> Sarah and Sophia.
> Shush, shush, my dears,
> now and forever.

The whole poem leads to that strong emotional statement in the last stanza; "Shush, shush, my dears, / now and forever," a statement which should reek of exaggerated emotion but which works because of the way it has been prepared for. The first stanza gives primarily the intellectual context, the second gives the physical and the third the emotional, while the juxtaposition of the three helps to create the narrative development.

An apparent weakness in the poem would seem to be the lack of information concerning the physical context of the first stanza and the actual story of the two sisters. That this doesn't bother us is partly due to the balance between the three stanzas, and because of how Kunitz takes us by surprise with the switch to second person and the mention of the two names. Mostly we proceed through a poem accumulating questions which we hope will be answered, but part of the effect of the surprise in the third stanza is that it distracts us from these questions.

Look at the poem "Outside Fargo, North Dakota" by James Wright:

> Along the sprawled body of the derailed Great Northern
> freight car,
> I strike a match slowly and lift it slowly.
> No wind.
>
> Beyond town, three heavy white horses
> Wade all the way to their shoulders
> In a silo shadow.
>
> Suddenly the freight car lurches.
> The door slams back, a man with a flashlight
> Calls me good evening.
> I nod as I write good evening, lonely
> And sick for home.

At first it seems that the poem is simply a clear physical description followed by a clear emotional description with little or no intellectual context. But then we see intellectual context appear in that odd line, "I nod as I write good evening," which makes us realize that the whole experience may be a memory which the narrator is recalling as he writes the poem. We also see intellectual context, although emblematically, in the line, "I strike a match slowly and lift it slowly," which seems to symbolize understanding or intellectual perception, like a lightbulb over a cartoon character's head.

Here again the emotional context is stated clearly at the end, but looking at the physical context we see it contains buried metaphors concerning the emotional state of the narrator. We realize that the narrator in his loneliness and isolation is like the sprawled body of a freight car and, secondly, that the three white horses wading into shadow are an image of companionship and love in the face of the unknown, creating an emblem of what the narrator yearns for.

What Wright is trying to do is make that last phrase "lonely / And sick for home" jolt us into recognition, but for that to work he has to set up a foundation which will justify that phrase, yet keep the reader from anticipating it. The reader proceeds through the poem trying to determine the reason for the description. Then, with that last phrase, it all becomes clear. At that point, however, the reader goes back into the poem and it is by considering the relationship between the three types of context and how they relate to the narrative that he comes to understand what Wright is doing.

As an example of a poem where the intellectual context predominates look at Wallace Steven's "The House Was Quiet and the World Was Calm."

> The house was quiet and the world was calm.
> The reader became the book; the summer night
>
> Was like the conscious being of the book.
> The house was quiet and the world was calm.
>
> The words were spoken as if there was no book,
> Except that the reader leaned above the page,
>
> Wanted to lean, wanted much most to be
> The scholar to whom his book is true, to whom
>
> The summer night is like a perfection of thought.
> The house was quiet because it had to be.
>
> The quiet was part of the meaning, part of the mind:
> The access of perfection to the page.
>
> And the world was calm. The truth in a calm world,
> In which there is no other meaning, itself
>
> Is calm, itself is summer and night, itself
> Is the reader leaning late and reading there.

The poem describes the nature of an unknown book and what it is like to read the book. All we know about the book is that the summer night is like its "conscious being" and that the reader wants to be like the book's author for whom the book is the "perfection of thought." At the beginning the reader becomes the book and at the end the book becomes the reader, while the emotional context is the reader's yearning for this unity. The yearning is also expressed in the physical description: "The reader leaned above the page, / wanted to lean, wanted much most to be / The scholar to whom his book is true." The poem gives us a wonderful interweaving of the physical and emotional dominated by the intellectual. In the end, we realize that the poem is not about the book at all; rather, it is about the reader's desire to transcend his physical nature and become pure idea — idea as beautiful and true as a summer night. We also see here an example of how one context can modify and heighten another: that if the physical context or summer night did not provide a metaphor for the intellectual, then the intellectual context would remain too abstract.

The French poet Mallarmé once said that to name is to destroy and to suggest is to create. I would agree with this even though I have now spent some time arguing that the poet should name clearly, meaning that he must give the reader sufficient information. Suggestion won't work until the reader has enough information to brood about. The poem begins to work when the reader is able to contemplate the relationship between its various parts. Ideally, the more he thinks about that relationship, then the more it is allowed to ramify and the more the poem gives back to him. But the reader cannot engage in that act of contemplation if necessary information is withheld or if he keeps interrupting that act with questions concerning information he should already have.

A poem has to obey the rules of simple discourse: information must be exchanged and understood. The purpose of that information is to bring the reader to a point where he suddenly confronts himself and sees himself anew. A poem is like an elaborate scaffold designed to entice the reader up to the highest level where he is then bumped over the side. One hopes that he will fly or at least glide a little, that he will be briefly freed from the cage of personality. Earlier, in discussing non-verbal perception, I said it had the side effect of momentarily taking us out of our isolation and joining us to some larger idea of the world. That, in fact, is the aim of the poem itself, and it is partly by balancing the types of information within the poem and by manipulating the non-verbal perception induced by metaphor that the poet can sometimes bring this about.

William Matthews

Ignorance

We like to talk about poetry as a form of knowledge, a way of knowing, as if it were good to be knowing. In the science fiction movies of the 1950's and 1960's, made in the stunned calm aftermath of the split atom, once the radiation-swollen monsters have been vanquished and the hero and heroine can pause for deep breath and thought, one of them is bound to say to the other that there are some things humans are not meant to know. But Pandora's box is to open.

And Pandora's box is to suffer opening. It is not accidental that such atomic- and, later, hydrogen-nightmare movies were made almost exclusively in America and Japan.

In Roger Corman's 1963 film, "The Man with the X-Ray Eyes," Ray Milland could see through the surfaces of things to their structures. He had conducted experiments on himself, against the advice of more cautious but drably conventional colleagues, to get this ability. Once won, it destroyed him. He was, to cite a Hitchcock title, "The Man Who Knew Too Much," which is a morally melodramatic Hollywood way to say "the man who knew dangerous things." It's not the quantity of what he knew that was a problem, but that he broke limits and taboos.

In one scene from the movie Milland is riding in a car. Modern buildings whir by. He wears sunglasses, the bright light of geometrical structure hurts his eyes so, and his heart and soul. It's like taking Blake for a spin around Houston; Newton has crushingly won the day. The world seems to be made of blueprints, and the structural principles for all the buildings are plagiarisms — not of some historical source, but of each other.

Milland's living hell has no surfaces: it turns out that beauty is only skin deep. Isn't it the light on the lawn that we love, and not the moles, the industrious worms, the fine hairlets of roots? Does a poem really have, as the textbooks say, "levels" of meaning (seven, like Troy!)? Or isn't what is miraculous about poems that they are only ink on paper, the way we live only on the surface of the earth, and the way lovers have, finally, only the surfaces of each other's bodies?

It's true, the viewer feels by the end of the Corman's stylishly tawdry movie, the Ray Milland character gave up everything valuable. At the end of the movie he takes off his sunglasses, and the screen, doused with light, goes bright white, as if blindness were, after all, too much light, the saturating flash of the split atom.

Here is an A. E. Housman poem.

> Crossing alone the nighted ferry
> With the one coin for fee,
> Whom, on the wharf of Lethe waiting,
> Count you to find? Not me.
>
> The brisk, fond lackey to fetch and carry,
> The true, sick-hearted slave,
> Expect him not in the just city
> And free land of the grave.

The first quatrain is so clumsily written there must be a reason, though not necessarily a good reason, for it. The gawkiness is especially puzzling, since Housman is a poet of glib effects.

The main clause of the convoluted first sentence begins (with its direct object) in line three, but six words (among them the sentence's second present participle) intervene before we get, first the verb, and next the subject, and then another verb in infinitive form, no less unfinished thereby than *crossing* and *waiting* were. Everything is up in the air grammatically and down in the underworld dramatically; time holds its breath. The grammar "imitates," a certain species of poetry handbook would say, the psychological situation. Is this the imitative fallacy? A kind of grammatical onomatopoeia?

As is so often the case, critical terminology creates new problems as fast as it solves old ones. There's a tension the lines can't quite accommodate, between the need of grammar to make knowledge from experience, and the need of experience to resist resolution into knowledge. This tension represents an accuracy, insofar as we imagine for poetry a relationship between knowledge and experience like that between a realistic painting and a landscape. And this tension represents a failure of making, insofar as we imagine for poetry a need for transmutation by which a poem becomes an experience, rather than a report of experience anterior to the poem. Of course poetry won't sit still (d'Annunzio: "Anatomy presupposes a corpse.") for this kind of talk, which is why we love and need it.

The second stanza is like the Housman poems we remember more readily than this atypical and interesting one. There's a contest in it, between Housman's classical education and utterly romantic sensibility, and the contest is poised. It's smoother and more "well written." But both stanzas are about the same thing. Here is a love in which the speaker is a slave, a lackey, fond (the word suggests dotage, sexual sentimentality and ineffectuality, all three at once), a kind of romantic pack animal; he hates it but can't have his love without it. It's one of the last things for him, the way love and death get intertwined when lovers can't imagine a future they can trust. You'll miss me when I'm gone, he seems to be taunting, who won't go until called. Death would make the two lovers finally equal, but it has been the contest for equality on which they have built their love. No less than death, such a love has one coin only. When the debts are cleared, in an ironic City of God, then the struggles of love are replaced by the good citizenship of moral victory and the loss of the wracked body.

I've paraphrased and elaborated, at a length far greater than Housman's poem, what the speaker "knows" about his situation. It isn't knowledge that translates readily to action, unless death be considered an action. The poem is also hollow threat, a loving invective. It's a kind of knowledge — the poem is neither mute nor stupid. But it's a kind of brave ignorance, too.

The poem reminds me of a definition of poetry by Eliot, whom we conventionally think one of our more cerebral poets. Poetry tells us "what it feels like." At just this point in musing about poetry and knowledge we could close down our curiosity by a trick of definition. We could say that "what it feels like" is itself a kind of knowledge, and smugly return to the platitude — half-true, according to the habit of platitudes — that poetry is a kind of knowledge (But "Money, too, is a kind of poetry," as Stevens said, and what does money know?). Knowledge about what? Poetry is "about" our experience, we could say, but it is made out of language. In poetry, experience has some of the intractability of matter. We don't know surely what it is and we know only a little about what use to make of it. And in poetry, language has some of the elusiveness and danger of energy, and likewise its own ineluctable laws.

Two passages from *The Aeneid* (in Allen Mandelbaum's translation) will suggest how much larger the scope of brave ignorance can be. If this were a contest between Housman and Virgil, we could complain about loaded dice. An epic can and had damn well better take on more than an eight-line lyric, and one of these poets is vastly more capable than the other. Each did what he could, and that's beside the point. In Housman's poem we find a vividly animated psychology, in which all its context must be, whether because Housman confined himself to eight lines or because his talent expired at the end of eight lines, "understood," as we used to say of missing parts of speech when we diagrammed sentences. Virgil is explicit.

In Book V of *The Aeneid* the conflict is temporarily concentrated to a duel of champions, Entellus and the far younger Dares.

> Entellus, rising, stretched his right hand high;
> but Dares, quick to see the coming blow,
> had slipped aside and dodged with his quick body.
> Enteluls spent his strength upon the wind;
> his own weight, his own force, had carried him
> heavy, and heavily, with his huge hulk
> down to the ground; just as at times a hollow
> pine, torn up from its roots on Erymathus
> or on the slopes of giant Ida, falls.
> The Trojan and Sicilian boys leap up;
> their shouting takes the sky; and first Alcestes
> runs to the ring; with pity he lifts up
> his friend, as old as he is. But the hero,
> not checked and not to be delayed, returns
> more keenly to the bout, his anger spurs
> his force. His shame, his knowledge of his worth
> excite his power; furiously he
> drives Dares headlong over all the field,
> and now his right hand doubles blows and now
> his left; he knows no stay or rest; just as
> storm clouds that rattle thick hail on the roofs
> at Dares, blow on blow, from every side.

Some of this is conventional battle stuff, but there is always in Virgil powerful interaction between action and comment, figure and ground, the conventions he observes and the torque by which he transforms them into components of a personal style. In such a poet, everything can be conventional and simultaneously thick with recognizably personal style.

"Entellus spent his strength upon the wind" is a formulaic line, but the wind is no less real for that. Entellus is about to make a comeback — force spurred by anger and power excited by "his shame, his knowledge of his worth." These could be two distinct items in a series of two, or they could be apposite, so that "knowledge of his worth" becomes a definition of "shame." Virgil's is a tragic and meditative psychology, not merely a dramatized one.

Entellus is a storm, who "knows no stay or rest; just as / storm clouds that rattle thick hail on the roofs, / so do the hero's two hands pummel, pound / at Dares, blow on blow, from every side." Wasn't it the sky the shouting of the Trojan and Sicilian boys took, for a second? Blows are doubled by the right *and* left hand, and then we get "stay or rest," and then "pummel, pound," and then "blow on blow," until this ferocity, doubling (like rhetorical momentum) at a geometrical rather than an arithmetical pace, surrounds us "from every side" with a hail of shame and worth and anger, and the very sky we thought for a second to touch has come into us, and our emotions are like weather.

The Aeneid is about love and war, fixed sentimentally in our time as alternatives by the injunction to make love and not war. The avoidance of the harsh word "but" in the formula tells us much about the ways we wanted to be moved when that phrase seemed like an epigram. If history has made war so repellent that we have trouble with the imaginative fusion Virgil made of love and war, that is a possible good omen for our politics, and when we need to remember how much of love is agression, we can find our texts in Freud, so long as we don't shrink "love and war" to "love and anger."

Love and war are linked continually by *The Aeneid*. In Book VIII Venus, fearful for her son, Aeneas, intercedes with her husband Vulcan. They are gods, and therefore they are the weather of humans, the way parents are the weather of children. But they are gods made in our image, and therefore they are themselves subject to weather.

In this passage Venus is "the goddess," and "he" is Vulcan, the blacksmith, so the flame is his own petard.

> The goddess spoke; and as he hesitates,
> with snow-white arms on this side and on that
> she warms him in a soft embrace. At once
> he caught the customary flame; familiar

heat reached into his marrow, riding through
his agitated bones— just as at times
a streak of fire will rip through flashing thunder
and race across the clouds with glittering light.
His wife, rejoicing in her craftiness
and conscious of her loveliness, sensed this.

Here the storm is habitual desire. Her arms are only two, and
they come "on this side and on that," but we sense the power of
desire that is "customary" and "familiar" (it is desire that includes
a family, and thus her son, and his), and know how Vulcan is surrounded (he is doubly surrounded, in fact: not only is desire
"around" him, like Venus's arms, but it is also spreading from the
inside out, from the marrow). Sexual love makes us weather, so
that we are the storm, the weight of our bodies and the diffusion
of the air, both, just as we are love and war, both, fighting by love
for a way to continue what love has made valuable to each of us.
In short, the whole weight of time, as humans know it, is on us,
and what time feels like; it is the need to have time be a central
character in such poems as *The Aeneid* that gives us so many
scenes in which the gods and humans intersect at pained cost to
all parties.

Perhaps to be knowing is to withhold, to hoard knowledge.
Eventually knowledge must be spent, or how else could one
demonstrate possession of it? But it may be that we never know
something so thrillingly as when we can, but have not yet chosen
to, disclose it.

"Morality is self-evident," wrote Freud (who also wrote in *The
Interpretation of Dreams* a sentence beginning "Personally I
haven't had an anxiety dream in years . . ."), but what is self-
evident is paradoxically difficult to discover, because it's not self-
evident until it's seen.

At a recent dinner I heard someone say of a couple we all — all
of us at the table — knew, "Everybody knows they're split up."

Let's stop to think about this short sentence, which doesn't
mean what it says or say what it means. If everybody knew it, why
say it? "Everybody" means "everybody in the know," and then
the sense of the sentence is tautological: "everybody in the know,
knows." Perhaps the structure of tautology accounts for what is
audibly smug and self-enclosed in this sentence.

By extension, the sentence asks "Are you an everybody or a
nobody?" Note how being an individual is excluded from the
possibilities. One of us at the table was by this measurement a nobody, and since she was also a close friend to both members of

the couple, she was alarmed for their pains, and she was hurt not to have heard even bad news about their lives from them before she heard it as gossip. You may have guessed already how this anecdote will finish. Later that night she phoned them, and woke them up, and what everybody knew was wrong.

I leave it to you to wonder if the moral of that anecdote is self-evident. The role I had in it leaves me few rights to wisdom. But here's what I propose: it's no better in poetry to be knowing than in civilian life, and it's as valuable to be explicit. For whatever you think you know — and you can be explicit about what you don't know —, you don't know you need to learn.

A writer who speaks of having something to say is almost always doomed by that obligation to bad writing, unless he or she is willing to append: "but I don't yet know what it is."

Here, from "Dry Salvages" in Eliot's *Four Quartets,* is a passage about what it can't say.

> For most of us, there is only the unattended
> Moment, the moment in and out of time,
> The distraction fit, lost in a shaft of sunlight,
> The wild thyme unseen, or the winter lightning
> Or the waterfall, or music heard so deeply
> That it is not heard at all, but you are the music
> While the music lasts.

To advertise "a passage about what it can't say" is to boast and disclaim at once. Taken as a whole, the *Four Quartets* could be said to be a poem about certain powerful psychological recurrences, and what great sense certain religious assumptions can make of those recurrences. And so as a whole long poem, the quartets raise questions of belief, at least tangentially, and face the dilemma (the analogy of musical structure is, I think, only a partial answer to the dilemma) of needing to return again and again to the psychological cruxes in order to activate the religious impulse. There is a sort of erotic compulsion, a continual re-creation of a powerful and mythological early scenario, in the poem.

But now we are looking at a brief excerpt only, and its argument, that we find it hard to be vividly present in our lives, and sense in a muffled and insulated way what we both fear and long to undergo more powerfully, is not a specifically religious matter. Where Eliot may be writing nonsense is when he speaks of "music heard so deeply / that it is not heard at all."

In logic, paradox is a way of giving up, of signing that the road ends here. I am not sure that I have ever had a paradoxical emotion, in the sense that an absolute equality between the weight of opposites obtains in a paradox. It may be that emotions don't come in opposites, but that "mixed feelings," as we gingerly call them, always contain some of each other. It seems to me possible that paradox is a way to acknowledge that logic, in order to be a useful faculty, must choose internal consistency rather than inclusiveness, when that choice is confronted, and simultaneously a way of saying that the choice is now confronted. Either the investigation gets carried on by other forms of curiosity, or is abandoned.

Eliot pushes on a little way only, but he writes so well in situations where what might conventionally be called subject matter is all fog and wisp that he knows how to do it, to give weight to both his ignorance and his longing to know. And "but you are the music / While the music lasts" is a magisterial stroke that galvanizes the whole passage; it's interesting to notice that until its very end, the whole sentence is slack and ungathered. It's when Eliot doesn't turn back, but pushes on into his ignorance, that the sentence grows taut and shapely.

"What," wrote R. P. Blackmur, "should we get rid of our ignorance, the very substance of our lives, merely in order to understand one another?"

James Wright's posthumously published book of poems, *This Journey,* has among its many beauties a wonderful poem called "The Vestal in the Forum."

In the 1950's our poetry was awash with poems on Italian statues and fountains written by poets holding a Prix de Rome or a Guggenheim, and the usual percentage held: few of them were good. So in the 1960's — the same decade in which Wright began publishing poems in a plain style, whose knowledge was hidden in and sometimes by, metaphor — in the 1960's there was a knowing joke in poetry life about how bad conventional poems about Italian statues and fountains were, as if the opportunity rather than the poems were dull.

It is typical of Wright's poetic strengths that he would, in a style hard-won and won partially by rebellion against the literary mannerisms of the 1950's which had most influenced him, rescue the emotional occasion. He is looking at a Roman statue.

> This morning I do not despair
> For the impersonal hatred that the cold
> Wind seems to feel
> When it slips fingers into the flaws
> Of lovely things men made,
> The shoulders of a stone girl

Pitted by winter.
Not a spring passes but the roses
Grow stronger in their support of the wind,
And now they are conquerors,
Not garlands any more,
Of this one face:
Dimming,
Clearer to me than most living faces.
The slow wind and the slow roses
Are ruining an eyebrow here, a mole there.
But in this little while
Before she is gone, her very haggardness
Amazes me. A dissolving
Stone, she seems to change from stone to something
Frail, to someone I can know, someone
I can almost name.

Among the "lovely things men made" are not only statues but the models for statues, humans in their bodies. Wright was dwindling to death from cancer when he wrote this poem. The poem's own "cold wind" is partly the poem's matter-of-fact tone, the ability Wright prayed for in an earlier poem, "to speak in a plain voice." Without the mediation of rhetoric, plain means in this context. But also it means, surely, stripped cruelly of flesh, eroded, pitted, cracked, on the way from the specific voluptuousness of flesh to the spare, skeletal, democratic shape the dying share. It's the shape time wins from us, even in statues which are by convention immune to time in ways no specific and beloved body can be. But posterity is not breath, and the urban chemistry of Rome is rotting statues and buildings faster than classical time or cold breath could dream of, if they dreamed. The Man with the X-Ray Eyes sees death, "clearer to me than most living faces." Than *most* living faces, he takes care to say, rather than pretend he can, like the roses, "grow stronger in support of the wind." I love and recommend the poem's last sentence especially.

A dissolving
Stone, she seems to change from stone to something
Frail, to someone I can know, someone
I can almost name.

What can be known is frail, and naming is not knowing. We love, we writers, the literary implications of Adam naming the animals in Eden, with their celebration of the power of names and the centrality of language to human knowledge and authority. Language is also central to human confusion and impotence, and Adam in Eden is also a vast baby hurling syllables from his playpen.

John Hollander has a poem, "Adam's Task," based on Genesis 2:20, and here are names of some animals in that poem's world, in which we also live: *glurd, spotted glurd, whitestep, implex, verdle, McFleery's pomma, grawl* (three types of these), *flisket, pambler, greater wherret* and *lesser wherret, sproal, zant, lily-eater,* and (tellingly) *comma-eared mashawk.* Here is a creation made from language rather than from mud and fire and language and clouds of swirling water.

In such a world as the one Hollander ingeniously and somewhat reluctantly, even tenderly, satirizes, most of our nostrums about "creative writing" are true. "No tears in the writer, no tears in the reader," wrote Frost, who may have meant by this maxim that the poet didn't suffer enough to earn any suffering in a reader, or may have meant simply, "Damn, this is a dull party." It isn't, I want to insist, what the poet earns or knows, but what he or she writes, that matters. "No surprise for the writer, no surprise for the reader," Frost went on to say, compounding a nonsense. I don't mean to suggest he wasn't addressing a serious and interesting truth about poems: they somehow contain traces of the urgency with which they were written, and this fact provides both poet and reader with opportunities (though they are different opportunities) for self-regard.

And we have silly urgencies. We surprise ourselves over and over with ordinary things, a way both to maintain our sense of wonder and to maintain our deeply narcissistic definitions of pleasure. Hollander's poem exercises his love of language and his love of its limitations by intertwining them, as if the tree of knowledge grew the fruit of ignorance. Probably it does.

Wright's poem ends, because it followed faithfully the luck of its beginnings, by acknowledging both the drive and the impossibility to know our lives, or to be ignorant of them. I think we are wrongly hopeful to speak of poetry as a kind of knowledge, and that we may be hoping for the wrong thing. It would be better, I imagine, to think of poetry as a kind of passionate and structured ignorance, like a dream.

William Stafford

Some Arguments Against Good Diction

> . . . it is with words mainly that we delineate the conceivable and
> if we never allow words to be a little eccentric, never allow
> ourselves to apply a word to any state of affairs actual or conceiv-
> able, to which it would not customarily be applied, we are
> without means to refer to any state of affairs for which there is
> not a word, any possibility undreamt of in our philosophy.*

Ordinary statements about diction and literature and the
process of writing often have such convenience and such easy
links to what we say about other activities, that we are tempted
to accept the superficial formula. This tendency — a kind of
Gresham's law of art discussion we have to guard against. Whatever is distinctive in some intricate activity is *felt* by the practitioners, but in talking about the activity with others (and even
in conceiving it to themselves), people accept quick formulations
that *generally* help. But the cumulative effect of the assumptions
thus woven into art discussion becomes misleading. To avoid such
misunderstandings, we try restating, but we have to use the
language, again full of distortions; so we do something like taking
off a rubber glove with one hand, and it is a glove that *wants to
stay on.*

One such topic confounded by Gresham's law is that of
diction. Apparently for many people the writer is conceived as a

---

*John Wisdom, *Paradox and Discovery* (Oxford: Basil Blackwell, 1965), p. 132.

person sitting at a big desk with cubbyholes containing all the words there are — or all the words the writer knows. The person writes his story or essay, or anything, by carefully reaching with long tweezers into the cubbyholes to get the right words (proper words in proper places — everyone knows that poems are made with words). *Le mot juste* is the slogan of excellence in writing.

Following the implied advice of such a picture and of those apparently helpful phrasings, a novice learns an adequate vocabulary, sits down at his desk with all the cubbyholes, and is a writer. But somehow he does not write *War and Peace*. That picture and those words have misled the would-be writer, and they can even menace the accomplished writer who lives perilously surrounded by such pleasant, simple concepts and sayings that superficially delineate his art.

The process of writing that I experience has little connection with the formulations I most often hear. Where words come from, into consciousness, baffles me. Speaking or writing, the words bounce instantaneously into their context, and I am victimized by them, rather than controlling them. They do not wait for my selection; they volunteer. True, I can reject them, but my whole way of writing induces easy acceptance — at first — of any eager volunteer. I want to talk about these volunteers, but first want to consider another reason for trying carefully to set the record straight, about attitudes toward language. The point concerns how a writer feels about language, in general. Many opine that a writer, and particularly a poet, for some reason, must love language; often there is even a worshipful attitude assumed. I have noticed this assumption with particular attention because it happens that insofar as I can assess my own attitudes in relation to others' I have an unusually intense distrust of language. What people say or write comes to me attenuated or thinned by my realization that talk merely puts into the air an audio counterpart of mysterious, untrustworthy, confused events in the creature making the sounds. "Truth," or "wonder," or any kind of imaginative counterpart of "absolute realities" — these I certainly do not expect in human communication.

An illustration of this distrust — an illustration that brings in contrary attitudes held by very imposing people, and hence is highly dangerous for my own case — came when I saw inscribed in gold on a pillar in the Library of Congress this saying: "The inquiry, knowledge and belief of truth is the sovereign good of human nature." To me, such a saying is hollow; I see it as demonstrating man's pathetic infatuation with an apparent power that is essentially just a redundancy. The highest we know is high for us, but its communication is an interior, not an absolute, phenomenon. And I cringe to realize that my own saying of my kind of truth is hazardous at best. Language — others' and my own — is very thin.

But back to diction. When we talk or write we venture into an immediate engagement with the language we happen to have. This accumulation of sounds and assumptions and automatic, unconscious logicings provides us with a progressing experience we feel as meaningful. If we find ourselves in a state of emergency when applying our natural language to the emerging opportunities, we can slog through words and make some kind of communication without necessarily feeling that the language is being helpful in any local way — we speak or write in a workaday fashion, and our language may not have any lift or "poetic" feeling. That is one way to use the language.

Another way is to let the language itself begin to shape the event taking place by its means. If it happens that at this time in history and at this place in our own experience we happen on a word with a syllable that reverberates with many other syllables in contexts that reinforce what the immediate word is doing, we have "powerful language." The internal reinforcements of the historically opportune language we happen to own come into something like focus or harmony. We speak or write poetry. Even if what we write is prose, we may speak of it as "poetical." This kind of link with poetry I take to mean that some kind of dynamism in the language itself — syllables, cadences, local or larger surges in sound or imagery — is carrying the *now*-conditioned reader or hearer into his own blissful redundancy inside his own experience. Like the philosophers who admire the scope of thought, the artists are **exhilarated by the "power of art."**

Let me try for a direct statement of what is disquieting about what ordinarily surfaces when we talk about "good diction." For a writer, it is not the past or present of words that counts, but their futures, and those futures are approaching by means of influences too various for rules or derivations to control or predict. When the poet says, "The fog comes pussyfooting along," or something like that, it isn't that the isolated words have been drafted, but that some kind of yearning connection among experiences has taken over. Reluctantly, the writer enters language and fearfully entrusts that limited and treacherous medium to keep from absolutely violating the feeling he has entrusted to it. In the ensuing transaction, language accomplishes several things at once.

1. It begins to distort, by congealing parts of the total experience into successive, partially relevant signals (just as this sentence is doing now).

2. It begins to entice the reader or hearer away into his own version or variation on the speaker's or writer's relations to the words.

3. But — and an important but — the transaction also begins to enhance the experience because of a weird quality in language: the successive distortions of language have their own kind of cumulative potential, and under certain conditions the distortions of language can reverberate into new experiences more various, more powerful, and more revealing than the experiences that set off language in the first place.

It is that cumulative potential in language that writers find themselves relying on again and again as they fearfully advance, leaving behind some of the purposes and aims they started with and accepting the wondrous bonuses that chance and the *realizing* elements of the future's approach allows them. *Le mot juste* does not exist. For people, the truth does not exist. But language offers a continuous encounter with our own laminated, enriched, experiences; and sometimes those encounters lead to further satisfactions derived from the cumulative influences in language as it spins out. That kind of language experience we grope for and identify with various tags. One of them is just a word — poetry.

Michael Ryan

On the Nature of Poetry

On a steamy night last week, after a rare Vermont day when it had been hot enough to lightning, I drove home from my office through a deep fog. It was nearly midnight; there was almost no light from the sky. I parked my car in the driveway, and began to sense my way to the front door, when I looked up and saw an enormous, black shape in the yard: the ninety-foot tree which I had watched in the sunlight with great pleasure now seemed awesome. Darker than the darkness, it was numinous, and impossibly huge, like a god. I came inside feeling stirred, feeling I had been touched beneath rationality, and since I was working on this talk and having a hard time writing it, I felt I had been instructed. I don't think my experience of the tree can be explained, and yet such experiences, in solitude and with others, are surely part of our lives; some people feel them as the most important part, informing the rest. I said that I had been touched beneath rationality, which I believe is true, but I would take it farther than that to say that I had been touched beneath personality; it was as if this profound feeling had nothing to do with me, personally, at least in the daily ways I think about myself.

Jung might have called this an experience of the archetype:

Do we ever understand what we think? We understand only such thinking as is mere equation and from which nothing comes out but what we have put in. That is the manner of working of the intellect. But beyond that there is thinking in primordial images — in symbols that are older than historical man; which have been ingrained in him from earliest times, and, eternally living, outlasting all generations, still make up the groundwork of the human psyche.

Jung, Neumann, Joseph Campbell and many others have demonstrated the recurrence of essential primordial images in the art and myth of cultures that could not have known of one another. Bastian called this phenomenon "elementary ideas," always rendered by way of local ethnic forms: Freud, while listening to his European and American patients speak out their anguish and fantasies, stared at an array of African carvings of gods. Whatever the metaphor — and for Jung the archetypes are not only images but a process, "persons" living in our personalities — much of our psyche seems to be beneath or beyond individual intellect; as human beings we share what Jung called the "collective unconscious," an impersonal personality, even if we have difficulty understanding it in itself or how it works in us individually.

This difficulty may arise not from its inherent obscurity but from our removal from it. We think of ourselves as rational beings, and ostensibly conduct the business of society according to rational premises, but our evolution as a species occurred over a long time before the evolution of rational intelligence. Just how long is shown by the calendar that compresses the fifteen-billion-year life-in-progress of the universe into a single year. On that calendar, the earth is formed about September 25, hominids appear at approximately 10:30 P.M. on December 31, and the whole of recorded human history takes place during the last ten seconds. This dramatizes both our recent arrival and the elements of our nature: there is much that made us that we don't know about. It's hard to imagine a "thoughtless" world, and easy to forget that we are thoroughly creatures of the universe, formed in the ooze for four billion years before we were able to write down how it feels to be human; the oldest specimens of written language date back only five thousand years, barely a moment in terms of evolution.

Lewis Thomas says in *The Lives of a Cell:*

Man is embedded in Nature . . . The uniformity of the earth's life, more astonishing than its diversity, is accountable by the high probability that we derived, originally, from some single cell, fertilized in a bolt of lightning as the earth cooled . . . We still share genes around, and the resemblance of enzymes of grasses to those of whales is a family resemblance.

And:

> A good case can be made for our non-existence as enti-
> ties. We are not made up, as we had always supposed,
> of successfully enriched packets of our own parts. We
> are shared, rented, occupied. At the interior of our
> cells, driving them, providing the oxidative energy that
> sends us out for the improvement of each shining day,
> are the mitochondria, and in a strict sense they are not
> ours. They turn out to be little separate creatures, the
> colonial posterity of migrant prokaryocytes, probably
> primitive bacteria that swam into ancestral precursors
> of our eukaryotic cells and stayed there. Ever since,
> they have maintained themselves and their ways, repli-
> cating in their own fashion, privately, with their own
> DNA and RNA quite different from ours. They are as
> much symbionts as the rhizobial bacteria in the roots
> of beans. Without them, we would not move a muscle,
> drum a finger, think a thought.

It might be argued, through Thomas, that Jung's archaic remnants
are a physiological fact; as further evidence, Joseph Campbell, in
The Masks of God, describes innate releasing mechanisms in animals — how a baby chick responds to the shadow of a hawk even
before it's all the way out of the shell — and one could also cite
the encoded transfer of genetic messages from generation to generation. But whether we live the archetypes, or the archetypes "live
us" (as James Hillman says), this nonrational, primitive *stuff*
reaches into everything we do and think and feel, perhaps powerfully enough at times to make contact directly: beneath rationality,
beneath personality. We may not be able to understand it through
analysis, which Hillman maintains is "a late manifestation of the
Western, Protestant, scientific, Apollonic ego," but we experience
it in the primordial image, in poetry and music and myth. With
Freud and Jung, we call it the unconscious (*unbewusst,* which also
translates as "unaware, involuntary, instinctive"); it informs our
sense of shape and all nonlinear, affective modes, which is most of
what we are and cannot say. The problem with talking about it is
the same as with defining God: one tends toward either tautology
or mysticism. Yet those four billion years, if they are contained in
the presence of a huge tree on a foggy night or the magnetism of
an attractive stranger, must also be part of language.

It seems undeniable that language, in conjunction with consciousness, is an evolutionary development; if so, its underlayers

are that from which it evolved, for which we have only negative terms: the preliterate and unconscious. This is implied by Chomsky's notion that the fact of many languages does not deny a unity at the depth of the species, a unity which manifests itself in universal language capability and the formal properties of language.

In making poetry, and in reading it, we give the formal properties of words, their sound and arrangement, a kind of attention we usually do not give them, because we are usually intent on the meaning of the words alone. As a result, something extraordinary may happen to the language: its shape becomes palpable, its cadence becomes definite, its meaning may range from common sense to the edge of intelligibility and hover there, and the whole arrangement of words is felt as a solid that shifts and changes.

I think if there is anything in us that is purely preliterate and unconscious, it is rhythm. We are subject to its influences incessantly, and our lives depend on it, our sense of timing. Night and day; the seasons; the beat of the ocean against the shore; the internal clocks which determine, among other things, the stages of sleep and dreaming; our heartbeats; our brain waves in alternating states of excitation and inhibition: these are just a few of the countless rhythms we are in the midst of, outside and within. Because they are so various and pervasive and deeply internal, they escape our attention, even as they enter our thoughts, our feelings, and our language.

I've never taught a poetry writing class that has not suffered my reiteration of Duke Ellington's line: "It don't mean a thing if it ain't got that swing." How can you describe the feeling of reading a Roethke poem, any one really, but especially the late poems in stanza forms such as "In A Dark Time" or "The Sequel," when the rhythm is so palpable it is as if the poem could be cupped in your hands? Those poems move great distances in meaning between sentences and yet they hold together, largely because of the sound. The same thing is operating in a song that makes you want to get up and dance. From the poet's point of view, the rhythm helps the poem to get written; the poet feels the right word, its sound tugging against its meaning, and doesn't *think* of it, at least in the ways we usually think of thinking. Rhythm and sound and arrangement — the formal properties of words — allow the poet to get beyond thought, or beneath it.

In the earliest poetry, rhythm was believed to indicate the presence of the divine. There's little doubt that what we write today would not be recognized by the ancients as poetry; theirs was much closer to song or chant. The Homeric bards would go into a trance as they recited hundreds of dactylic hexameter lines;

it was said of Archilochus that he could provoke suicide through the power of his iambic abuse. Julian Jaynes says

> The association of rhythmical or repetitively patterned utterance with supernatural knowledge endures well into the later conscious period. Among the early Arabic people the word for poet was *sha'ir,* "the knower," or a person endowed with knowledge by the spirits; his metered speech in recitation was the mark of its divine origin. The poet and divine seer have a long tradition of association in the ancient world, and several Indo-European languages have a common term for them. Rhyme and alliteration too were always the linguistic province of the gods and their prophets.

Jaynes is interested in early poetry as evidence of what he calls the bicameral mind, essentially a separation between right- and left-hemisphere brain functions, rhythm being a right-hemisphere function and, according to Jaynes, the crucial ingredient of the language in which gods dictated their wills to men. The poet was the shaman-healer, the most important member of the tribe, and even as late as ancient Greece the poet was given great respect as the bearer of the preliterate roots of the race. The way he was able to say extraordinary things was through entering rhythm, and thus his words harked back to the beginning even if plain talk did not. Because of this, the poet was an authority dangerous to civilization, in which language is to be used according to the dictates of reason, to formulate the moral agreements institutionalized as laws that will insure good order if the citizenry understands them and agrees to them. So it's no accident that Plato, in constructing his idea of a civilized society, devotes the last book of the *Republic* to banishing the poet from the state. Rhythm, rhyme, alliteration — the formal properties of words — allow the gods to speak because, as impulses, they deflect the tyranny of reason as the sole criterion for word-choice. Their speech is prerational, preliterate and compelling; their wills are capricious, their power absolute.

Emily Dickinson said, "If I feel physically as if the top of my head were taken off, I know this is poetry." The poem begins and ends in the body, all those years inside us. And yet, paradoxically, it's because of language that we can't feel the world purely physically, immediately — as Stanley Burnshaw says — "seamlessly." Language makes its own relationship to the world and interacts with·our physicality; this enmeshed mode of perception and thought and feeling is still unique among the beasts, despite Lana's and Washoe's linguistic inventions and the communication system of dolphins, though perhaps they will be the next race of poets. Language is linkage: the word-as-thing. But it's also not-the-thing or, more exactly, a thing-in-itself. Thus an iconic theory of language can't account for our linguistic capacity, because of the room in language for seemingly infinite flexibility, discovery, and self-reference — in short, for a great variety of play, just to see what it will do.

Perhaps the inclination to play, common to mammals, derives from the desire to reproduce in small the randomness-into-form and variations-within-form that are the fifteen billion years of our generation; recreation: *re-creation*. The first act of poetry seems to come from entering this "playful" relationship to language, when the writer learns how, in Mallarme's phrase, to "yield the initiative to the words." Early in my introductory poetry writing classes, I try to help my students break down their accustomed way of using language — rationally, as reference, as an indicator which disappears once the intended meaning is communicated. I try to get them to listen to the words, to hear their music, to feel their arrangement, to "lose control," if necessary, in order that the language itself jar them into new **meanings** they could not have "thought" of otherwise.

Their success at doing this depends on a feeling for form that can be awakened but can't be taught; it seems to me a genetic endowment that is probably, as Stanley Kunitz says, a "prehensile thing." **Julian Jaynes writes**:

As you listen to an address, phonemes disappear into words and words into sentences and sentences disappear into what they are trying to say, into meaning. To be conscious of the elements of speech is to destroy the intention of the speech.

Yet at climactic moments of real or rhetorical passion, a speaker may enact the cadence with his hands and arms and body, as if he would call upon all the resources of the language. The form of verse is an announcement to both the writer and the reader of precisely that intention — that words will be used here in all their richness, not only for reference and meaning, as linkage, but also for their formal properties, as things-in-themselves.

Of course, the form of the poem is more than an announcement; it allows the interaction of formal properties, the play of the language to take place, without everything getting out of hand or nothing happening at all. This is why Frost thought writing free verse is like playing tennis with the net down: without form there is no game, no order, no possibility for discovery.

But form need not mean conventional or received forms, and the Modernist distrust of them, or more precisely Pound's and Eliot's distrust during their Imagist phase, derives from the conviction that conventional forms allow only certain kinds of poems to be written, the kinds of poems that are the monuments of English literature and which had fallen into decadence at the beginning of this century. It's fascinating to imagine a psychology inherent in the iambic pentameter line, in which some 70 percent of English poetry has been composed: why that duration, that specific number of beats, to tighten the formal attention? Or to speculate why a fourteen-line, strictly end-rhymed verse with a contextual turn (the volte) between the octave and sestet seems to be an apt form for lyric utterance, especially directed to a human or divine beloved. The advantage of conventional forms is obvious: they insist that there be an interaction of the formal properties of the words used, even if that insistence is as gentle as a ten-syllable pattern of predominantly alternate stress; therefore, theoretically at least, they push the poem away from talk or prose cut into lines, and try to influence some slight jarring into new meaning. Their disadvantage, from our vantage in literary history, is even more obvious: conventional forms cannot accommodate all formal impulses; or — to look at it from another angle, the angle of the poem's generation — the interaction of formal properties of words is too multifarious to be standarized. In Pound's view (about 1912), conventional forms promoted bad writing because they didn't allow the writer to say what he would "in the stress of some emotion, actually say." As with the Romantics, most of the complicated formal innovations of the Modernists were based on the simple need to reform poetic diction. Yeats, partially due to Pound's influence, changed his diction, but rhyme and meter were to him invaluable aids to composition; he could write no poetry without the forms of verse.

Frost was right in thinking free verse is a contradiction in terms; as Delmore Schwartz said of Williams's prosodic notion of a variable foot, it's like an elastic inch. Good "free verse" is really formal improvisation. The words interconnect and interact formally every bit as thoroughly as in the strictest sonnet. The difference is that no pattern of interaction, however slight, is set at the beginning, to allow for a greater richness of formal interaction, not a lesser, to allow for a greater instrumentality of the language.

The fact that this is usually not the result of "permissiveness" has no bearing on the potential for an unmetered but rhythmical, unrhymed but sound-linked form of poetry. Many of the best poems of this century have been written in this "free verse" form. There's no reason why poems can't continue to be written in conventional forms as well — in fact, some that now aren't probably should be — but I doubt that we will ever go back to a time when all of them are. Historically, in terms of form, poets have never been in a better position, though such adages of contemporary poetry as the one Charles Olson attributed to Robert Creeley — "form is never more than an extension of content" — are simplistic and misleading. The form of the poem is the way the poem tells the poet what it wants to be; the poet, once he has absorbed this way of feeling language and responding to its form, may stand as a kind of censor, rejecting the impulses that aren't *right* in every possible way, in meaning as well as sound and arrangement. Auden, thinking mostly about content, wanted to extend the Censor to a Censorate including "a sensitive only child, a practical housewife, a logician, a monk, an irreverent buffoon and even, perhaps, hated by all the others and returning their dislike, a brutal, foul-mouthed drill sergeant who considers all poetry rubbish." One begins writing poems as program notes to his personality, and maybe they should always retain that early ardor of self-expression; but a poet cares about the poem as a made thing as much as about what it says, and to him the two are as inseparable as a word from its sound.

Whether we are aware of them or not, the formal properties of language make their own complex patterns which are followed and, to some extent, fulfilled in all language usage, even in discursive prose. The most scholarly article researched and outlined in advance, will probably come out with a few surprises in it for the writer; writing at the top of page one, he can't predict the exact words he will use at the bottom of page two. E. M. Forster has the old lady exclaim "How can I know what I think until I see what I say?" This is one source of the joy of using language, but for the writer it's the source of no end of fretting as well.

The poet, released from most of the responsibilities of the scholar, in the end has others that are much more onerous. As Frost said, "The poem begins in delight and ends in wisdom." That is a large demand. On another occasion, Frost put the same formula in different terms: "Poetry begins in trivial metaphors, pretty metaphors, 'grace' metaphors, and goes on to the profoundest thinking that we have." Like many of Frost's remarks about poetry, both of these emphasize the writing as a journey of discovery, but "the profoundest thinking that we have" *is* metaphorical thinking and it is taking place as soon as the poem begins.

For the act of making metaphor is inherent in the linguistic act, as well as in all of our most important operations of mind. The foundation-blocks of science are metaphors (as in the term foundation-blocks): chemical "bonding," the properties of light as "waves" and "particles," the "conscious" and "unconscious" (a term that did not exist in any language until the eighteenth century). The words we use are the results of particular historical currents ("currents") — we can hardly speak without metaphor. Yet we act as if these words refer to real things because of our habit of using language-as-linkage, and we even use them to explain metaphor itself when in fact they are themselves metaphors.

In this way, language can become self-referential and jargon-ridden; too much inbreeding causes it to lose vitality. The significance of metaphor, Stevens argued in *The Necessary Angel,* always derives from its reference to reality. The root of metaphor — *metapherein* — means "carry over" or "bear across," and implies a conceptual movement, a translation between worlds: at its most profound, perhaps, a translation from the world of our wordless origins into our own.

That first world resides in all of us. Mnemosyne, the goddess of memory, is the mother of the muses. Poetry puts wordlessness into words. Blake exhorted us to "cleanse the doors of perception": not the windows, the doors, that which allows exit and entrance. Physiologically, we see more with our brain than with our eyes, according to expectation and habituation; the same might be said of metaphorical seeing with the brain of cultural expectation and linguistic habit.

"No surprise for the writer, no surprise for the reader"; we want the poem to change our way of seeing. Yet, for the sake of survival, the brain programs itself to limit vision, in both senses. One of the symptoms of schizophrenia is sensory overload; the brain can't process all the data presented to it by the body. It functions properly more by exclusion than inclusion — like art, through a selection of detail. But there always remains the central human and aesthetic question about *what* is being excluded. Auden said, "A poem may fail in two ways: it may exclude too much (banality), or attempt to embody more than one community at once (disorder)."

If Richard Leakey is right in *Origins,* that language arose out of the need to communicate shared tasks in order to survive, then its original function was to exclude from attention what was unimportant to the task at hand, thereby providing an ordering of the experience of the world. That exclusion, which characterizes rationality and discursiveness, is also necessary and useful to poetry, because it is in the balance between order and inclusion that poems are made. As Stevens said, "The poem must resist the intelligence *almost* successfully." The rage for order must win in the end because it is that rage that allows us to survive. However, if the battle against it — by the world, by nature, by the unconscious and preliterate, by the sound and rhythm of the words — is not a raging battle, the poem will not embody the richness and strife of our origins.

At the same time that we are a part of nature, we are *apart* from it because of our consciousness of it and of ourselves. It's significant that one of the first things Adam does in Eden is to name the animals: that act of naming distinguishes us. It's as amazing to imagine a languageless world as a thoughtless world, since the two are so intimately connected in us, but one can picture the psychological change when the hunters are able to plan the hunt. Suddenly, there is a future; and with it, leisure; and with leisure, play; and with play, culture.

But a future also brings anxiety and a foreknowledge of death. All Occidental mythologies include some notion of the Fall, and trace the human condition to a separation from God and his Perfection. Of course, that separation is a metaphor for birth; the rubric of the myth parallels our experience of the first nine months of life, when our needs are met immediately and presumably we feel no isolation or desire. In the womb we are languageless, not having developed the cortical tissue that performs linguistic functions. But even if language were possible it would not be necessary, if it's tied to survival and consciousness of the self as distinct from the world. Language promotes self-consciousness, and vice versa, the bite of the apple from the Tree of Knowledge is the source both of human ingenuity and human anguish.

Perhaps this is one reason why so many of the greatest poets are poets of isolation (such as Dickinson, Frost, and Stevens, to name three Americans): at the heart of the linguistic act is self-consciousness and separation from the world. And visionary poetry, that would articulate our nonrational identity with the universe, may be difficult to write successfully for the same reason; such articulation would elude language if it is designed to delineate, define, and exclude.

But even if we can't imagine what the hominids thought or felt during those four million years or so before they began recording how they lived, much less what the cells that formed their structure thought or felt for the four billion years before that, all that time inside us has at least as much weight and influence on our psyche as the five thousand years we know about. Language is creative in this sense; it continuously, amazingly extends its province, even to precede its origin. All myths of origin, of both East and West, point back to a preliterate time, when the world was womb and life was an eternal moment, the *in illo tempore* of primitive sacred rites. Erich Neumann, in *The Origins and History of Consciousness,* calls this primal image of origin the uroborus.

> In Egypt as in New Zealand, in Greece as in Africa and India, the World Parents, heaven and earth, lie on top of the other in the round, spacelessly and timelessly united, for as yet nothing has come between them to create duality out of this original unity. The container of the masculine and feminine opposites is the great hermaphrodite, the primal creative element, the Hindu *purusha* who combines the poles in himself . . . . This perfect state of being, in which the opposites are contained, is perfect because it is autarchic. Its self-sufficiency, self-containment, and independence of any "you" and any "other" are signs of its self-contained eternality. . . . The perfection of that which rests in itself in no way contradicts the perfection of that which circles in itself. Although absolute rest is something static and eternal, unchanging and therefore without history, it is at the same time the place of origin and the germ cell of creativity. Living the cycle of its own life, it is the circular snake, the primal dragon of the beginning that bites its own tail, the self-begetting uroborus.

The impulse to poetry is the same as the impulse to myth: to construct an image of the discursively unknowable. In ritual, the myth is enacted, and the participants go through the sacred movements in order to feel the myth and know its way of knowing. When a dancer puts on the mask of a god, he *is* that god; there is no pretending about it. Language has that same function when used to tell mythic tales; the reality it communicates is to primitive people more genuine than that which can be seen and touched. The mythic world infuses the physical world, and both physical and metaphorical vision are informed by it. The result is an animistic world, in which looking at the tree one sees its spirit. The roots of poetry are in this way of using language; the whole enterprise is "as if," but there is finally no "as if" about it. Poetry, as Stevens believed, is a way of knowing the world.

The uroborus is the oldest mythic image we have. For Judeo-

Christian culture, the beginning was the Word, but the uroborus is before the Word, both in the historical sequence of creation myths and in our psyche. It addresses the preliterate, the psychology in the womb, the experience of pattern joined to the sequential-linear-analytical mode that dominates our culture, our way of using language, and our seeing.

The thesis of Stanley Burnshaw's *The Seamless Web* is that the primary human drive, manifesting itself in art and poetry as well as in myth and religion, is to recover this "seamlessness," this "primary organic unity with the rest of creation." It's a wonderful book and everyone interested in poetry and language would enjoy it. But Burnshaw's thesis seems to me slightly off center. Whether or not this "primary organic unity" was ever an actual historical condition (as the calendar of the life of the universe implies) and is now a physiological remnant (as argued by Thomas's *The Lives of a Cell*), the drive to consciousness is also intimately connected to our survival, and therefore to our being, as a species. The joy of learning is a physical pleasure of growth; new engrams are formed in the brain as ideas connect, which allow that electrical path to be traveled more easily in the future. We desire consciousness, as well as seamlessness, and would not give up its pleasures and benefits; otherwise, civilization and its cultures could never have developed. Although Neumann's model of human nature is the same as Burnshaw's, he takes exactly the opposite tack:

> Fixation in unconsciousness, the downward drag of its specific gravity, cannot be called a desire to remain unconscious; on the contrary, *that* is the natural thing. There is, as a counteracting force, the desire to become conscious, a veritable instinct impelling man in this direction.

In poetry, the drives for seamless organic unity and for consciousness exist hand in hand, enriching rather than contradicting each other. As in myth, which presents terms for human nature at its depths, poetry enacts its marriage of these drives as "a balance or reconciliation of opposite or discordant qualities," whereas elsewhere we feel their collision and entanglement as conflict and ambiguity. The poem brings the previously unknown and unformed to consciousness. It communicates, in the root sense of that word (to make common), as fully as any discourse, while it embodies the manifold patterning which characterizes the preliterate, nonrational mode of the psyche. Poems proceed in two ways at once: in time, insofar as the first word is read first, the second word second, and so on; and *in illo tempore,* as a pattern being filled in as we read the words. This is indicated by our sense of closure — as Yeats said, "The poem comes right with a click like a closing box" — we feel a sequence and pattern join and complete itself. So each word must not only promote its own interest, to stir us out of our linguistic habits into new vision, but it must also engage us in the pattern emerging. This may be why we are unsatisfied by a string of brilliant images, no matter how amazing or amusing each is in itself, if that's all the poem is; and are at least as unsatisfied by poems whose individual moments are predetermined by an obvious logic, whose pattern seems mechanical or static. We want richness, evocation, connections too various for analysis. We want to feel the poem as we feel the atmosphere when entering a room where so many things are happening we can't possibly isolate them. We aren't smart enough to do this by ourselves. The poem does it through the instrumentality of the language used in profound conjunction, not just according to the dictates of logic: conjunction made possible by form. The mode of logic, or discursiveness, as Burnshaw points out, is only one mode that a poem may include within it; there is an opportunity for "plurality of modes of thought" and "both common and uncommon sense together." As Hart Crane said, every poem makes a "new word," a joining of language and psyche which then becomes a public fact of language and culture, a "making common," a communication.

In closing, I want to return to the first two sentences of the passage from Jung I quoted at the beginning:

Do we ever understand what we think? We understand only such thinking as is mere equation and from which nothing comes out but what we have put in.

In this isolation and ignorance is one of the difficulties of being human. But the form of poetry allows us to enter language, as language enters us, and gives us a way of thinking beneath and beyond thought that returns much more than we are able to put in: "a momentary stay against confusion," which is embodied and which we may fully understand.

Ramon Fernandez, tell me, if you know,
Why, when the singing ended and we turned
Toward the town, tell why the glassy lights,
The lights in the fishing boats at anchor there,
As the night descended, tilting in the air,
Mastered the night and portioned out the sea,

Fixing emblazoned zones and fiery poles,
Arranging, deepening, enchanting night.
Oh! Blessed rage for order, pale Ramon,
The maker's rage to order words of the sea,
Words of the fragrant portals, dimly-starred,
And of ourselves and of our origins,
In ghostlier demarcations, keener sounds.

Lisel Mueller

Two Strains

For someone like myself, who writes in a language she was not born into, the second language assumes and retains a special fascination. We absorb our first language long before we speak it, and we learn to speak it fluently without ever becoming conscious of the learning process. The second language—in my case English, learned during adolescence—is different, and the consciousness of the difference is enhanced by a European school background which stresses grammar, spelling and etymology. It's true that after some time in a new country the process of learning the language also becomes unconscious: you are suddenly aware that you are no longer translating, but are thinking and even dreaming in the adopted language. And for many of us it is the native language that recedes and becomes the "second language." Nevertheless, the exoticism of a language learned at a distance remains for the non-active; it hovers in the back of one's mind, to surface on certain occasions.

Translating invariably provides such occasions. It's impossible to translate anything from one language into another without thinking of the natures, and/or structures, of these languages, the differences in their traditions, for example, and in their syntactic approach to expressiveness. The translator of poetry is forced to think hardest of all. The considerations in this essay ultimately proceed from such hard thinking about a poem by Marie Luise Kaschnitz, which I was translating from German into English. The problem started with the title, "Die Lander, die Meere," which could be rendered equally correctly as either, "The Countries, the Oceans," or "The Lands, the Seas." The choice is beyond accuracy; it comes down to sound, as well as very fine differences—vibrations, almost—of connotation. "The Countries, the Oceans" reproduces the syllabic and stress patterns of the German; on the other hand, "The Lands, the Seas" gives us words that are Germanic in origin. The similarity of *Lander* and *lands* as to sound is tempting. The words *countries* and *oceans* have connotations of geographic entity, while *lands* and *seas* have an additional generic sense of earth and water. As translator, I had to decide which of these connotations was closer to the poet's intention.

In the body of the same poem, I had to deal with the phrase "schlafende Griechin," which refers to the remains of an antique female statue on the coast of Sicily, but refers also to the poet herself, since the poem deals with the fluidity of past and present in the memory of old age. My first translation of the phrase as "sleeping Greek statue," though technically correct, bothered me. I knew *sleeping* was not quite the word I wanted, but I couldn't find the right one, the one I knew was hiding somewhere. Days later someone in my family made some mention of dormant plants, and my word jumped out at me. *Dormant,* from French *dormir,* means *sleeping,* of course, but tradition had endowed the word (ever since *La Belle au Bois Dormante?*) with a future, the implied certainty of an awakening. Though our experience tells us that sleeping creatures will most likely wake up, the word *sleeping,* unlike *dormant,* offers no such certainty. In the context of the Kaschnitz poem, the built-in expectation, with its suggestion of a doze rather than a deep sleep, was just what I wanted, and I marveled again at the richness of the language which allowed me such delicious choices.

It's a commonplace, of course, that English is the richest European language, and that it got that way because of a series of invaders into the British Isles, who left successive layers of language. English words remind us of the presence of Celts, Scots, Romans and Danes, but their two dominant strains derive from the 5th century invasions of the Angles and Saxons, two Germanic tribes, and the conquest by the French-speaking Normans in the 11th century. The amalgam makes English both less "pure" and more abundant than other languages; compare the sizes of dictionaries.

In many areas we have virtually a dual language, with words from both strains interchangeable as to meaning, though not necessarily "feeling" or "flavor." Because of custom and convenience, I will refer to the two strains as "Germanic" (i.e., Anglo-

became the official language. No wonder then that English has few Germanic words that refer to the intellectual life, virtually none for concepts in the sciences, and in the case of the arts, only for their simplest forms and aspects. Even in the areas of cooking, dress, furniture and manners, the language relies heavily on French-derived words. On the other hand, the plain, short Anglo-Saxon words for the necessities of a simple, agricultural life, for basic relationships, for our bodies and their organic processes, and for the natural world, have stuck: *birth, death, growth, sickness; earth, water, sun, moon; mother, father, child, love; hammer, nail, wrench; wall, door, window; hand, foot, bone, blood, breath, hair, tooth; sheep, cow; tree, wheat.* Except for the technical terms of science, we have no Latinate equivalents for most of these nouns, though we do have Latinate adjectives that refer to them: *native, mortal, terrestrial, aquatic, lunar, solar, corporeal, dextrous, pedestrian, bovine, aboreal,* etc.

Languages change. When we consider the enormous changes that occurred between the writing of *Beowulf* and Chaucer, and again in the two centuries between Chaucer and Shakespeare, it is astonishing that, four centuries later, we understand Shakespeare as well as we do. English, a Germanic language, is heavily stressed and employs the Germanic mode of syntax. Nevertheless, despite its Germanic roots and patterns, English has shifted its vocabulary heavily in the direction of Latinate words during the past two centuries. This shift has been accelerating in our own time. The inroads of general education, of science, technology and the social sciences all favor such a shift. Certainly the language of Shakespeare and the author of the King James version of the Bible (who did not use words like *solar, aquatic* and *pedestrian)* was much more clearly Germanic in its vocabulary, as well as in the use of certain constructions. One thinks of the many Germanic words that must have disappeared from usage, in addition to those we still know; words like *dale,* now taken over by *valley,* and *reckon,* which has become *figure.* One thinks of the *flower* which once was a *bloom,* and of the *deaf-and-dumb* who have become *deafmutes,* because of the more recent equation of dumb with stupid. And surely English must have had Germanic nouns for such basic concepts as "innocence" and "jealousy" and "mystery" at one time.*

One has only to listen to talk shows and interviews on radio and television to be made aware of the influx of Latinate words in

---

*It seems ironic that the word *tradition* is Latinate. But of course the very awareness of tradition, and hence the coinage of such a word, implies a self-conscious, sophisticated society.

Saxon and Scandinavian) and "Latinate" respectively, even though "Latinate," while accommodating all the Romance languages, technically leaves out English words deriving from Greek roots, of which there are many, especially in science and philosophy. (It's also true that some Germanic words ultimately go back to the Latin.)

There is no real difference in meaning between *amiable* and *friendly, forbid* and *prohibit, respond* and *answer, purchase* and *buy, gift* and *present, vivacious* and *lively*, but the feeling of the Latinate words is somewhat more formal, more "educated." Sometimes the difference in feeling is greater. A *forest* is more impressive than the *woods, climate* is more inclusive than *weather*, a *chamber* is more elegant than a *room*, a *mansion* is a very large *house*, an *object* is slightly more exalted than a *thing*, a *breeze* is a gentle sort of *wind*. A *corpuscular, mendacious monarch* is a puffed-up *fat liar* of a *king. Foliage*, a collective noun, encompasses a mass of leaves and so is more abstract than the simple plural *leaves*, but it keeps us from experiencing the visual and tactile image of that word.

Sex is Latinate, but the so-called four-letter words for specific sexual parts and acts are Anglo-Saxon nouns and verbs. Writers (and non-writers) know the difficulty of finding an appropriate "language of love" in English, since the Germanic words still offend many people and the Latinate ones feel "clinical." Euphemisms are all we have to fill the gap. We all remember D. H. Lawrence's attempt, in *Lady Chatterley's Lover*, to "purify" the taboo sexual words by using them in a work of literature. It's not surprising that he failed. A writer may have a great, and nearly instantaneous, influence on the literary style of his period, but he cannot singlehandedly change deeply embedded attitudes toward words, especially when they carry with them age-old associations of fear and shame. Preference for Latinate over Germanic words connected with bodily functions applies even where the Germanic words are permissible. *Fragrance, perfume* and *odor* are "nicer" than *smell*, and it's more genteel to *perspire* than to *sweat*.

We don't have synonyms for everything, of course. The Norman and Plantagenet kings and their aristocracy super-imposed on the Anglo-Saxon society a culture different in kind and broader in scope, a culture which moreover acted as a natural conduit for literature, architecture, science, philosophy and music from the European continent. While Latin remained the language of the law and the Church, French was the language of the ruling class and the schools until the 14th century, when the fusion we call English

everyday speech. But I am ultimately concerned with the words that poets use, and how they use them. I think it's safe to say that Pound's insistence on the plainest word (that modernist with the purist heart!) is not their foremost aesthetic concern. It may well be that poetic diction is changing, but if so, it is still at a much slower rate than general speech. Poets are conservators of language. They have no use for jargon, which much of our current speech consists of, and they like words that have been invested with history and weighted with feeling; words that have overtones, reverberations; words that set off a chain reaction of associations. And they have traditionally dealt with birth, death, love, the natural world and the humbler aspects of human existence. But the natural world is becoming less and less available as a subject, and that fact coupled with the move away from metered verse may additionally change poetic diction. It's too soon to tell.

Germanic nouns and verbs (except in the -ing formations) are words of one or two syllables. We think of them as strong, simple, immediate, visceral. They touch our elemental nature. We connect Latinate words with exoticism, sonority, decorum, wit and education; with the expression of ideas, and a high degree of conceptualization. The suffixes we use to extend words in order to express quality, process and states of being are Latinate: *moderation, radiation, bondage, sexuality, happiness.* *Word(s)* is Germanic, but *vocabulary* is Latinate, and *wordiness* a mix of a Germanic root word with a Latinate suffix. Such suffixes add to the number of syllables, of course, and we do indeed tend to equate "Latinate" with "polysyllabic," ignoring the huge number of short, specific words which had acquired the same status of common household words that we connect with Germanic ones. It's true, though, that words of more than two syllables in English are almost without exception Latinate. Most four-syllable words, and some three-syllable ones, receive two stresses, usually a primary and a secondary one: *estuary, memorandum, eternity, recognize.* Obviously, sound, including weight, is as much a factor as sense in word selection. A poet who wants to cluster stresses, who hammers away as Hopkins did, has to rely on a heavily Germanic diction, while a writer of light verse or social sature may choose a long, lightly accented line.* When Richard Wilbur has Pangloss tell us about the joys of venereal disease, which is after all a gift from Venus, and when he translates Moliere's sophisticated comedies of manners, the cultivated artifice of the society is made

---

*All histories of versification in English tell us of the overwhelming preference for the disyllabic, especially iambic, foot over the anapest and dactyl.

abundantly clear in the tripping meter and the witty feminine rhymes. Such lines as

> Since women are (from natural reticence)
> Reluctant to declare their sentiments,
> And since the honor of our sex requires,
> That we conceal our amorous desires

leave no doubt as to the spirit in which they are to be taken. And when Edward Dorn begins his poem "Song" with the lines

> Again, I am made the occurrence
> Of one of her charms. Let me
> Explain. An occupier
> Of one of the waves of her intensity

he sets the tone, telling us to expect a love poem which is elegant and keeps its distance.

In *The Truth of Poetry*, Michael Hamburger mentions Yves Bonnefoy's discussion of French, as compared to English, poetry. The tradition of French poetry, Bonnefoy says, is abstract; it deals with essences. French poets want generic words, unlike English ones, who want the specific. He thinks the difference arises from the languages themselves. As a result, those French poets whom English-speaking ones have particularly admired for their concrete imagery, rank low in the esteem of their countrymen. Surely Bonnefoy's discoveries show some parallels to our feeling about Latinate and Germanic words and underscore the Germanic tradition of poetry in English.

I have been looking at some well-worn anthology pieces by 20th century poets, curious to see what I would discover about their vocabulary. English being by definition a fusion of languages, it would of course be impossible to write a purely Latinate poem, at least one that used syntax, since conjunctions, articles, numbers and auxilliary verbs are Germanic. It would be much easier to write one in an exclusively Germanic vocabulary, but it wouldn't be likely to come about unless the poet consciously worked at it. In "Richard Cory," the first poem I looked at, Robinson reserves all the "fancy" words for Cory. The common people, of whom the speaker is one, they who "went without the meat and cursed the bread," are uniformly endowed with short, chiefly Germanic, words, and the Latinate ones, like "bullet," "pavement," "place" and "human," are of the sort that by now feel quite common. But Richard Cory, the rich man of the town, is *"imperially* slim," "clean *favored,"* "quietly *arrayed"* and *"admirably* schooled in every *grace."* The shoe fits.

Dylan Thomas, that lover of strong, old words, whose "tumble-down tongue" retrieved so many of them from obscurity, does something similar in his poem "In My Craft Or Sullen Art." Richard Cory is a man set apart by money and position and, it turns out, by some grief or terror so great it drives him to suicide. Thomas' poet-speaker, who "labour(s) by singing light" to praise the quotidian lovers, who "lie abed/with all their griefs in their arms" and are unaware of his existence, is also a man set apart. Thomas' diction throughout consists of short, simple words (including the Latinate, but common, rhyme words "rages," "stages," "wages," "pages," and "ages"), except when he refers to the possibility of fame,

> Not for ambition or bread
> Or the strut and trade of charms,
> On the ivory stages,

and to his work, which is *exercised in the still night.*" "Refusal to Mourn the Death, by Fire, of a Child in London," that magnificent poem, whose first thirteen lines are one driving, on-rushing sentence made up of one and two-syllable words of primarily Germanic origin (emphasized by the heavy alliteration), stuns the reader with its exceptions. Besides the religious words, there is the line "The *majesty* and burning of the child's death," followed by the statement that the poet refuses to demean this majesty "With any further/*Elegy* of *innocence* and youth." Any-one who has looked at Thomas' notebooks has seen the long lists of alternative words he used to write in the margins, and so knows the extreme care with which he chose his vocabulary. For this reader, "majesty" seems inevitable, the only word large, solemn and authoritative enough to do what Thomas wants it to do here. It is something of a public word, carrying overtones of great and stately ceremony. On the other hand, "Elegy" and "innocence" become pejorative in this context, take on an air of sentimentality and artifice that would trivialize the child's death. The poet's statement of refusal is followed immediately by the wonderful, simple line, "Deep with the first dead lies London's daughter," a line whose sound and sense tell us everything about the poet's feeling toward this death.

Wallace Stevens is often cited as a poet with a heavily Latinate diction. One thinks of such titles as "The Auroras of Autumn," "Memoirs of a Magnifico" and "The Revolutionists Stop for Orangeade." One thinks of the exuberantly witty use of words in "The Comedian as the Letter C," of the luxurious exoticism of "Sea Surface Full of Clouds," and the flavor of romantic alienation in "Esthetique du Mal," with lines like

> The tongue caresses these exacerbations,
> They press it as epicure, distinguishing
> Themselves from its essential savor,
> Like hunger that feeds on its own hungriness

But the fact is that Stevens' vocabulary is chosen for the occasion of each poem. "A High-Toned Old Christian Woman" is a splendid example of how he plays off Latinate against Germanic words. The poem is a kind of mock-battle, a joyous, frisky contest between sound effects. "Sunday Morning" and "Peter Quince at the Clavier," poems which are at once philosophical and sensuous, consists of that inimitable blend of flavors and textures which makes Stevens' language so truly marvelous. But there are many short poems whose language is quite plain. In *Harmonium,* for example, a large number of them come close to the Imagist ideal, as far as diction is concerned. The famous Tennesseean jar, for one. (Sometimes the titles are foolers. The only thing "foreign" about "Memoirs of a Magnifico" is its title.) Throughout Stevens' work, and especially in the posthumous poems with their revealing and disarming simplicity, we find poems of predominantly Germanic diction. I think that it's the placement, rather than frequency, of exotic words, as well as their flamboyance, that shocks the reader into regarding Stevens' vocabulary as more Latinate that it actually is; for example, the piling-up and juxtaposition of "caliper," "divine ingenue," "companion," and "fragrance of vegetal" in the first stanza of "Last Looks at the Lilacs," and the sudden extravagance of words like "inflections," "innuendoes," "barbaric glass" and "bawds of euphony" in the otherwise spare and chaste "Thirteen Ways of Looking at a Blackbird."

Theodore Roethke's diction is heavily Germanic, as befits a poet who wrote about the humblest forms of organic life and the naked life of feeling. In "Elegy for Jane," this applies not only to the verbs and nouns, but to the adjectives—and Roethke's poems are filled with adjectives. Such adjectives as "pickerel," "spiny," "maimed" and "bleached" (in conjunction with "valleys") are hard to find elsewhere in modern poetry. Significantly, the only line in which the total verb-noun combination is Latinate, is "And she balanced in the delight of her thought." The other Roethke poem known to every undergraduate is, of course, "My Papa's Waltz." Looking at that poem freshly, from my new perspective, turned into a happy surprise for me. Not only does the poem, with its triple-stressed lines, beat time in our heads, as Roethke's father did on that of his son, but its language instructs us abundantly about the nature of the activity and the attitudes of the participants. There is not a word of more than two syllables in the poem, except one, *countenance;* and look what it accomplishes:

> The whiskey on your breath
> Could make a small boy dizzy;
> But I hung on like death:
> Such waltzing was not easy.
>
> We romped until the pans
> Slid from the kitchen shelf;
> My mother's countenance
> Could not unfrown itself

Roethke needed no more than a single word to tell us how the mother felt about such goings-on.

A few old favorites, chosen at random, out of curiosity, with no intention of proving anything. But something has been proven for me after all: the persistence of how we feel towards words, the endurance of our sense of their associations, their surfaces, their taste—in short, our sense of their rightness for our purposes.

We can't always be sure whether we are responding to sense or sound. We think of *earth* and *breath,* for example, as strong, affecting words. But that is because of what they mean—because we connect them with our mothers and fathers, with our own organic life, our most basic needs—or is it because our earliest excursions into language, or perhaps some factors in our nervous system, determine our feeling about short, explosive words? In *How Does a Poem Mean,* John Ciardi presents a paraphrase of Williams' "A Sort of Song." What he calls paraphrase is virtually a translation of Williams' simple words, precise in meaning and frictive in sound, into blurrier, more general and more archaically "poetic" ones. The object of Ciardi's deliberately "bad" poem is, of course, to emphasize the importance of word choice in the overall effect of a poem, since its denotative meaning, the "message," is not altered. Beyond this intention, the paraphrase makes evident once again the wealth of the English vocabulary, as well as the receding of some once common words into archaisms. Williams' "wait," "split" and "rocks" become Ciardi's "bide," "cleave" and "crags." All six are Germanic, but only Williams' are in common usage now. Ciardi substitutes "spiritual and material" for Williams' "the people and the stones," a substitution of philosophical, non-specific, polysyllabic adjectives for Williams' nouns. The effect is one of greater remove from the

Robert Pack

Silences, Sighs, Caesuras, Elipses, Ohs, and Ahs

In his line, "As if we saw our feeling in the object seen," Wallace Stevens succinctly describes two essential aspects of metaphorical language. First, there is a perceived correspondence between an inner, subjective feeling and some physical reality out there. And, second, the perceiver is aware that this correspondence does not exist except in his "as if" assertion of its existence. Metaphorical seeing always involves making believe and the awareness — somewhere on the fine line between consciousness and subconsciousness — that one is making believe, so that the projection of a feeling onto an object can take place.

When one sees a beautiful sunset, for example, one sees the beauty of the sunset as if the beauty were inherent in the sunset itself. Thus the phrase "a beautiful sunset" is in effect a metaphorical statement. Metaphorical language is so natural to ordinary speech that usually one is not aware of it as such. When one says "She is a cold woman," or when Grandma says to Grandson, "You are so sweet that I could eat you," the listener knows, without being warned, that "cold" and "sweet" are not to be taken literally. They describe subjective feelings about people that are assumed to correspond to physical experience.

Robert Frost's description of metaphor, like Stevens', emphasizes the connection of inner and outer: "It is just saying one thing in terms of another . . . matter in terms of spirit, or spirit in terms of matter, to make the final unity." This unity may be further described as one of place and person, or of world and mind, and it cannot exist without its expression in language, so that the felt (experienced) correspondence of feeling and object depends on the metaphor that brings the two together. Frost calls this unifying effect of language a "gathering metaphor." For the "gathering" power of the poem is its design, a sort of megametaphor which holds the whole together and extends in complexity and nuance the various and discrete metaphors the poem contains. Yet as a structure of words, the poem is metaphorical in another way. The words themselves on the page become an object, and, to vary Stevens' line, it is as if in reading them, we hear our feelings in the sounds a human voice would make in speaking them. Every poem creates the illusion of a speaking human voice, and the reader may choose to think of that voice as belonging to an invented character or to the poet himself. But even if the latter assumption is made, the poet, through selection, has represented only an aspect of himself — one mood among many — and thus has fictionalized himself.

The feelings that the poem as verbal structure invites the reader to project upon the poem are never only the feelings appropriate to the subject of the poem itself — feleings such as sorrow, regret, sympathy. Inseperable from such subjective emotions is the pleasure the poem must always provide as poem. No matter how sorrowful the subject matter of a poem, a good poem will not make a reader feel sad. The reader does not experience sorrow, but the poem of sorrow, the pleasure of the poem of sorrow, even though the reader is reminded that indeed real sorrow exists in the world. Auden expressed succinctly this paradox of pleasure in poetic sorrow: "O happy grief is all sad art can say." The reader experiences the illusion of a human voice, knowing that it is an illusion, and therefore experiences this voice as metaphor. And it is the implied voice qualities of the written words — tone, pitch, speed, roughness or melodic ease — which are an essential part of the poem's gathering design and which can evoke this sense of human presence.

The essence of metaphor, then, is not merely the correspondence between inner and outer, between subject and object, but rather the verbal design itself, embodied as voice, which holds the two together, for the design is always more than the connections that it makes. Metaphorical design always evokes a sense of mystery — the mystery of connectedness and connection — and in particular the mystery of language without which the connections of inner and outer do not exist. The essence of metaphor, seen in this way, is innuendo, implication, and the awareness of possibility. Preceding language and idea is the human cry — the body's voice of sounds without words. For our cries like our words are both preceded *and* followed by silence. Yet silence too may become articulate because of the context in which it is placed — as with a musical rest note. We hear the silence of a rest note because it is contained within a musical phrase. In this sense, the mystery of the evocative power of metaphor may be compared to the delineated silences, the pauses within a poem, that are suggested by a shift in rhythm, for example, or a line break, or a missing syllable when two syllables are expected to complete a foot. In fact, the metaphorical center of a poem may be found in the implications of its silences.

In Robert Frost's "Hyla Brook," for example, we are listening to a brook that has lost its song.

> By June our brook's run out of song and speed.
> Sought for much after that, it will be found
> Either to have gone groping underground
> (And taken with it all the Hyla breed
> That shouted in the mist a month ago,
> Like ghost of sleigh bells in a ghost of snow) —
> Or flourished and come up in jewelweed,
> Weak foliage that is blown upon and bent,
> Even against the way its waters went.
> Its bed is left a faded paper sheet
> Of dead leaves stuck together by the heat —
> A brook to none but who remember long.
> This as it will be seen is other far
> Than with brooks taken otherwhere in song.
> We love the things we love for what they are.

The poem, in effect, is a response to and a celebration of the silence of the brook. The poem opens with the implication that there is a specific listener for this poem, since the speaker refers to "our brook," and that intimate "our" suggests the auditor may be his wife. By the end of the poem it has been clear that this is indeed a poem about the strengthening of the bond of love through the mutual metaphorical viewing of an object in nature just as the woman says in Frost's "West-Running Brook":

> As you and I are married to each other,
> We'll both be married to the brook. We'll build
> Our bridge across it, and the bridge shall be
> Our arm thrown over it asleep beside it.

Hyla Brook possesses two qualities which are named as "song and speed." But while the brook's speed is literal, a material quality, the quality of song is not inherent in the brook itself and thus necessarily implies a subjective beholder which thinks it sings.

The poem moves backward in time, for it is a poem after all about seeing the past, the signs of which have physically vanished so that a present absence gives way here to a past presence. Paradoxically, the brook's absence is seen and heard again in the poem as if it were once again early spring when the Hyla frogs were there, and, further back even, to a ghostlier winter, with its "ghost of sleigh-bells in a ghost of snow." The brook moves one way and the weeds another, just as the speaker's mind both remembers and looks ahead to the future. Again as in "West-Running Brook," love is defined as having the power to embody and affirm contraries, male and female, past and present: "It must be the brook / Can trust itself to go by contraries / The way I can with you — and you with me."

All the speaker actually sees in "Hyla Brook," from June on, is a bed of dry leaves, so that someone not familiar with this landscape would not see a brook at all and would not know that Hyla frogs ever lived there. Only by virtue of memory, by cherishing what has been there before, can the mind bring to the eye what is now gone and thus give body to absence: "A brook to none but who remember long." Filling the silence, seeing into the past, are then projected into the future as a bond of understanding between the speaker and his wife. Frost gives the reader a lesson on how to surpass literal sight as he assures us: "This as it will be seen is other far / Than with brooks taken otherwhere in song," for the bond between the man and the woman in this poem requires that the past be contained even in the radically changed present and continued into the future. This is precisely what ongoing love must accomplish. Frost is teasing his reader with a subtle boast, saying in effect that any other poet would write a poem about a brook that is a brook while he has the wit to write a poem about a brook that is not a brook, except by someone who knows the landscape well enough to remember what it was.

In order to love a brook that is no longer a brook, the speaker must incorporate the past, as if it still existed, into the way he now sees "dead leaves stuck together by the heat" so that the absent brook can become a metaphor for the continuity of love against the passage of time itself. The poem's final line, "We love the things we love for what they are," which at first reading seems so solidly committed to a literal and factual reality, can now be seen as reverberant with innuendo and implication. For the brook is both what it once was — a brook — and what it is now — merely dead leaves stuck together. To love things for what they *are* must include loving them as well for what they are not or once were, and for what they still may become. Reality will not be fixed in a simple, declarative "they are." What things are for Frost is what the mind can make of them. And so Frost transforms his brook which is no more into a metaphorical brook which continues to flow in the speaker's memory, the mind's "underground," a promise to go on loving even when his wife is no longer present, a promise flowing even into the silence that follows speech.

Wallace Steven's "The Snow Man" is another poem about beholding what "is not there." Yet unlike Frost's speaker who tries to remember spring in June, Stevens' Snow Man tries to see only winter in the winter landscape. As if the world could be observed objectively, like a purely physical fact, the Snow Man resists all metaphorical thinking. He will not allow himself to hear the wind as if it were expressing any human feeling like "misery." "One must have a mind of winter," he insists,

> not to think
> Of any misery in the sound of the wind,
> In the sound of a few leaves,
>
> Which is the sound of the land
> Full of the same wind
> That is blowing in the same bare place . . . .

This speaker wants to behold the landscape as *it* is, adding nothing of himself to what he sees. When Blake says, "We are led to believe a lie / When we see with not through the eye," he defined in wholly negative terms the "winter mind" of Stevens' Snow Man who sees "with" the eye, for to see *with* the eye is to perceive the world as an object apart from the beholding self. To see "through" the eye, however, is to perceive the world with one's mind — to associate objects with feelings and ideas, to behold the landscape as metaphor. Like Blake, Stevens is a celebrator of the imagination, seeing through the eye, yet he also knows how easily metaphor passes over into fantasy or illusion. For this reason, seeing with the eye, with the winter mind, is a necessary corrective or balance for the imagination. For Stevens, the literal eye provides the mind with a constant reminder of external reality.

Just as there are two ways of perceiving reality, with and through the eye, so there are two observers in Stevens' poem: a Snow Man who sees only what is objectively present, and a narrator-observer who regards the Snow Man and is keenly aware of what the Snow Man is *not* thinking. For this subjective narrator-observer beholds not only the visible, but the invisible as well. For him, the *idea* of

258

absence and silence has its own being and content, so that his language approximates winter stillness in the steadily repeating sibilants that hiss like dried leaves across the floor of this poem, "expressing silence / Of a sort" as Stevens says elsewhere of a pond in early winter. Although "The Snow Man" seems to be a poem about total winter desolation, it is of particular significance that the scene is filled with evergreens and that it has its own pristine beauty, free of the mind's association of "misery" with wind and coldness. Furthermore, the month is January, the commencement of a new year and the turning toward spring. In effect, Stevens suggests that this is not a poem merely about the diminished mind of the Snow Man who can no longer make any human connections with the landscape, the end of metaphorical imagining, but about a beginning as well. In order for the mind to begin again, however, to perceive the landscape in a human way, it must imagine energetically the ending of the imaginative effort that preceded it. As Stevens says in "The Plain Sense of Things," "the absence of imagination had itself to be imagined."

For the poem's narrator, imagining the Snow Man's winter mind involves imagining the absence of imagination. The Snow Man hears monotonous sound, almost like silence itself, but from the narrator's point of view there is a paradoxical fullness to this description of emptiness in which a winter scene is "Full of the same wind." The Snow Man sees things as things, facts as facts, but to the more imaginative mind of the narrator, objects may also be seen as metaphors, and therefore, for him, to perceive winter as an objective, physical fact and not as a symbol of misery betokens a failure of the imagination. Still, he realizes, there is the intractable sound of the wind which is merely itself only one step removed from silence. For the Snow Man is the best perceiver of a nothingness that does indeed exist. As close as we can get to the sense of silence in the repetitions of the sounds of sameness and monotony, so too do we approach unmediated reality as we postulate its independent existence prior to any metaphorical imposition upon it. Nevertheless, Stevens' whole poem becomes a metaphor, since absence, when well imagined, encompasses its opposite — the presence of the *idea* of absence, the idea of non-being.

The poem's narrator, beholding the Snow Man, realizes by implication that perception is nothing — it is empty — until human associative thought (of things that are not there) transforms objects into metaphors. But this nothing does exist as "the nothing that is," though only the narrator and not the Snow Man can know this. What the Snow Man *sees* is what the narrator *knows*, for the narrator encompasses the *idea* of nothing, and that idea quickens his desire for the renewal of metaphorical perception. As Stevens says in a later poem: "And not to have is the beginning of desire, / To have what is not in its ancient cycle." This renewal of the desire for metaphor is suggested by the approach of the distant sun as the year turns toward spring. With the realization that "nothing" must be confronted, we hear a kind of gasp — a flash of silence one might say — in the penultimate line, the only line in the poem that ends with an enjambment:

> nothing himself, [the Snow Man] beholds
> Nothing that is not there and the nothing that is.

Only through metaphor can the absence of metaphor be imagined. A world without metaphor is nothing, yet this is true for Stevens in both a literal and metaphorical sense, and thus the poem both partakes of silence and is about silence — silence as natural fact and silence as possibility.

Human reality — emotion, mood, need — cannot be expressed denotatively as fact because it is always changing, fluid, open to further possibility. So human love, for example, is composed as much of memory and hope as it is of physical desire. Love is an idea of obligation and responsibility wedded to, inseperable from, a bodily need for touch and sexual release. As Yeats said: "love would be [no] more than an animal hunger but for the poet."

In William Blake's poem, "Never Seek to Tell Thy Love," we have a story about a traveler's amorous, wooing sigh, and is itself the sigh of the rejected narrator after he has failed to win the lady with the direct declaration of his love. Here is the poem:

> Never seek to tell thy love
> Love that never told can be;
> For the gentle wind does move
> Silently, invisibly.
>
> I told my love, I told my love,
> I told her all my heart,
> Trembling, cold, in ghastly fears,
> Ah! She doth depart.
>
> Soon as she was gone from me
> A traveller came by
> Silently, invisibly —
> He took her with a sigh.

In contrast to the blunt and forthright narrator, the traveler's sigh is the epitome of language as suggestion and connotation. Blake implicitly compares human breathing and nature's breathing, the "gentle wind," and thus conveys to the reader the emotions of the narrator and the traveler in terms of how the poem breathes evenly or catches its breath through rhythmical shifts. The radical metrical interruption in the refrain line, "Silently, invisibly," for example, characterizes the interrupted breathing, the sigh, the anxiety of the narrator, and also suggests his subconscious identification with the traveler.

The narrator begins urgently — almost all his lines start with stressed syllables: "Never seek to tell thy love," and a strong rhythmic pattern quickly is established. But that pattern breaks abruptly in the fourth line: "Silently, // invisibly." The two missing stresses in this poem of four beats per line must be read into the caesura in the middle of the line. In the comma, like a musical rest note, we hear a doubly stressed pause — a sigh, an intake and exhalation of breath, invisible and approaching silence. The narrator is compared to the easy movement of nature itself in the figure of the gentle wind which provides us with an image of nature's breathing, open and ongoing in contrast to the narrator who seeks to limit love by thinking to tell "all his heart." Love is destroyed, Blake implies, by placing it within mental boundaries, as though one could ever capture it. As Blake says elsewhere: "He who bends to himself a joy, / Does the wingèd life destroy, / But he who kisses the joy as it flies, / Lives in eternity's sunrise." The woman who hears the narrator's declaration of love is aghast because love has been limited in its unmetaphorical telling, and we hear her dismay echoed in the extended sigh, the outcry of the narrator: "Ah, she doth depart." Better to speak, like the wind, the language of innuendo and suggestion. Unlike the narrator's sigh of despair and defeat, the traveler's sigh is one of pleasure and of promise, love opening the senses and the mind to the mystery.

If the traveler's sigh corresponds to the "gentle wind," nature's benevolent power, then the gasping, anxious sigh of the narrator corresponds to a failed imagining of nature and thus a constricted sense of bodily desire and of love. These opposing sighs constitute the central metaphor of Blake's poem, and they remind us of the nature of metaphor itself, the language that enables us to see things, not merely as they are, but in the fullness of their open possibilities, always there to be realized through the marriage of inner and outer, mind and nature. "If the doors of perception were cleaned," he reminds us in "The Marriage of Heaven and Hell," "everything would appear to man as it is, infinite."

Another of Frost's poems, "The Road Not Taken," can be read as a series of sighs for one's divided selves: the life one lives and the life one might have lived.

Two roads diverged in a yellow wood,
And sorry I could not travel both
And be one traveler, long I stood
And looked down one as far as I could
To where it bent in the undergrowth;

Then took the other, as just as fair,
And having perhaps the better claim,
Because it was grassy and wanted wear;
Though as for that the passing there
Had worn them really about the same,

And both that morning equally lay
In leaves no step had trodden black.
Oh, I kept the first for another day!
Yet knowing how way leads on to way,
I doubted if I should ever come back.

I shall be telling this with a sigh
Somewhere ages and ages hence:
Two roads diverged in a wood, and I —
I took the one less traveled by,
And that has made all the difference.

The impossible wish for more than one life leads the speaker to seek consolation in the belief that the choice of his actual life has at least had some positive significance. The speaker's first palpable sigh for the recognition of mortal limitation can be heard in the line, "And be one traveler, // long I stood," where the heavy pause after the comma carries over into the stress on the word "long." A sigh of regret is unmistakable in the speaker's voice, whose varying intonations constitute the fundamental metaphor of the poem. For that voice is far more complex and self-revealing than the relatively simple allegorical image of the two roads would suggest. In fact, the speaker tries to persuade himself that the two roads can be distinguished, that a real choice was made, but he soon catches himself up and corrects that rationalization. Actually, both roads turn out to have been the same: "And both that morning equally lay / In leaves no step had trodden black." The speaker cannot convince himself that a meaningful choice took place, and there is an extended sigh in that recognition in the stressed "Oh" that opens the subsequent line against the flow of the iambic meter: "Oh, I kept the first for another day!"

The "first" road is kept by the poem itself, surprisingly, in its title, despite the later claim that the road he *did* take has made "all the difference." After all, the poem itself is what he will sigh for in the future when he will again look back, for he tells us that "I shall be telling this with a sigh." In effect, the telling has already told, but here the poem is projected into an indefinite future. When and where is "Somewhere ages and ages hence"? Is the speaker imagining that he might be reciting this poem perhaps to his grandchildren as an intentionally misleading and therefore subtly comic parable about looking for meaning in life where none is to be found because choice was after all an illusion? Or is the speaker imagining an after-life in which the purpose of the journey of life, even in distant retrospect, will still be obscure to him? If so, will his sigh then express eternal uncertainty? The reader can only follow the speaker's meaning here in speculation. The speaker, however, returns to the objective fact. "Two roads diverged in a wood," though now even the detail "yellow" has dropped away, suggesting the increased remoteness of his/her perspective. The line break places another pause, another sigh, between the double self: "And I — // I took," separating one "I" from the other, reinforcing the reader's sense of the sorrow of the speaker's divided consciousness. We hear his melancholy tone for being limited to "one" life in the breaking of his voice. His sighs, his troubled breathing, however we interpret them, are more concrete than any meaning the speaker can impose upon his experience.

The apparently affirmative and individualistic claim, "I took the road less traveled by," then, is contradicted by the facts of the poem. The two roads "equally lay," indistinguishable except for the historical fact that he took one and not the other. He cannot know what another life might have been, nor can he make a useful comparison. His statement, as he fully recognizes, is ironic, and that perhaps accounts for the prolonged sigh which is the very "telling" of this poem — for it is a sigh which must go unrelieved in any future retellings wherever "ages hence" they may take place.

As in many of Frost's poems, the experience presented here is one of non-revelation. The wish for a revealed meaning or a proven significance, as in the making of a choice, is disappointed, and the reader can hear that disappointment in the speaker's voice in the constrained ironic bitterness of the last line. Frost put it this way once: "A good sentence does double duty: it conveys one meaning by word and syntax and another by the tone of voice it indicates." So, while the words of the final line, "And that has made all the difference," denote that a meaningful and positive choice has been made, the very tone of voice undermines and reverses that assertion. In this steadily iambic poem with only few variations, the final two metrical feet are reversed; they are trochees which give a falling effect — "all the difference" — and in them the reader can hear the diminishing of the speaker's voice. The last line is the only one in the entire poem to end on an unstressed syllable, an exhalation of breath, a sigh fading into silence. So the voice that speaks this poem, filled with the mysterious inflections of a sigh, is the true metaphor corresponding to the narrator's experience of nostalgia for a revelation that never took place.

The voice that speaks a poem, as implied by the written words, is itself a metaphor; what the reader learns or surmises from that voice may provide the crucial information of the poem. Voice inflections like pitch and speed and voice qualities like harshness or mellifluousness may be suggested, for example, by rhythm, rhyme or the emphasis on vowel or consonantal patterns. Yet there is nothing more expressive in a poem than its pauses, its silences, for they evoke the bodily sense of breathing, easy or hard, and they may correspond to the *idea* of silence as absence or, at the other extreme, to an *idea* of silence as mental or spiritual inwardness.

Howard Nemerov's exquisite and poignant lyric, "During a Solar Eclipse," relates the silence of reflective thought, "we stand bemused," with the silence of the cessation of individual life in the light of cosmic change:

The darkening disk of the moon before the sun
All morning moves, turning our common day
A deep and iris blue, daylight of dream
In which we stand bemused and looking on
Backward at shadow and reflected light,

While the two great wanderers among the worlds
Enter their transit with our third, a thing
So rare that in his time upon the earth
A man may see, as I have done, but four,
In childhood two, a third in youth, and this

In likelihood my last. We stand bemused
While grass and rock darken, and stillness grows,
Until the sun and moon slide out of phase

And light returns us to the common life
That is so long to do and so soon done.

Nemerov speaks his poem in the collective "we," since watching a solar eclipse is a public and communal event which unites us for a moment in "our common day." His individual voice enters only in the second stanza, "A man may see, as I have done," and quickly passes back into the indistinguishable "we." The speaker, observing a cosmic event beyond himself, turns inward as his thought deepens and becomes still with the repetition of "We stand bemused," which leads immediately to the image of the darkening "grass and rock" and to the increased heaviness of meditative silence as the "stillness grows."

Within this silence, however, there is a pause, a breathful sigh, in which the individual self, Nemerov speaking as "I," holds to this reflective instant of his own life as he watches in quiet inspiration ("bemused") the "reflected light" beyond him. The pause is felt profoundly in the stressed word "this," enjambed doubly by line *and* stanza. Nemerov dwells on "this" rare moment of sight as if his life could somehow be prolonged a little in its contemplation. If this pause is heard as a sigh, it is a sigh of possession and at the same time an acknowledgment of loss in the inexorable "turning" of time. The phrase, "as I have done," suggesting the recapitulation of his individual life, passes over into the final phrase "and so soon done," making more precious "the common life" whose shared light the speaker will cherish for whatever time remains to him. Finally, the sigh of the poem is released in the subdued lament of predominating "O" sounds, "so long to do and so soon done," whose melancholy is equalled only by its loveliness.

Life merges from silence and stillness and returns to them. The connecting interim is composed of sound and movement, and Stevens' "Life is Motion" may be read as a little parable on this theme. In this poem, Stevens employs and distinguishes two aspects of language; language as image and language as abstraction, which correspond to physical presence and conceptual thought: the word as sound-object and the word as idea. The letter O and the sound O are introduced doubled in the word "Motion." Person, dress and place are related by having a prominent O letter and their implied sounds. Bonnie's and Josie's names have their O; their state, Oklahoma, is filled with O; they are dressed in calico; and their cry, "Ohoyaho," which sounds like a cave-man's version of Oklahoma, is a primative warbling on the variants of the vowel O. Here is a whole world in nine lines:

In Oklahoma
Bonnie and Josie,
Dressed in calico,
Danced around a stump.
They cried,
"Ohayaho,
Ohoo" . . .
Celebrating their marriage
Of flesh and air.

The first two words of the title, "Life Is," prepare the reader for an abstract and general proposition, and the word, "Motion," completes the concept. Although "Motion" as a word evokes only an idea, not an image, it directs the reader's attention to the physical world of concrete, moving things, and Stevens will not return to abstract language until the poem's concluding two lines. For Stevens, every poem contains by implication the origin of language itself — the physical cry of the human voice not yet shaped into a word. As Stevens says in "The Man with the Blue Guitar," "The poem is the cry of its occasion"; inherent in the words and the design of the poem is the sound made by a rush of breath from the lungs, through the throat, directed by the tongue, against the teeth of the lips. This is the breathing voice that cries out "O" either in pleasure or in pain. The letter "O" presents the idea of this sound and, in essence, makes manifest what Stevens calls "the poem of the idea within the poem of words," to which we should add, on Stevens' behalf, "within the poem of sounds," for as Stevens says (in his essay, "The Noble Rider and the Sound of Words"): "above everything else, poetry is words; and words, above everything else, are, in poetry, sounds."

The setting of the poem, suggested by the calico clothing, is the nineteenth century American frontier. A farming family has taken time out from work for a celebration, probably a wedding. The expansion of the country westward and the clearing of the land for farming suggest life-affirming activity and energy, yet the image of the stump which appears at the dead center of the poem (eleven words before and after), produces a counter effect. The reader hears and witnesses a physical dance accompanied by a primal, incantatory poetry around the central "stump" of death. Creation and destruction are thus seen as inseparable. The cry "Ohoyaho, / Ohoo," is breath itself, pure voice unmediated by linguistic meaning. An emphatic breath pause is indicated by the ellipses, and in that moment, as cry trails off into silence, the reader-listener is invited to make the connection between the expressiveness of bodily voice sounds and the mind's power to conceptualize, to articulate ideas such as the idea of "marriage." The poem thus presents the idea of celebration and *is itself a celebration* of the idea of marriage: the marriage of person and place, of life and death, of body and mind, and, above all, of sound and poem. The poem is a metaphor for itself, celebrating itself, wedding the body's cry with the mind's linguistic design; it is a metaphor for the literal human voice transformed into poetic speech, according to Stevens' faith — "poetry, exceeding music, must take the place of empty heaven and its hymns" — that in the beginning was the letter "O" and its breathful sound. The poem is itself the unified and musical cry (as in the pun on "air") of the body and the mind-spirit, truly a "marriage of flesh and air."

William Carlos Williams' "The Sea-Elephant," is a poem spoken by a variety of voices. We hear the voice of a circus barker, an animal trainer, a lady at the circus, the sea-elephant, the poet-narrator, and the partially remembered voice of an anonymous poet returning from the distant past.

Trundles from
the strangeness of the sea —
a kind of
heaven-

bearded
to the surface-and
the only
sense out of them

Ladies and Gentlemen!
the greatest
sea-monster ever exhibited
alive

is that woman's
Yes
it's wonderful but they
ought to

the gigantic
sea-elephant-O wallow
of flesh where
are

put it back into the sea where
it came from.
Blouaugh!

there fish enough for
that
appetite stupidity
cannot lessen?

Swing-ride
walk
on wires-toss balls
stoop and

Sick of April's smallness
the little
leaves

contort yourselves-
But I
am love. I am
from the sea-

Flesh has lief of you

enormous sea
Speak!
Blouaugh! (feed

me) my
flesh is riven-
fish after fish into his maw
unswallowing

to let them glide down
gulching back
half spittle half
brine

the
troubled eyes-torn
from the sea.
(In

a practical voice) They
ought
to put it back where
it came from.

Gape.
Strange head-
told by old sailors-
rising

Blouaugh!
there is no crime save
the too heavy
body

the Sea
held playfully-comes
to the surface
the water

boiling
about the head the cows
scattering
fish dripping from

the bounty
of . . . and Spring
the way
Spring is icummen in-

The two primary voices, however, are those of the sea-elephant who cries out in frustration, hunger and desire, and the poet-narrator who in effect translates the sea-elephant's expressive sounds into the language of conceptual speech as when the poet as circus trainer says, "Speak!" and the sea-elephant replies "Blouaugh," which the poet then interprets as "feed / me."

The sea-elephant's "Blouaugh" suggests the primal cry out of which, eventually, all speech will come. We hear an echoing resemblance of its sliding "O" vowel in the poet's exclamation, "O wallow / of flesh," even before the sea-elephant speaks in the poem. The sea-elephant is on show, but so too is Williams in composing his poem; both in a sense are out of their element and have to struggle to perform in a new medium, the sea-elephant on land, the poet in language. For the poet, identifying himself with the sea-elephant as a fellow creature, only language heightened into poetic design can lighten the weight of the "too heavy / body." The "crime" of flesh, its voracious hungers, requires relief through the expression of itself in voice and finally in poetry.

Like the sea-elephant out of the sea which has been for him "a kind of heaven," since it gives buoyancy to his body, human consciousness alienates us from the demands of our bodies, our unappeasable "appetite." For the poet that alienation may be overcome through his sympathetic and accepting identification with the sea-elephant, an emblem of his bodily desires. So too their languages must merge into one, equally concrete and abstract. The poet's conceptual, declarative statement, "But I / am love," speaks for both himself and the sea-elephant. This identification becomes explicit in the following line, "I am / from the sea," and reminds the reader of the common evolutionary heritage of all creatures. Thus the repeated cry, "Blouaugh!" also belongs to both the sea-elephant and the poet as it exists simultaneously as bodily cry and metaphorical word. Expressing the carnal and the mental need for satisfaction and love, the poet's human language is both voice and meaning, both physical gesture and idea.

At the end of the poem, the poet-narrator describes the sea-elephant in his natural element, water, evoking again the imagery of his appetite for food and love as he "comes / to the surface / the water / boiling about the head the cows / scattering / fish dripping." This power of appetite and desire is the creature's "bounty," as the variety of conjured voices, gathered together by the poem, have been the poet's bounty, his circus performance of verbal images as if he were balancing "on wires" or "toss[ing] balls." This final description, "fish dripping from / the bounty / of . . ." slows down and breaks off into a sigh or a deep pause, a silence. At that moment the cultural past of poetic tradition floods back into his mind so that the poet speaks not only in a creature's voice, not only in his own voice, but in a voice recalling the long history of poetry and of desire. The poem cannot end by drifting off into silence as the ellipses suggests, for as Williams says in "Asphodel that Greeny Flower," "Silence can be complex too, / but you do not get far / with silence. / Begin again."

So Williams' poem begins again at the end, out of silence, returning to the thought of "Spring" and an early memory of the tradition of poetry in English. His own contemporary voice merges with a voice from the past, just as his human voice merged with the animal voice of the sea-elephant. The design of the poem, gathering these separate voices together, is itself a single metaphor, both making connections and expressing the idea of connectedness and continuity. The human voice of words and sounds, surrounding and giving shape to silence, fixed in the poem's design, is the metaphor that also creates the continuity between Nature and Art, as if Nature had found a voice in which she could express herself. Although the "rest is silence" into which our lives will vanish, the moment of art may realize and thus make real the illusion of life as extended and intensified, an illusion in which we see ourselves truly as our own metaphorical creation.

A poem is of the body as much as of the mind; a poem is physical as the human voice is physical. It comes from the chest and the throat and the lips and the tongue and the teeth. It is fast or slow, loud or soft, steady or wavering; it embodies sobs and sighs and laughter. As Stevens says, the poem of the mind "is a violence from within that protects us from a violence without. It is the imagination pressing back against the pressure of reality. It seems, in the last analysis, to have something to do with our self-preservation; and that, no doubt, is why the expression of it, the sound of its words, helps us to live our lives." It is not just the words that help, but also the *sound* of the words, the words as voice, the voice as physical utterance. "The poem is the cry of its occasion," Stevens rightly insists, whether that occasion be sorrowful or joyous.

When Goethe's Faust looks into his soul and sees a fundamental division there, a longing for both heaven and earth, his anguish spills over from his words into his cry, "Ach!": "Zwei Seelen wohnen, ach!, in diese Brust." And when Gerard Manley Hopkins envisions the descent of the Holy Ghost in the image of the dawn, figured as a dove, his ecstasy is given voice, beyond intellectual formulation, in the prolonged, breathful cry of an "Ah!" breaking into the midst of the final phrase of the poem: "Because the holy ghost over the bent / World broods with warm breath, and with Ah! bright wings." And at the end, at the edge of a final silence, when King Lear kneels over the body of hanged Cordelia, even though his reason knows that she is dead — "And thou no breath at all? Thou'lt come no more." — mercifully Lear has the illusion that he sees her lips stir, and his outcry then constitutes his final lines in the play: "Look on her! look! her lips / Look there, look there! O. O. O. O." We, as audience, cannot tell whether it is joy or grief or some inscrutable combination of the two that breaks his heart and releases him from the rack of the world — just as Gloucester died, "his flawed heart . . . Twixt two extemes of passion, joy and grief, / Burst smilingly."

Lear moves beyond us into some ultimate emotion; so too his language moves beyond words into pure sounds and silence — silence which is both the end and the beginning of speech. Silence as nothing and silence as replete with emotional implication, just as the fool had said to Lear early in Act I, "Now thou art an O without a figure. I am better than thou art now; I am a fool, thou art nothing." Having borne witness to Lear emerging from the O of nothing into the mysterious fullness of his final "O. O. O. O," we are left behind, with Edgar, to console ourselves, to find the words to live by — not merely the meaning of words, but the sounds of their emotions, the voice and cry of the human heart. Edgar says:

> The weight of this sad time we must obey;
> Speak what we feel, not what we ought to say.

This plea for the merging of feeling and language is a plea, finally, for metaphorical speech.

Denise Levertov

On the Function of the Line

Not only hapless adolescents, but many gifted and justly es-
teemed poets writing in contemporary nonmetrical forms, have
only the vaguest concept, and the most haphazard use, of the line.
Yet there is at our disposal no tool of the poetic craft more important, none that yields more subtle and precise effects, than the
line break if it is properly understood.

If I say that its function in the development of modern poetry
in English is evolutionary I do not mean to imply that I consider
modern, nonmetrical poetry "better" or "superior" to the great
poetry of the past, which I love and honor. That would obviously
be absurd. But I do feel that there are few poets today whose
sensibility naturally expresses itself in the traditional forms (except for satire or pronounced irony), and that those who do so are
somewhat anachronistic. The closed, contained quality of such
forms has less relation to the relativistic sense of life which un-
avoidably prevails in the late twentieth century than modes that
are more exploratory, more open-ended. A sonnet may end with a
question; but its essential, underlying structure arrives at *conclusion*. "Open forms" do not necessarily terminate inconclusively,
but their degree of conclusion is — structurally, and thereby ex-
pressively — less pronounced, and partakes of the open quality of
the whole. They do not, typically, imply a dogmatic certitude;
whereas, under a surface, perhaps, of individual doubts, the
structure of the sonnet or the heroic couplet bears witness to the
certitudes of these forms' respective epochs of origin. The forms

more apt to express the sensibility of our age are the exploratory, open ones.

In what way is contemporary, non-metrical poetry exploratory? What I mean by that word is that such poetry, more than most poetry of the past, incorporates and reveals the *process* of thinking/feeling, feeling/thinking, rather than focusing more exclusively on its *results;* and in so doing it explores (or can explore) human experience in a way that is not wholly new but is (or can be) valuable in its subtle difference of approach: valuable both as human testimony and as aesthetic experience. And the crucial precision tool for creating this exploratory mode is the line-break. The most obvious function of the line-break is rhythmic: it can record the slight (but meaningful) hesitations between word and word that are characteristic of the mind's dance among perceptions but which are not noted by grammatical punctuation. Regular punctuation is a part of regular sentence structure, that is, of the expression of completed thoughts; and this expression is typical of prose, even though prose is not at all times bound by its logic. But in poems one has the opportunity not only, as in expressive prose, to depart from the syntactic norm, but to make manifest, by an intrinsic structural means, the interplay or counterpoint of process and completion — in other words, to present the dynamics of perception *along with* its arrival at full expression. The line-break is a form of punctuation *additional* to the punctuation that forms part of the logic of completed thoughts. Line-breaks — together with intelligent use of indentation and other devices of scoring — represent a peculiarly *poetic,* a-logical, parallel (not competitive) punctuation.

What is the nature of the a-logical pauses the line-break records? If readers will think of their own speech, or their silent inner monologue, when describing thoughts, feelings, perceptions, scenes or events, they will, I think, recognize that they frequently hesitate — albeit very briefly — as if with an unspoken question — a "what?" or a "who?" or a "how?" — before nouns, adjectives, verbs, adverbs, none of which require to be preceded by a comma or other regular punctuation in the course of syntactic logic. To incorporate these pauses in the rhythmic structure of the poem can do several things: for example, it allows the reader to share more intimately the experience that is being articulated; and by introducing an a-logical counter-rhythm into the logical rhythm of syntax it causes, as they interact, an effect closer to song than to statement, closer to dance than to walking. Thus the emotional experience of empathy or identification plus the sonic complexity of the language structure synthesize in an intense aesthetic order that is different from that which is received from a poetry in which metric forms are combined with logical syntax alone. (Of course, the management of the line in *metrical* forms may also permit the recording of such a-logical pauses; Gerard Manley Hopkins provides an abundance of evidence for that. But Hopkins, in this as in other matters, seems to be "the exception that proves the rule"; and the alliance of metric forms and the similarly "closed" or "complete" character of logical syntax seems natural and appropriate, inversions notwithstanding. Inversions of normal prose word order were, after all, a stylistic convention, adopted from choice, not technical ineptitude, for centuries; although if utilized after a certain date they strike one as admissions of lack of skill, and indeed are the first signs of the waning of a tradition's viability.) It is not that the dance of a-logical thinking/feeling in process *cannot* be registered in metric forms, but rather that to do so seems to go against the natural grain of such forms, to be a forcing of an intractable medium into inappropriate use — whereas the potential for such use is implicit in the constantly evolving nature of open forms.

But the most particular, precise, and exciting function of the line-break, and the least understood, is its effect on the *melos* of the poem. It is in this, and not only in rhythmic effects, that its greatest potential lies, both in the exploration of areas of human consciousness and in creating new aesthetic experiences. How do the line-breaks affect the melodic element of a poem? So simply that it seems amazing that this aspect of their function is disregarded — yet not only student poetry workshops but any magazine or anthology of contemporary poetry provides evidence of a general lack of understanding of this factor; and even when individual poets manifest an intuitive sense of how to break their lines it seems rarely to be accompanied by any theoretical comprehension of what they've done right. Yet it is not hard to demonstrate to students that — given that the deployment of the poem on the page is regarded as a score, that is, as the visual instructions for auditory effects — the way the lines are broken affects not only rhythm but pitch patterns.

Rhythm can be sounded on a monotone, a single pitch; melody is the result of pitch patterns combined with rhythmic patterns. The way in which line-breaks, observed, respectfully, as a part of a score (and regarded as, say, roughly a half-comma in duration), determine the pitch pattern of a sentence, can clearly be seen if a poem, or a few lines of it, is written out in a variety of ways (changing the line-breaks but nothing else) and read aloud. Take, for instance, these lines of my own (picked at random):

Crippled with desire, he questioned it.
Evening upon the heights, juice of the pomegranate:
who could connect it with sunlight?

From "4 Embroideries: II, Red Snow"

Read them aloud. Now try reading the same words aloud from this
score:

Crippled with desire, he
questioned it. Evening
upon the heights,
juice of the pomegranate:
who
could connect it with sunlight?

Or

Crippled
with desire, he questioned
it. Evening
upon the heights, juice
of the pomegranate:
who could
connect it with sunlight?

The intonation, the ups and downs of the voice, involuntarily
change as the rhythm (altered by the place where the tiny pause or
musical "rest" takes place) changes. These changes could be recorded in graph form by some instrument, as heartbeats or brain
waves are graphed. The point is not whether the lines, as I wrote
them, are divided in the best possible way; as to that, readers must
judge for themselves. I am simply pointing out that, read naturally
but with respect for the line-break's fractional pause, a pitch
pattern change *does occur* with each variation of lineation. A
beautiful example of expressive lineation is William Carlos Williams's
well-known poem about the old woman eating plums.

They taste good to her.
They taste good
to her. They taste
good to her.

"To a poor old woman"

First the statement is made; then the word *good* is (without the clumsy overemphasis a change of typeface would give) brought to the center of our (and her) attention for an instant; then the word *taste* is given similar momentary prominence, with "good" sounding on a new note, reaffirmed — so that we have first the general recognition of well-being, then the intensification of that sensation, then its voluptuous location in the sense of taste. And all this is presented through indicated pitches, that is, by melody, not by rhythm alone.

I have always been thrilled by the way in which the musicality of a poem could arise from what I called "fidelity to experience," but it took me some time to realize what the mechanics of such precision were as they related to this matter of pitch pattern. The point is that, just as vowels and consonants affect the music of poetry not by mere euphony but by expressive, significant interrelationship, so the nuances of meaning apprehended in variations of pitch create *significant, expressive melody,* not just a pretty "tune" in the close tone-range of speech.

One of the ways in which many poets reveal their lack of awareness about the function of the line-break is the way in which they will begin a line with the word "it," for instance, even when it is clear from the context that they don't want the extra emphasis — relating to both rhythm and pitch — this gives it. Thus, if one writes,

He did not know
it, but at his very moment
his house was burning,

the word "it" is given undue importance. Another example is given in my second variant of the lines from "Red Snow." The "it" in the third line is given a prominence entirely without significance — obtrusive and absurd. When a poet places a word meaninglessly from the sonic point of view it seems clear that he or she doesn't understand the effect of doing so — or is confusedly tied to the idea of "enjambment." Enjambment is useful in preventing the monotony of too many end-stopped lines in a metrical poem, but the desired variety can be attained by various other means in contemporary open forms; and to take away from the contemporary line its fractional pause (which, as I've said, represents, or rather manifests, a comparable minuscule but affective hesitation in the thinking/feeling process) is to rob a precision tool of its principal use. Often the poet unsure of any principle according to which to end a line will write as if the real break comes after the first word of the next line, e.g.,

> As children in their night
> gowns go upstairs . . . ,

where *if one observes the score* an awkward and inexpressive "rest"
occurs between two words that the poet, reading aloud, links
naturally as "nightgowns." X. J. Kennedy's definition of a run-on
line is that "it does not end in punctuation and therefore is read
with only a *slight pause* after it," whereas "if it ends in a full pause
— usually indicated by some mark of punctuation — we call it *end-
stopped*" (my italics on "slight pause"). Poets who write nonmetrical poems but treat the line-break as nonexistent are not even
respecting the traditional "slight pause" of the end-stopped line.
The fact is, they are confused about what the line is at all, and
consequently some of our best and most influential poets have
increasingly turned to the prose paragraph for what I feel are the
wrong reasons — less from a sense of the peculiar virtues of the
prose poem than from a despair of making sense of the line.

One of the important virtues of comprehending the function
of the line-break, that is, of the line itself, is that such comprehension by no means causes poets to write like one another. It is a
tool, not a style. As a tool, its use can be incorporated into any
style. Students in a workshop who grasp the idea of accurate scoring do not begin to all sound alike. Instead, each one's individual
voice sounds more clearly, because each one has gained a degree
of control over how they want a poem to sound. Sometimes a
student scores a poem one way on paper, but reads it aloud differently. My concern — and that of his or her fellow students once
they have understood the problem — is to determine which way
the author wants the poem to sound. Someone will read it back to
him or her as written and someone else will point out the ways in
which the text, the score, was ignored in the reading. "Here you
ran on," "Here you paused, but it's in the middle of a line and
there's no indication for a 'rest' there." Then the student poet can
decide, or feel out, whether he or she wrote it down wrong but
read it right, or vice versa. That decision is a very personal one and
has quite as much to do with the individual sensibility of the
writer and the unique character of the experience embodied in the
words of the poem, as with universally recognizable rationality,
though that may play a part, too. The outcome, in any case, is
rather to define and clarify individual voices than to homogenize
them; because *reasons* for halts and checks, emphases and expressive pitch changes, will be as various as the persons writing. Com-

prehension of the function of the line-break gives to each unique creator the power to be more precise, and thereby more, not less, individuated. The voice thus revealed will be not necessarily the recognizable "outer" one heard in poets who have taken Olson's "breath" theory all too literally, but rather the inner voice, the voice of each one's solitude made audible and singing to the multitude of other solitudes.

Excess of subjectivity (and hence incommunicability) in the making of structural decisions in open forms is a problem only when the writer has an inadequate form sense. When the written score precisely notates perceptions, a whole — an inscape or gestalt — begins to emerge; and the gifted writer is not so submerged in the parts that the sum goes unseen. The sum is objective — relatively, at least; it has presence, character, and — as it develops — needs. The parts of the poem are instinctively adjusted in some degree to serve the needs of the whole. And as this adjustment takes place, excess subjectivity is avoided. Details of a private, as distinct from personal, nature may be deleted, for example, in the interests of a fuller, clearer, more communicable whole. (By private I mean those which have associations for the writer that are inaccessible to readers without a special explanation from the writer which does not form part of the poem; whereas the personal, though it may incorporate the private, has an energy derived from associations that are shareable with the reader and *are* so shared within the poem itself.)

Another way to approach the problem of subjective/objective is to say that while traditional modes provide certain standards for objective comparison and evaluation of poems as effective structures, (technically, at any rate) open forms, used with comprehension of their technical opportunities, *build unique contexts* which likewise provide for such evaluation. In other words, though the "rightness" of its lines can't be judged by a preconceived method of scansion, each such poem, if well written, presents a composed whole in which false lines (or other lapses) can be heard by any attentive ear — not as failing to conform to an external rule, but as failures to contribute to the grace or strength implicit in a system peculiar to that poem, and stemming from the inscape of which it is the verbal manifestation.

The *melos* of metrical poetry was not easy of attainment, but there were guidelines and models, even if in the last resort nothing could substitute for the gifted "ear." The *melos* of open forms is even harder to study if we look for models; its secret lies not in models but in that "fidelity to experience" of which I have written elsewhere; and, in turn, that fidelity demands a delicate and precise comprehension of the technical means at our disposal. A general recognition of the primary importance of the line and of the way in which rhythm relates to melody would be useful to the state of the art of poetry in the way general acceptance of the bar line and other musical notations were useful to the art of music. A fully adequate latitude in the matter of interpretation of a musical score was retained (as anyone listening to different pianists playing the same sonata, for instance, can hear) but at the same time the composer acquired a finer degree of control. Only if writers agree about the nature and function of this tool can readers fully co-operate, so that the poem shall have the fullest degree of autonomous life.

Marvin Bell

The "Technique" of Re-Reading

God knows, there exist more techniques for writing than are usually acknowledged. Probably, each of us uses a hundred or more all at the same time. Some of them may occur before a word is put to paper. For example, you go for a walk because you have noticed that afterwards you feel like writing. Or you stay up extra late at night because you have noticed that after midnight you somehow elude the more banal levels of rationality. Or you begin to get up earlier than the rest of the family because you have noticed that, by afternoon, the poetry you might have written has gone into caring for the children. Or you sharpen twelve pencils because a better first line seems to emerge after a little stalling. Or you use a fountain pen, or a typewriter, or examination bluebooks or yellow paper or lined pads, or a quill pen. You smoke or drink coffee. You don't smoke or drink coffee. Like Hart Crane, you drink cheap wine and play Ravel's "Bolero" on the phonograph. You walk about. You pull your hair. You eat your beard. You sit in the corner of the cafeteria during lunch hours. You sit at the kitchen table after breakfast. You hide in a studio out back in which you scheme to build a trap door and a tunnel to the sewers of Paris. These are "Writing Techniques." If you are lucky and talented, you may not need much else. You will be able to do your best work by following the method suggested for writers by W.M. Persig in *Zen and the Art of Motorcycle Maintenance:* "Make yourself perfect and then write naturally."

Certainly, that seems a worthy goal: gradually to replace labor with inspiration, to achieve in maturity that condition in which poetry arrives as easily, as Keats would have it, as leaves to trees.

In the meantime, which is where most of us find ourselves, we need among our stores of writing techniques a method for noticing the little things in language, and for seeing how others did, consciously or unconsciously, all that we hope to do later by nature.

That method is re-reading. Not reading but *re*-reading. We all know readers who have looked their way through great libraries of books without absorbing any. On first reading, such readers may experience a poem as fully as any of us, but their experience of the poem is perforce limited to the least experience of reading and to the associations a text may stir as one's thoughts wander.

Reading as a writer is another matter. Language is a reflexive medium, even for the most unconscious of poets. In addition, writing usually assumes a strong linear base — one word at a time. Self-reflexive and linear, a poem read once has not been fully read. To learn from language itself and from poetry, we think about *how* it says what it says, as well as *what* it says. You must know and, knowing, you must be able to say. If you cannot say it, you probably don't know it.

There is another side to this. Learning to re-read your own work and others' is an absolute necessity because it is crucial to those of you who intend to go on writing that you learn how to continue to educate yourselves in the absence of teachers. Everyone knows that conferee in search of answers which would at once kick his or her writing up a level. In applications to the program in which I teach, we sometimes note that an applicant has studied with A through M in school, and also N through Z for periods of a week or two during summers. Teaching *can* make a difference, but only for the essentially self-reliant.

Sometimes a student brings me poems that have already been discussed by another teacher. In such cases, the poet must be taking votes, right? "The other guy said this poem was bad but you like it, so it must be a good poem after all." Or, "The other guy liked it, so what does it matter if you don't? I was just checking your taste."

I get questions about revising poems that are based on there being a "correct" way to say a thing, or to lineate a free verse poem, or to begin or conclude or . . . But you know the questions. Not one of them has an answer. The plain truth is that, except for mistakes that can be checked in the dictionary, almost nothing is right or wrong. Writing poems out of the desire to find a way to be right, not wrong, is the garden path to dullness.

You have to learn to learn, if you're serious about writing. It's not that hard. First, you should realize that no teacher is ever going to tell you all that he or she knows. Second, however much he or she tells, you will only hear as much of what is said as you are able to at the moment. You can take from a given teacher a few tricks, perhaps one or two ways of writing, but what you might better seek beyond that, for the long haul, is an attitude toward writing and an attitude toward how to read as a writer.

Reading as a writer is not the same as reading as a non-writer. The writer is looking for what he or she can use. The writer reads on the edge of his or her chair. The writer goes slowly, and doubles back.

Teachers were my teachers when I went to school, but poems have been my teachers since. I don't say *books,* but poems — one by one. Reading, or perhaps just scanning, entire books of poems is what the critic does when he or she discusses style and theme. In an ideal world, I sometimes think, we would not review books at all — as if individual poems did not have content. We would write reviews of single poems. Come to think of it, sometimes students do that. Is it possible that students are smarter than reviewers?

Nor need you wait to be "tempted," like they say, to re-read poems. Poems are not movies; one doesn't lie back in the dark and demand stimulation. You go forward. At least, you lean a little. In part, that's what poetry is: a quality you experience because you pay it a special attention.

Richard Wilbur's poem "The Writer" is an accomplishment of sanity and intelligence. It is also a fine example of how one small move in the language can lead to others and how poetic showmanship can lead to serious concern.

THE WRITER

In her room at the prow of the house
Where light breaks, and the windows are tossed with
    linden,
My daughter is writing a story.

I pause in the stairwell, hearing
From her shut door a commotion of typewriter-keys
Like a chain hauled over a gunwale.

Young as she is, the stuff
Of her life is a great cargo, and some of it heavy:
I wish her a lucky passage.

But now it is she who pauses,
As if to reject my thought and its easy figure.
A stillness greatens, in which

The whole house seems to be thinking,
And then she is at it again with a bunched clamor
Of strokes, and again is silent.

I remember the dazed starling
Which was trapped in that very room, two years ago;
How we stole in, lifted a sash

And retreated, not to affright it;
And how for a helpless hour, through the crack of the
      door,
We watched the sleek, wild, dark

And iridescent creature
Batter against the brilliance, drop like a glove
To the hard floor, or the desk-top,

And wait then, humped and bloody,
For the wits to try it again; and how our spirits
Rose when suddenly sure,

It lifted off from a chair-back,
Beating a smooth course for the right window
And clearing the sill of the world.

It is always a matter, my darling,
Of life or death, as I had forgotten. I wish
What I wished you before, but harder.

Wilbur's poem is accentual — three stresses apiece in the first and third lines of each stanza, and five apiece in the middle lines — but I haven't chosen it to discuss meter. Rather, I'd like to look at how it begins, continues and ends.

That's a simple enough first line, isn't it? *We* can write that, can't we? Imagine yourself writing it out: "In her room at the front of the house . . ." No, not "front," but "prow." One word has been changed in a phrase any of us might utter over coffee or on the telephone. Instead of "her room at the front of the house," Wilbur says, "at the *prow* of the house."

Why? Well, any reason will do, and it's possible that the poet simply thought to jazz it up a bit, to be figurative because poetry derives at times from figurative language and because this poet has a talent for making figures. It's even possible that the poet's house vaguely resembles a boat in its shape. My own suspicion is that this is simply one more example of a poet using what comes to mind. Wilbur is a sailor; he served in the Navy; he vacations in Key West on the Atlantic. To him it's natural to identify the front of a house with the prow of a boat.

Lines two and three announce the place and the plot. What could be more straightforward? "My daughter is writing a story." And what could be more natural but that the proud father, a writer himself, pause in the stairwell to listen? He stands outside her door and hears the typewriter going, and how does he describe it? First, as "a commotion of typewriter-keys." That's more figure-making, at first blush an elementary sort, the kind of prepositional phrase figure-making we were asked to list on the blackboard in grade school — an "enigma of elephants," and so forth — except that this one contains nothing made-up. What he hears is, in fact, a noisy commotion, in which the clamor of the keys additionally seems to express the commotion of the creative turmoil going on inside her room.

Here Wilbur decides to extend the figure with a simile. Well, the poem must continue to listen to itself and to give visible in-dications of listening to itself. Hence, having likened the front of the house to the prow of a boat, he chooses another nautical item to which to liken the sound of the typewriter: the sound of a chain being hauled over a gunwale. Is she, then, pulling up anchor?

Stanza three, likewise, is witty and showy. If the house is a ship, why then her life in it carries cargo, some of it heavy, and one may wish her a lucky passage — both in her story and on the seas of life. That's easy: serious but easy.

The poem is still listening — re-reading — itself. And what has it heard so far? It has heard a proud father saying the usual things, albeit with grace and flair. And so we come to the second part of this poem, in which the father will realize how casually one may say good luck. Please notice, by the way, that he didn't write, "But now it is she who pauses, to reject my thought and its easy figure." No, that would have been mere fancy. He can't know what the silence means, and so he writes, "*as if* to reject my thought and its easy figure." His simile was an easy figure for her typing; his metaphor was an easy figure for her writing and her life; *he* is, likewise, an easy figure pausing for a moment outside her door, calm against the clamor of her keys.

At this point in the poem, it might seem that there is nothing further to say, at least not if one is able to resist the siren call of one's abstract ideas and bald statements of feeling. It is time to look elsewhere, and the poet looks, as poets will, into memory. For when the poem listens to itself, the poet has been listening to *himself,* and listening to oneself is itself an act of listening to the past. Language can eat the future but it lives off the past.

He remembers a trapped bird, in that very room it happens, who had to try and try. When it fell, he tells us, it fell "like a glove," sometimes to the "desk-top," and one thinks of the writer's hand slumping from the keys to the desk in between sentences. But there is more to the parallel. The bird grew humped and bloody in its effort. Its success in getting out of that room depended on its wits, or brains, and it had to learn the hard way on its own.

Finally, it makes it, "clearing the sill of the . . . window." No, the "sill of the *world.*" If we didn't get it, we do now: his daughter's writing a story is part of her growing up and away. She too will someday clear the sill of their world: the world of the family and of her room at the prow of the house.

Guess what? This is serious business after all. The triumph of this poem, the big thing which depends on all the little things along the way, lies in the speaker, the father, taking his daughter more and more seriously. Finally, he says it: "It is always a matter, my darling, of life or death, as I had forgotten. I wish what I wished you before, but harder." One thing that poems do is to give a phrase or sentence or thought more meaning. Or to find out how much more it meant all along. "I wish what I wished you before, but harder."

When I re-read this poem, I see many reassuring things for a writer. I see that simple details can have meaning beyond furnishing a world or telling a story. I see that the past may relate to the present and vice-versa. I see that what begins in word-play may end in honor. I see again how the very essence of a poem may be to arrive at that spot at which the speaker may call his daughter his darling.

Okay, that's groundwork. How is my reading of it affected by my being a writer? Primarily, in this way: that, having read it and first been taken by the reality and clarity of its feelings, I go back to see how the poem might have been written. I try to imagine myself freely arriving at the same words, images, associations, thoughts in the same order.

You know, it's a truism that one learns to write by reading. But not necessarily by *wide* reading. Rather, by *deep* reading. One might read a few things over and over, perhaps over a period of years, and so be more lastingly influenced than by a slighter acquaintance with more.

Of course one may read and re-read happily without thinking about it, hoping to learn by intuition, and certainly some poems are less discussable than others. I have a theory — just one of many theories that come and go, depending on the context — that the great achievements of American poetry have been essentially rhetorical, those of rhetoric rather than of image and metaphor, or of imagination, structure and vision. In American poetry, as you all know, great emphasis has been placed on an individual tone of voice. The great Mommas and Daddies of modern poetry in English are enormously distinctive, one from the other. The great generation of American poets now in its fifties and sixties contains individuality of style and tone of voice in profusion. From the late Fifties until the late Sixties, it seemed as if no two books dared to have anything of method in common. Method, mind you, and language, not content, which I dare to say retrospective analysis will find far less individuated than styles among the poets in question. Nonetheless, the Imagists had said that a new cadence meant a new idea, essentially a defense of formalism, whether in traditional forms, variants of them or so-called free verse. Not a new imagination, mind you, a new *idea.* The emphasis on ideas, baldly stated or only insinuated, in American poetry, has meant an emphasis on those aspects of a poem which are essentially rhetorical. The secrets of tone are, for the most part, those of syntax and words without meaning, so-called "function words" which indicate relationships: subordination, coordination, conjunction, opposition, etc. Syntax is logic, or the appearance of it, and a new logic inevitably produces a new tone of voice.

In the classroom, we tend to marvel at rhetoric, and to discuss most freely poems held together by rhetoric, poems in which, however frontal the narrative, however rich in objects, images or metaphors, however insistent the vision, the poem is primarily a set of rhetorical maneuvers.

It is harder, much much harder, to learn from poems which skip that rhetorical level, and which present themselves as associational texts in which the reasoning is in between the lines, while the lines themselves present only the emblems of experience and, sometimes, of epiphany.

TO THE SAGUARO CACTUS TREE
IN THE DESERT RAIN

I had no idea the elf owl
Crept into you in the secret
Of night.

I have torn myself out of many bitter places
In America, that seemed
Tall and green-rooted in mid-noon.
I wish I were the spare shadow
Of the roadrunner, I wish I were
The honest lover of the diamondback
And the tear the tarantula weeps.

I had no idea you were so tall
and blond in moonlight.

I got thirsty in the factories,
And I hated the brutal dry suns there,
So I quit.

You were the shadow
Of a hallway
In me.

I have never gone through that door,
But the elf owl's face
Is inside me.

Saguaro,
You are not one of the gods.

Your green arms lower and gather me.
I am an elf owl's shadow, a secret
Member of your family.

James Wright's poem may seem "farther out" than Wilbur's "The Writer." Its images seem to lie on the page as if disconnected, each from each. If by rhetoric the poem establishes its tone of voice and hints at connections, nowhere do we come on anything so bold as, "It is always a matter, my darling, of life or death, as I had forgotten." Instead we get, "I have never gone through that door, but the elf owl's face is inside me."

Look back at the first three lines. From the writer's point of view — that is, from the point of view of a thief — what's to notice? The basic sentence is a simple statement of fact: the elf owl creeps into the saguaro at night. But Wright says "secret" of night. "Secret" is one of James Wright's words. It shows up often in his last three books. From its recurrent use we can see that it holds symbolic and visionary overtones for Wright, much like certain words in the poems of Emily Dickinson: such words as "grace," "noon," "seal," "purple" and "circumference." From the canon of Wright's poetry we might see that his use of the word "secret" arises from a fierce belief that a man's life is something inside, out of view of others, not one's public life at all — something private, personal and intimate. But of course you don't have to know any of that. The phrase here, "secret of night," makes perfect sense all by itself. Night is the great cover. The elf owl *creeps* secretively into the tree.

The other tiny "extra" in what would otherwise be a plain sentence of desert lore is the rhetorical maneuver at the start: "I had no idea." That's immediate involvement: the voice of the poem is at once strong and engaged. A stance has been taken. While such small maneuvers may come to be second nature to any one of us, using them is quite as much a matter of technique as is calling a part of one's house by the name for a part of a boat.

From here on, the poem will be an expression of increasing identification with the elf owl. Wright says that he has had to tear himself away from many places that seemed to be, like the cactus tree that is home to the elf owl, tall and green-rooted. But they were not. Like Whitman, he thinks he could turn and live with the animals; he wishes he were something of nature without the self-consciousness of a man. But, being a man, he wasn't able to live in a cactus tree. His desert was that of the factories where he worked and quit.

Still, there is in each of us a secret life. A life in which we identify with the elf owl and in which we see ourselves living at night in a cactus tree in the welcome desert rain. And so he says, addressing the tree, "You were the shadow / Of a hallway / In me." And while, being a man, he has never gone through that door, he can say of himself that he carries the elf owl's face inside.

The poem listens to itself. That is how it arrives at tall and green-rooted places in mid-noon, to echo and parallel a cactus tree in the desert. That is how it finds its way to factories which are themselves scorched deserts.

But the poem does not merely repeat itself. Try out the last stanza without its second line. Without "You are not one of the gods," it would merely be more of the same. What is added? For one thing, in case you were wondering, no, he is not according the tree divinity. Moreover, it contains a certain insistence on facts and this world, the sort of insistence we saw four lines earlier when he said, "I have never gone through that door." Without such moves, a poem turns into mere fancy: a story, say, about a man who could live inside a cactus and talk to elf owls. No; it is not a story at all, but an expression of a secret identification and a longing to be naturally at home.

From the first time I came upon this poem, it held my interest as a writer. Wright, as you probably know, began writing as a formalist, indebted to the poems of Edwin Arlington Robinson. With the book, *The Branch Will Not Break,* his writing underwent a sea-change, apparently influenced by his reading and translating of Spanish poets and the German expressionist poet, Georg Trakl. Thereafter, Wright was always said to be a surrealistic image-maker. In later books, he put back the open rhetoric he had forsaken in *The Branch Will Not Break* but continued also to write great flourishes of surrealistic imagery. In this poem to the saguaro, the landscape is made surreal — it helps to be in the desert among The Friends of Salvador Dali — but it is not fanciful. Everything here is real.

We should all, I would think, want to be able to write such lines as "You were the shadow / Of a hallway / In me," and "I am an elf owl's shadow, a secret / Member of your family." It may help, therefore, to notice how Wright gets to such lines and fills them with meaning. You don't get to "You were the *shadow* of a hallway in me" unless you first see in the cactus tree a hallway for an elf owl. One of the things poems do is add meaning to what has already been said: "I wish what I wished you before, but harder."

Now pause a moment over the last two lines of the poem. There are the words "shadow" and "secret" again. Are the images in these lines just vague emotional equivalents to the speaker's feelings, or do they make sense based on what "shadow" and "secret" meant when he used them earlier? I'll put it in terms of simple logic: if the cactus tree was a hallway to the elf owl in the desert, and was therefore the shadow of a hallway to the worker in the hot factories, then the worker can become the shadow of the elf owl. Each is a part of the other. The elf owl doesn't live exclusively in the cool tree but also in the burning desert. Indeed, he "creeps" into the tree, a secret act in the night. Nor does the worker's entire life take place in the brutal light of factories. He has his naturally cool places, his secret life. The living elf owl and the living man are one, more so than the speaker realized, perhaps, when he wished openly to be the shadow of the roadrunner, the lover of the diamondback, and the tear wept by the tarantula. He is, in a sense, all of those things — the more so if he knows it. If the green arms of the saguaro do not lower and gather him *in fact,* in his mind he is able to rise to embrace them and to affirm his identification with all the world and with all its forms of life.

Sometimes, at the end of a poem, the world is larger and the speaker is less alone.

After awhile, James Wright started to write pieces of short prose. He explained that he "wanted to learn to write prose." Are they prose or prose-poetry, or are they poems that happen to have been set down in paragraphs? I would say that it is a sign of the times — some would say a bad sign, others would say a good sign — that we need not linger on the question. Our various technical definitions and technical standards for poetry have been greatly added to by a larger, untechnical standard and definition based on the quality of imagination in poetry, and on what we might call "poetic structure": how the writer moves from one thing to another and how meaning is apprehended, enlarged or diminished.

Our American poetry, and the ways in which we speak about it, have been changed in the last ten to fifteen years not as much by the examples of our own best poets or by those who have been brought to our shores from other English-speaking countries aboard barrages of East Coast publicity as much as by poetry in translation. Not just the finest, most considered and most accurate translations (for example, Mark Strand's translations of Alberti and Andrade, or Charles Simic's versions of Vasko Popa, or Alastair Reid's of Pablo Neruda, or translations of Zbigniew Herbert by Czeslaw Milosz and Peter Dale Scott, or Edmund Keeley and George Savidis' versions of Cavafy) — not just the finest and also most accurate, but also those which, like Ezra Pound's translations of Li Po, take liberties with literal accuracy to render, perhaps even exaggerate, the spirit of the poem (for example, Robert Bly's versions of Neruda, Lorca, Jiménez, Rumi, Rilke, Martinson, Ekelop, Tranströmer and so many others, and W.S. Merwin's translations from both Eastern and Western languages) — and not just the very best of the anthologies of poetry in translation (of which I will mention Mark Strand and Charles Simic's *Another Republic,* Czeslaw Milosz's *Postwar Polish Poetry,* Hardie St. Martin's *Roots and Wings: Poetry from Spain, 1900-1975,* and that hoary old favorite, perhaps now forgotten, Robert Payne's anthology of Chinese poetry, *The White Pony,* first published in 1947 and seemingly added to on re-publication in 1960) — not only the finest, most accurate, the most conscious of spirit and imagination, nor the best gathered books of translations have influenced us to think more broadly about poetry, but so also have translations by poets who have done merely a little of this or that, using a "pony" and a dictionary to translate a few Persian ghazals or one or two poems by the Spanish poet, Unamuno, say. In every translation, there comes to us a new wave of permission, an increased sense of freedom. Is it because we are forced to abandon our prejudices and personal likes and dislikes if we are to enjoy travel? Is it because other cultures do not share our over-whelmingly technical view of things? Is it because the pressures of empire, even a crumbling empire involved in a desperate holding action, affect our point of view? No doubt it is all these things and others. One thing is certain: every literature has grown fresh, and every great writer been made greater, by writers looking to other cultures and languages for new words and renewed permission.

So, if we look at a short poem by Tomas Tranströmer, trans-lated from the Swedish by Robert Bly, we have to adjust our way of learning. Let's read it.

AFTER A DEATH

Once there was a shock
that left behind a long, shimmering comet tail.
It keeps us inside. It makes the TV pictures snowy.
It settles in cold drops on the telephone wires.

One can still go slowly on skis in the winter sun
through brush where a few leaves hang on.
They resemble pages torn from old telephone
 directories.
Names swallowed by the cold.

It is still beautiful to feel the heart beat
but often the shadow seems more real than the body.
The samurai looks insignificant
beside his armor of black dragon scales.

The poem is titled, "After a Death." One could easily mis-remember it as, "After a Shock," for that is what it is about. It is not an elegy. We are told nothing about the person who has died nor even his name. We read that the death was a shock. There is a mention of television. Perhaps it was someone famous. Perhaps it was an assassination. Perhaps it was the killing of John F. Kennedy. In fact, it was. Tranströmer says so. But I have taken note again and again that he does not say so in the poem nor even offer a dedication or an epigraph *in memoriam.* The poem is more general than that. Indeed, Tranströmer says that an uncle died around the same time and that the deaths combine in the poem. In my mind I contrast it with the American rush to dedicate poems, to mention the names of famous friends and to publish elegies for poets before the ink has dried on their obits.

Of course, our rush to identify and dedicate is not born of bad intentions. We want everything to be particular. We love particulars. We have faith in particulars. We honestly believe that, if we can get the particulars correct and in the right order, our job will be done and the poem complete.

Perhaps we favor particulars in part because our choice has long seemed to lie exclusively between particulars and rhetorical explanation. We therefore, and for important reasons, favor the concrete over the abstract, the particular over the general, presentation over explanation, showing over telling.

Yet so much poetry from other cultures exhibits both the tensile strength of the particular and the active force of the general. How does this happen?

I can notice elements in this Tranströmer poem that line up with the question. Conventionally, we can say that a long, shimmering comet tail is a fine metaphor for the sudden, fiery grief that exploded in front of us when Kennedy was assassinated and then streaked into darkness. Or for any death that comes as a shock. But I notice also the first thing, which is simply the poet's leap into the heavens and then his sudden drop back to earth and the domestic: "It keeps us inside," a wonderful detail; "It makes the TV pictures snowy." Do these things make sense emotionally? Obviously. Do they make sense physically, in the world of current physical theory? Yes, for a comet tail might be thought to affect electronic reception. If it's exaggeration, it only imitates in hyperbole the extreme emotions of shock and grief. And the fourth line — "It settles in cold drops on the telephone wires" — continues the images of difficult communication, messages, all in the air. If the telephone lines themselves sweat cold beads, what effect must the news have on human beings?

Some kind of thinking must have taken place between stanzas one and two. I can imagine it. While the poet was asking himself, unconsciously, "What next?" for his poem, he came to the same question about his subject. For there is nothing notable to say about the anatomy and biology of death which would advance this poem. The rest of the event is only news.

This is another way in which a poem can listen to itself. The poem does not merely listen to itself so that it can gain applause by showing that it did. No, it listens for clues. "What next?" Imagine this. You are sitting at your kitchen table, writing. You have written four lines. You read those four lines as if you were someone else, someone who asks a question or expresses disagreement. Now you know what to say next.

After a shocking death, one can still go out into the same world, on skis if you are in the right country for them, but the world will seem changed. The few leaves hanging on winter brush will resemble pages. And here we notice something perhaps having no basis in the original language of the poem: that the English plural of "leaf" is "leaves." But pages of what? The poem is still paying attention to itself. Remember those telephone wires in line four? "Pages torn from old telephone directories"; hence, "names swallowed by the cold." Cold drops on the wires, names swallowed by the cold, a lump in the throat — as separate as the images may seem when we first come upon them, they live in one neighborhood.

When I look at how the final stanza of this poem begins, I am reminded of the distance between our poets and many of our critics. Few of our critics would care for a line like, "It is still beautiful to feel the heart beat." Half of our poets and most of our critics write as if they believe that, since life ends in death, we are essentially dead. Hence, they believe, sometimes without knowing it, that *any* uncomplicated emotion about life is excessive: therefore, sentimental. If you take away nothing else from this Conference, let me give you this one idea to chew on: Poetry, because it is written by the living to be read by the living, is a way of *life.* It is always about *living,* even in the shadow of death. The samurai's armor of black dragon scales, which Tranströmer saw in the Stockholm Museum, overshadows the swordsman, and the shadow often "seems more real than the body," but it is "still beautiful to feel the heart beat." Without line nine, the poem would be different. Without line nine, it would not be wisdom but complaint.

Now this Tranströmer poem, in translation, does not show a certain vibrancy of language I myself favor, nor a fiercely idiomatic character, nor a sharply etched individual tone. It comes to us in a neutral tone, an impersonal voice, yet I find in it a certain intimacy regardless — perhaps because of the very objects in the poem (tv, telephone, brush and leaves), and perhaps because it asks the question most of *us* would ask, "What next?" And perhaps in part simply because it actually employs the word "us."

And it accomplishes extra meaning in its last sentence, just as the Wilbur and Wright poems did. That the suit of armor dwarfs the samurai might be merely a museum fact, something which moves us to say, "Look at that!" Put where it is in the poem, however, we are more likely to say, *"Think* about that!" Thus the writer has given a detail from a showcase an emotional weight it always possessed but which had to be released by those acts of imagination which preceded it in the poem. I find this quality in poetry from other countries more often than in American poems: the quality, that is, of releasing from objects the emotional force they hold in quiet.

Now I'd like to strengthen or weaken my case, and add a dimension to it, by confessing that I sometimes read, in private, my own poems. And that I read them, after awhile, the same way — to see, as much as is possible, what occurred in the process of writing them.

You might think I ought to have known all that at the time, but what we first do consciously later becomes second nature, and in any case, I believe in inspiration, spontaneity, association, accident and temporary insanity. During the interminable time of a writing block, I employ a rubber stamp which reads, "Temporarily Deceased."

I'll read through "To an Adolescent Weeping Willow."

TO AN ADOLESCENT WEEPING WILLOW

I don't know what you think you're doing,
sweeping the ground. You
do it so easily, backhanded, forehanded.
You hardly bend. Really, you sway.
What can it mean
when a thing is so easy?

I threw dirt on my father's floor.
Not dirt, but a chopped green
dirt which picked up dirt.

I pushed the pushbroom.
I oiled the wooden floor of the store.

He bent over and lifted the coal
into the coalstove. With the back of the shovel
he came down on the rat just topping the bin
and into the fire.

What do you think? — Did he sway?
Did he kiss a rock for luck?
Did he soak up water
and climb into light and turn and turn?

Did he weep and weep in the yard?

Yes, I think he did. Yes,
now I think he did.

So, Willow, you come sweep my floor.
I have no store.
I have a yard. A big yard.

I have a song to weep.
I have a cry.

You who rose up from the dirt,
because I put you there
and like to walk my head in under
your earliest feathery branches —
what can it mean
when a thing is so easy?

It means you are a boy.

Right away, I notice things. It seems to me that this poet did
something sincere but also tricky to start the poem. He challenged
the tree. Even before he told us one thing about it, he got worked
up. Immediate emotion. Condition *Now*. A rhetorical maneuver,
in the idiomatic language of common people, similar to the beginning lines of certain favorite poems by James Wright: "The Old
WPA Swimming Pool in Martins Ferry, Ohio," for example, which
begins, "I am almost afraid / To write down / This thing." Or "To
the Saguaro Cactus Tree in the Desert Rain," which begins, "I had
no *idea* . . . ." Influence? More likely, something of experience and
language held in common but not always welcomed into one's
writing unless, sometimes, one first notices it elsewhere.

I can hear the poem listening to itself, using the rest of the
first stanza to explain the challenge of the first line. And I can see,
now, that the poet simply turned his back on the question he had
posed: "What can it mean when a thing is so easy?"

For this poet, poems are not about what one already knows so
much as they are about what one didn't know one knew. To find
out what one doesn't know one knows, one must sometimes look
elsewhere. It's a process similar to going to bed to sleep on a
problem and waking with the answer. Physicists do it all the time.
Freud did it. Will it matter *where* one looks while looking away?
It probably does, but another question occurs to me to undermine
that one: Could one possibly look away *without* intuitive reference
to what has been on one's conscious mind and surely still lingers

beneath it at the moment one turns away? I think not. The self has a coherence, and the poet, good or lucky or both, can retrace those connections later on.

Looking back, it all seems patently obvious. The willow stands swaying easily in dirt. The speaker in the poem, the poet as it happens, once did something with dirt that might have been easy to do but which seems, at first glance, to contain the seeds of unease — so much so that the poet immediately retreats to explain. He wasn't bad, he didn't make trouble for his father; he was good, he helped.

In fact, he did more. He swept up and oiled the floor.

"Yes," says that invisible reader, lurking behind the writer's shoulder but never in the direction in which the writer looks for him, "Yes, but what did *he* do while you were handling your childhood chores? Didn't he do the harder things? Let's name a couple to remind you."

And that's enough of *that.* Is this a poem about running a five-and-ten? No, we don't know what it's going to be about, mostly, finally, but it won't be that. "Don't forget," says the second self, "you're talking to a tree. You asked it a question, so far un-answered. Can you answer it or not? No, not yet? Then why not ask the tree some more questions?" *Hotshot tree, doing everything so easily . . . Do you think my father was like you? Did he sway, kiss a rock, soak up water and climb into light?* And now comes a lucky moment in the language. It's not just any old tree; it's a willow, a *weeping* willow. "Did he weep and weep in the yard?" That means one thing for the tree and another for one's father. Asked about a tree, it's a light piece of wit, but it's damn serious when asked about the father.

Suddenly, the poet is forced to answer his own seemingly rhetorical questions. When he began his questions directed towards the tree, they were questions to suggest differences. One expected them to be answered with "No's" but it turns out the answer was "Yes" all along, particularly to the first and last question.

So now the weeping willow — at the beginning bothersome, even offensive, in its ease — can be accepted. The poet has asked his challenging question and, though he has yet to answer it, has bled the confusion and confrontation from it. The willow and his father have something in common.

The differences, however, are still at issue. *Willow, come sweep my floor. I have no store but I have a yard. I do the father's singing and crying now. Not only that, I planted you there.*

So what, then, of the question posed in lines five and six: "What can it mean when a thing is so easy?" Looking back at this poem, trying to imagine myself at the time of writing it, it seems to me that by writing the poem I found the answer to what I meant by the question — to what *I* meant, not to what the same question might mean when asked by one of you. The question itself had to be given more meaning by the poem, meaning that lurked underneath when the poem began.

It takes the poem to answer the question. Then it takes only one sentence of six monosyllabic words to deliver the answer. The willow is an adolescent. That is why some things are easy for it. Moreover, the seeming ease of youth is characteristic of the distance in time between any father and any son, not the distance of not getting along but the distance of cold fact: the son knows little of the consciousness of the father. The son hangs around, sweeps the floor. He thinks it's more or less the same for his father, who fires the coalstove and kills rats in the basement. He doesn't know, like they say, shit. Not because he is stupid or unsympathetic. It means only that he is not a man, but a boy. He will know the difference when he is a man.

I am reassured when I look again at this poem. It says to me that I can pose a question and not answer it while the poem goes on, confident that an answer will arrive. It says to me that I can talk to one person (or tree) about another. I see, as I have always suspected, that I feel a heightened and immediate engagement when I address someone or some thing directly — that, in that sense, I want the poem to matter because someone is listening. I see that, when I ask a question, I want it to be answered. I suspect that I could derive from this poem a method by which to write others. The method would require a challenging remark, some description of what is being addressed, a question to be answered at the end, and a set of memories set down one after the other until a connection is achieved between memories and the thing being addressed, a welcome in place of the initial challenge, and the answer. I'm not interested in applying such a method myself, if it is one, but I see that it might be done, and that something similar might be done with any poem one admires sufficiently. I know one poet who writes her poems primarily by extrapolating requirements from other people's poems. After all, your own obsessions and language will surface regardless.

In conclusion, I'd like to talk about what it takes besides talent and perseverance to make the big leagues. Everyone knows that, no matter how good you are in your home town, at some point you have got to play with and against the best. If your kid is really that talented with the violin, he needs a world-class teacher. It's no accident that a large share of the best basketball players in the country come from a few well-known schools and playgrounds, or that hotshot high school baseball players and tennis players head for those particular warm climates where the other hotshots have gone. Louis Armstrong and Miles Davis didn't get to play that way by stepping on the football field with the high school band to play simple marches. You want to be a carpenter, you've got to apprentice yourself to a good one. You want to be a tailor, it helps to know at least one person who can make a suit.

Well, one can't always give up everything and go off to hang around the right playground or teacher. But, in literature, it's different: one *can* hang out with the best. It's all right there in the library.

Still, the books are not the process. What's in the books is the end result. It's as if one saw the ball going through the basket again and again, without ever seeing the moves that made the shot possible. Consequently, if you are to learn from what is given you, the poem itself, you must put yourself into it again and again, imagining the process — nay, *inventing* the process by which the poem may have come to be. More often than not, what you invent will be sort of what the poet did.

From re-reading, you will grow up and go free. Then, getting your poems written will depend on need, luck and perseverance. The rest is genius.

MFA
WRITING PROGRAM

AT
VERMONT COLLEGE

Intensive 12-Day Residencies

August and January on the Vermont campus

• Workshops, classes, readings
• Planning for 6-month projects

Non-Resident 6-Month Writing Projects

Individually designed during residency

• Direct criticism of manuscripts
• Sustained dialogue with faculty

Faculty

Dianne Benedict
Mark Doty
Mekeel McBride
Jack Myers
Sena Jeter Naslund
Mark Smith
Gladys Swan
Leslie Ullman
Gordon Weaver
Roger Weingarten
David Wojahn

Visiting Writers

Glenda Adams
Carolyn Chute
Andre Dubus
Stanley Elkin
Daniel Mark Epstein
Leslie Epstein
Laura Furman
Diana O'Hehir
Mary Oliver
Pattiann Rogers
Susan Stewart
Charles Wright
John Yount

Degree work in poetry, fiction and non-fiction. Plus a post-graduate writing semester for those who have already finished a graduate degree with a concentration in creative writing. For further information:

Roger Weingarten
MFA Writing Program
Box 515,
Vermont College
Montpelier
Vermont 05602

Other opportunities for graduate and undergratuate writing study are also available at the college. Vermont College admits students regardless of race, creed, sex or ethnic origin.

The Coordinating Council of Literary Magazines

is pleased to announce

THE GENERAL ELECTRIC FOUNDATION AWARDS for YOUNGER WRITERS

FOR LITERARY ESSAY . . . . VICKI HEARNE
"Talking With Dogs, Chimps, and Others"
published in *Raritan*, New Brunswick, NJ

FOR POETRY . . . . AUGUST KLEINZAHLER
Eleven Poems
published in *Sulfur*, Pasadena, CA

ALICE NOTLEY
Six Poems
published in *Ink*, Buffalo, NY

LUIS OMAR SALINAS
Six Poems
published in *Revista Chicano-Riqueña*,
Houston, TX

FOR FICTION . . . . ROBERT SHAPARD
"Tosteson's Dome"
published in *Cimarron Review*,
Stillwater, OK

ROLAND E. SODOWSKY
"Landlady"
published in *Sou'wester*, Edwardsville, IL

The Awards include prizes for winning writers and
companion prizes for the literary magazines which nominated their works.
They recognize excellence in younger and less established
writers while supporting America's literary magazines.

Judges: Doris Grumbach • Elizabeth Hardwick • Kenneth Koch •
James Alan McPherson • Gary Soto

For information on the
1984 General Electric Foundation Awards for Younger Writers,
write to CCLM, 2 Park Avenue, New York, NY 10016.

CRAZYHORSE

poetry & prose

Lee K. Abbott
Jon Anderson
John Ashbery
Marvin Bell
Robert Bly
Philip Booth
Christopher Buckley
Jerry Bumpus
Michael Burkard
Frederick Busch
Raymond Carver
Michael Cimino
Philip Dacey
Nicholas Delbanco
Stephen Dobyns
Norman Dubie
Andre Dubus
Stephen Dunn
Pam Durban
Russell Edson
John Engels
Carolyn Forche
H.E. Francis
James Galvin
Eugene K. Garber
Albert Goldbarth
Joric Graham
Linda Gregg
Jonathan Holden
Richard Hugo
Mark Jarman
Laura Jensen
Denis Johnson
Erica Jong
Donald Justice
Galway Kinnell
Maxine Kumin

Denise Levertov
Philip Levine
Larry Levis
Gordon Lish
William Logan
Thomas Lux
William Matthews
Jerome Mazzaro
Sandra McPherson
Robert Mezey
Lawrence Millman
Steve Orlen
Greg Pape
Stanley Plumly
Leon Rooke
Vern Rutsala
Reg Saner
Sherod Santos
Charles Simic
Louis Simpson
Dave Smith
Gary Soto
Marcia Southwick
David St. John
William Stafford
Gerald Stern
Maura Stanton
Pamela Stewart
James Tate
Leslie Ullman
Diane Wakoski
Miller Williams
Richard Wilbur
Susan Wood
Charles Wright
James Wright
Paul Zimmer

Please enter my subscription to CRAZYHORSE for [   ] one year, $8.00;
[   ] two years, $15.00; or [   ] three years, $22.00.

Name _____

Street _____

City _____ State _____ Zip _____

Make your check payable to "CRAZYHORSE Assn./UALR Alumni Assn."
Dept. of English, UALR, 33rd and University, Little Rock, AR 72204.

The Alabama Poetry Series
new in 1984 . . . .

The Arctic Herd JOHN MORGAN

"These poems are strong and full of carefully controlled feeling. They are tender and precise evocations of the moral and sensory life of man."—Annie Dillard

The Invention of Kindness LEE UPTON

"Lee Upton's poems are uniquely rich and full of surprises. The people, the characters in her poems, speak in voices painfully and hilariously recognizable. Their lives are captured in the sureness of this poet's instinct.

"Whatever strange turns these poems may take seem just right, because these people, as American as any you are likely to meet, are in a very special state of grace: that is, they have the love and care of their author. This is a marvelous book."—James Tate

---

Also in the Alabama Poetry Series

Sandra Gilbert, *In the Fourth World*
Rodney Jones, *The Story They Told Us of Light*
Mary Ruefle, *Memling's Veil*
Mariève Rugo, *Fields of Vision*
Brian Swann, *The Middle of the Journey*
Alberta Turner, *A Belfry of Knees*

The University of Alabama Press
Box 2877, University, Alabama 35486

MR

MISSISSIPPI REVIEW
SOUTHERN STATION
BOX 5144
HATTIESBURG, MS 39406
$10/$18/$26 1/2/3 YRS

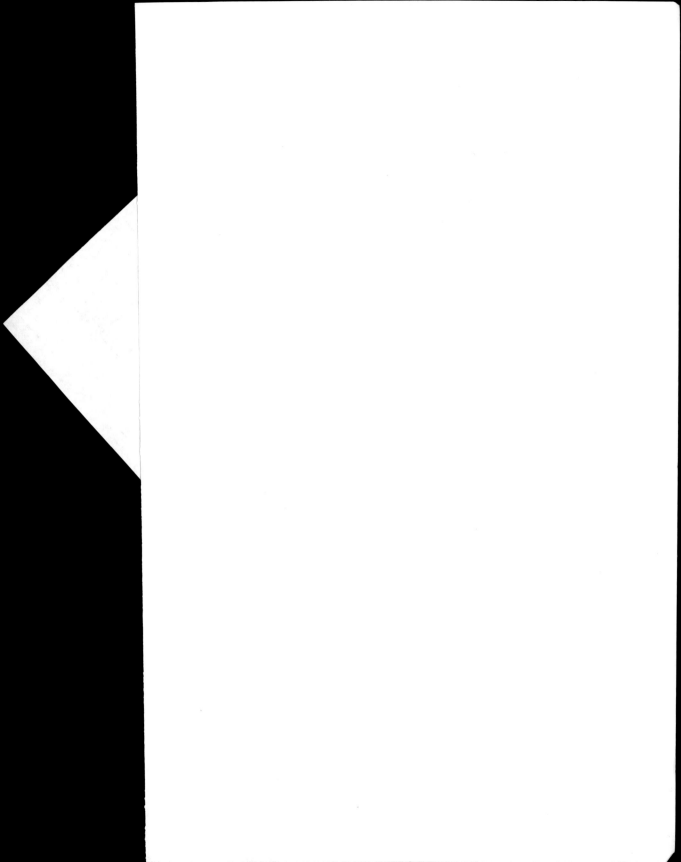

DATE DUE

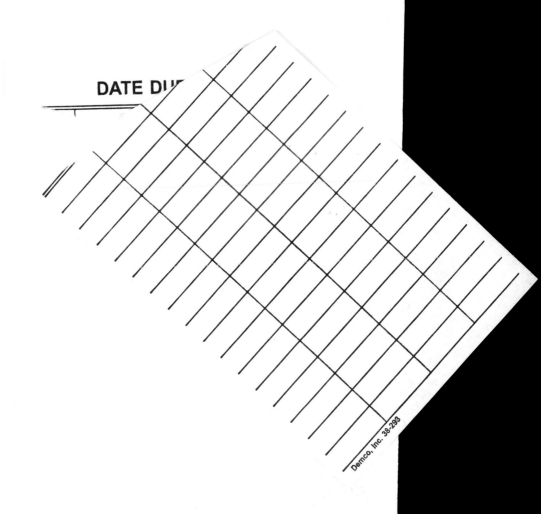

Demco, Inc. 38-293